PIONEERS OF
THE REFORMATION IN ENGLAND

SMITHFIELD MARTYRS MEMORIAL CHURCH
(This church was destroyed during the 1939-1945 war)

PIONEERS OF
THE REFORMATION
IN ENGLAND

By

The Right Reverend
MARCUS L. LOANE, M.A., D.D.
Sydney

LONDON
THE CHURCH BOOK ROOM PRESS

First published 1964

© Marcus L. Loane.   1964

PRINTED IN GREAT BRITAIN BY
BILLING AND SONS LTD.
GUILDFORD AND LONDON

"And what shall I more say? for the time would fail me to tell of . . . the prophets who through faith subdued kingdoms, wrought righteousness, obtained promises, . . . quenched the violence of fire, . . . out of weakness were made strong."

Hebrews 11: 32–34.

To

PHILIP EDGCUMBE HUGHES

M.A., B.D., D.LITT.

and

DAVID BROUGHTON KNOX

B.A., M.TH., D.PHIL.

Friends and fellow students of
The English Reformation

"God, once again having pity on this realm of England, raised up His prophets, namely William Tyndale, Thomas Bilney, John Frith, Doctor Barnes, Jerome, Garret, with divers other, which both with their writings and sermons, earnestly laboured to call us unto repentance that by this means the fierce wrath of God might be turned away from us. But how were they entreated? How were their painful labours regarded? They themselves were condemned and burnt as heretics, and their books condemned and burnt as heretical. O most unworthy act!"

THOMAS BECON,
Preface to "The Flower of Godly Prayers"
in *Prayers and Other Pieces*
(Parker Society), p. 11.

FOREWORD

by the Rev. J. R. W. Stott, M.A.
Rector of All Souls, Langham Place

THOSE OF US WHO ARE CHURCHMEN in the Anglican Communion need to be better informed both about the theological issues of the Reformation and about the calibre of the men who championed it in life and death. It is sometimes said that we must not fight the battles of the Reformation again. This would be true if the battles then bravely fought had been decisively won. But, alas! some of the very doctrines for the repudiation of which the Reformation martyrs died are gaining the ascendancy in the Church again. The evangelical faith is in jeopardy in the Church of England in the twentieth century, as it was in the sixteenth. Latimer's candle is in danger of being snuffed out.

It is good, therefore, that the Christian public should be confronted by the issues afresh, and that in the best possible way, namely in the words and deeds of the Reformers themselves. When Bishop Loane's earlier volume, *Masters of the English Reformation*, was published, I myself greatly profited from reading it and have since given or lent it to many people. *Pioneers of the Reformation in England* contains biographical sketches of four less well known figures. It was not their fault that they did not rise to greater eminence. They showed considerable promise, but they were not honoured by men, and their lives were cut short by martyrdom. Nevertheless, their witness lives on in these pages, as Bishop Loane enables us to come to know them largely through their own writings.

Two lessons have impressed my mind in reading the MS. They concern two qualities which these four men shared, and which are sorely needed in the same cause today. The first is their learning. All four were Cambridge graduates who, having embraced the gospel, sought to commend it to others by thoughtful preaching and writing. They were not afraid to engage in controversy. They believed passionately in the truth which had been revealed to them. They had themselves been won over from the old religion, and they were sure that others could be won over too. So they searched the Scriptures, and the fathers, and endeavoured to convince the nation of the truth of the gospel. Although none of them became a leader of the Reformation, we can watch in this book the help which they gave to the leaders— Frith to Cranmer, Rogers to Tyndale, and Bradford to Ridley. Each could have echoed Bradford's noble words, "I am certain and able, I thank God, to defend by godly learning my faith".

The second quality they all displayed was courage. True, they were men of frailty and of like passions with us. Barnes, who had a smaller discernment of doctrine and a greater intemperance of language than the others, began to vacillate when cruelly threatened. But all four suffered imprisonment and death by fire, and endured most valiantly to the end. They were not men-pleasers. Bradford was the bravest; even the heavy pressures of a primitive attempt at brainwashing did not overcome him. His mind was set upon pleasing God. "Life in His displeasure is worse than death", he said; "and death in His true favour is true life." It was this deep longing to serve and glorify God which made these reformers scornful of the praise of men. "Stick to His Word", was Bradford's exhortation to others, "though all the world should swerve from it".

The Church of England will not be recaptured for the truth of the gospel without both learning and courage. May God use this book to raise up among us a new generation of scholars and martyrs!

JOHN R. W. STOTT

AUTHOR'S PREFACE

THE WORK OF JOHN WYCLIFFE and the witness of the Lollards meant that England was like "a field ploughed and prepared" for the good seed of the Reformation.[1] Persecution had driven the Lollard movement off the stage of national cognisance, but the law "de heretico comburendo" had not destroyed its underground survival and vigorous influence in many corners of England. Wycliffe's Bible was still distributed, and the reading of that Bible in the mother tongue of England fed the souls and strengthened the faith of the Lollards for nearly a hundred and fifty years before Tyndale's translation of the New Testament appeared. This love of the Bible was one of the bridges between Wycliffe's movement and the Reformation. Modern historians differ on the question as to how far Lollard thinking may have contributed to the insights of the Reformation in matters of doctrine. Persecution had deprived the Lollards in the main of their books, and their teaching was handed down by word of mouth. This may explain why the records of the Lollard trials show that the Lollards often differed among themselves on points of faith. But a constant feature of the Lollard trials was the fact that they denied purgatory and the bodily presence of Christ in the Sacrament, and this must have had a bearing on the minds of men like Frith who were to deny the same doctrines in the reign of Henry VIII.[2] Tyndale was to publish two old Lollard tracts in order to prove that the theology of the Reformation was not some new-fangled teaching as its opponents insisted. Perhaps it was less in formal doctrine than in religious attitude that the Lollards were true precursors of the Reformers; this would help to explain why so many Lollards who came into contact with the Lutheran "heresy" at the outset of the Reformation were won by its teaching.

[1] D. B. Knox, *The Doctrine of Faith in the Reign of Henry VIII*, p. 138.
[2] Ibid., p. 94.

ix

It is impossible to tell how soon such a Reformation would have come to England if it had not received that great Lutheran stimulus. The old Lollard congregations in the country districts were to remain at first outside the reach of the Reform movement, but the works of Martin Luther and his friends had begun to find their way into eager hands by the end of the second decade. English merchants were in touch with printing houses on the Rhine and in the Low Countries, and a new and adventurous traffic sprang up in the transportation and sale of these books. They came in through ports like Lynn and London and soon found a willing market in Cambridge and Oxford. Thus in 1521, Warham could complain to Wolsey that "divers" in Oxford "were infected" with heresy.[1] And in 1523 Cuthbert Tunstall made a significant comment on the spread of Lutheran influence in a letter to Erasmus: "It is no question of some pernicious novelty; it is only that new arms are being added to the great band of Wycliffite heretics."[2] G. M. Trevelyan has summed up the situation very clearly: "Although the new doctrines scarcely differed at all in essentials from Lollardry, they appealed better to the politician and the man of learning. The orthodox instantly took alarm. King Henry wrote his famous Defence of the Faith, and Cardinal Wolsey in that same year issued orders to seize all Lutheran books. Here then ends the history of Lollardry proper, not because it is extinguished but because it is merged in another party. The societies of poor men who met to read the Gospel and Wycliffe's Wicket by night, suddenly finding Europe convulsed by their ideas, seeing their beliefs adopted by the learned and the powerful, joyfully surrendered themselves to the great new movement for which they had been waiting in the dark years so faithfully and so long."[3]

Wycliffe died in peace in 1384, but the Lollard movement was fruitful in heroic martyrdom. Death by fire is so horrible to contemplate that we cannot blame the men who shrank from such an ordeal; but the destiny of a heretic in the hell of mediaeval theology was so much more terrifying that it is not hard to see why many were induced to recant. There was no hope for them either in this world or the world to come if the Church were

---

[1] G. M. Trevelyan, *England in the Age of Wycliffe*, p. 350.
[2] Ibid., p. 349.   [3] Ibid., p. 350.

right and they were wrong. It was this fear which caused the long chain of recantations from the time of Purvey in 1401 to the time of Cranmer in 1556, and it sheds a bright new lustre on those who in spite of fear were steadfast. In March 1401, William Sawtrey was burned in the Cattle Market because he taught that "after the consecration by the priest, there remaineth true material bread".[1] In 1410, John Badby, a west country Lollard, was brought before the two Archbishops, eight Bishops, the Duke of York and the Lord Chancellor. He would not swerve from his belief that "Christ sitting at supper, could not give His disciples His living body to eat".[2] He was sentenced to death and the faggots were piled round his stake at Smithfield. The Prince of Wales was in the crowd which had come to look on, and he could not unmoved watch him as he went to his fate. "He argued with him long and earnestly, making him promises of life and money if only he would recant. It was a remarkable and significant scene. The hope and pride of England had come in person to implore a tailor to accept life, but he had come in vain. At last the pile was lit. The man's agonies and contortions were taken for signals of submission. Henry ordered the faggots to be pulled away and renewed his offers and entreaties, but again to no effect. The flames were set a second time, and the body disappeared in them for ever. Henry the Fifth could beat the French at Agincourt, but there was something here beyond his understanding and beyond his power, something before which Kings and Bishops would one day learn to bow."[3]

The roots of the Lollard movement had been buried in the soil of Oxford, but the seed-bed of the Reformation was in Cambridge. From the time when Little Bilney found peace of heart in 1519 to the time when Elizabeth came to the throne in 1558, Cambridge was the cradle of this great new spiritual movement for all England. Bilney was burned to death in the Lollards' Pit near Norwich in 1531; John Hullier of King's died at the stake on Jesus Green at Cambridge in 1557. There were in all twenty-five men who were sons of Cambridge and who died in the cause of the Reformation. Some bore names that are now justly famous; others were hardly known outside their own circle.[4]

[1] Ibid., p. 334.   [2] Ibid., p. 335.   [3] Ibid., p. 335.
[4] See Rupp, *Studies in the Making of the English Protestant Tradition*, p. 197.

The strength of the movement within Cambridge can also be measured by the number of her exiles during the reign of Queen Mary. Miss C. H. Garrett has listed a total of 472 exiles and has shown that no less than seventy-six of them were nurtured in the schools of Cambridge. They were drawn from every College except Magdalene, and they numbered forty-four who were or had been Fellows. H. C. Porter adds the names of twelve more exiles who had come from Cambridge but whose College has not been traced. "So", he says, "the list of Cambridge exiles can with propriety contain about ninety names, a fifth, that is, of the total number listed by Miss Garrett."[1] Seven of these exiles, including Sir John Cheke and William Turner, had gone up to Cambridge between 1519 and 1530, the years when the White Horse Inn had been the centre of the movement. Cambridge was the home of nearly all the leaders of the English Reformation, though they may not have been original thinkers such as Wycliffe had been. "But they had great ability", as D. B. Knox points out, "for restating in forceful idiomatic English the theology of the Continent";[2] and they sealed their testimony with the loss of all things in death or in exile for the glory of God.

Thomas Bilney, shy and gentle as he was by nature, through grace became the true spiritual progenitor of the Cambridge leaders of the Reformation. In the unfolding history of this movement, there was a straight line from that "most sweet and comfortable" word of Scripture which brought peace to his soul to the "comfortable words" which Cranmer chose from St. Paul in his liturgy for the Communion. Bilney's two most famous converts were Robert Barnes and Hugh Latimer: Barnes was to convert Richard Bayfield, and Latimer was to convert John Bradford; Bayfield was to work in closest bonds with Tyndale, and Bradford was to prove the dearest friend of Ridley. These men were all valiant in fight, and they loved not their lives unto the death. The voyage of Columbus into unknown seas which lay beyond the setting sun was not half so grand or brave as the venture of these men through the flames of death into a yet untried eternity.[3] Frith and Bradford, Barnes and Rogers may be less well known than Bilney and Tyndale, Ridley and

---

[1] H. C. Porter, *Reformation and Reaction in Tudor Cambridge*, p. 78.
[2] Knox, op. cit., p. 138.   [3] H. S. Darby, *Hugh Latimer*, p. 39.

Cranmer, but as in the case of the great Masters of the English Reformation, their death left an impact which that generation could not forget. "And in our time", so Bale recalled, "George Bainham in the fire did never complain; John Frith never showed himself once grieved in countenance; Barnes never moved, as his enemies do report; Peter Frank in Colchester sang joyfully to the Lord; the three young men in Suffolk rejoiced at the death; with such other many. And how far shall they be from pains after this, the great day of the Lord shall declare."[1] Wise are they who still keep in mind the words of the aged but resolute Latimer as he cheered his fellow martyr with the immortal utterance which has outlived all his sermons: "We shall this day light such a candle by God's grace in England as I trust shall never be put out!"[2]

[1] John Bale, *Select Works*, p. 586.   [2] *John Foxe*, Vol. VII, p. 550.

CONTENTS

THE BURNING OF JOHN FRITH
(with Andrew Hewitt)

JOHN FRITH

1503–1533

"Brother Jacob, beloved in my heart! there liveth not in whom I have so good hope and trust, and in whom my heart rejoiceth, and my soul comforteth herself as in you; not the thousandth part so much for your learning and what other gifts else you have, as because you will creep alow by the ground and walk in those things that the conscience may feel; . . . in fear, and not in boldness; in open necessary things, and not to pronounce or define of hid secrets, or things that neither help nor hinder, whether it be so or no; in unity and not in seditious opinions: insomuch that if you be sure you know, yet in things that may abide leisure, you will defer, or say till others agree with you, 'Methinks the text requireth this sense or understanding'. Yea, and if you be sure that your part be good, and another hold the contrary, yet if it be a thing that maketh no matter, you will laugh and let it pass, and refer the thing to other men, and stick you stiffly and stubbornly in earnest and necessary things."

—WILLIAM TYNDALE to John Frith in January 1533. See *John Foxe*, Vol. V. pp. 133-134.

J OHN FRITH WAS BORN IN KENT AT
Westerham in 1503 and grew up at Sevenoaks where his parents
moved while he was a child. There is only the most meagre store
of material from which we can draw to form a picture of Frith
in his adolescence or young manhood; this is perhaps the first
full-length attempt to set out all the known facts of his life in a
connected narrative. His father, Richard Frith, kept an inn at
Sevenoaks and was able to send him to school at Eton. He followed
the pattern of so many Eton school boys and went up to Cambridge as a member of King's College. We do not know the year
in which he was enrolled at King's, but Sir Thomas More was
to note that he had been taught by Stephen Gardiner. Honour
and power in Church and Realm still lay before Gardiner, but
his star was already in the ascendant. He had become a Doctor of
Civil Law in 1520 and of Canon Law in 1521; he was to become
one of Sir Robert Rede's Lecturers in 1524 and Master of Trinity
Hall in 1525. Thus the future Bishop was a Tutor in the early
twenties, and Frith was "a scholar of his".[1] These were the years
in which the winds of New Learning had begun to refresh and
invigorate the climate of study at Cambridge, and Frith was to
respond to the impulse with the alacrity of one who was born for
academic success. All who knew him were to agree that his
capacity to learn, his promptitude and alertness of mind, were of
quite an exceptional order. Foxe said that he was not only a lover
of learning, but that he was himself truly learned.[2] He made himself
expert in the Classics and could recite at length in his later years
from Greek and Latin poets alike. It was said that scarcely could
his equal be found among all his fellow students at the time when
he took his degree in 1525.[3]
There were winds of spiritual change as well as of New Learning during the years when Frith was a student, and Cambridge
had become the centre of Reformation thought in England. In
March 1519, Erasmus had brought out a second edition of the

[1] More, *Apology*, p. 140.   [2] Foxe, Vol. V, p. 4.   [3] Ibid., p. 3.

Greek New Testament which he called the Novum Testamentum.[1] It was through a copy of this book that Thomas Bilney of Trinity Hall grasped the secret of his personal acceptance with God through faith in Christ alone. Bilney gathered round him a group of like-minded scholars for the study of the New Testament, and the Reformation found its cradle in the meetings which they held in the White Horse Inn. This Inn had a postern door which opened on to Milne Street, or Queen's Lane as it is to-day, and was especially convenient for men who came from King's and Queen's.[2] Perhaps one of them was William Tyndale who had transferred from Oxford to Cambridge during the year 1516 and who pursued his studies there until 1522. His sojourn in Cambridge was long enough to overlap with Frith's first term, and it may have been then that the two men met and grew to love each other. Foxe said that it was through Tyndale that Frith "received into his heart the seed of the Gospel and sincere godliness."[3] In Daye's folio, this is assigned to London in 1525; but the narrative at this point is somewhat confused.[4] Mozley points out that the only place in England where we know that they both were at the same time was Cambridge; if they did not meet there, we cannot say where it took place.[5] It is reasonable to fix the year 1522 as the time when they first met in Cambridge and to assume that through Tyndale Frith would join those who met at the White Horse Inn.

Meanwhile there were other forces at work which were to play their part in his career. Thomas Wolsey, Cardinal and Lord Chancellor, was at the height of his magnificence and power. Hampton Court and York Place (renamed Whitehall after his death), as well as great country seats like The More, all bear witness to his love of wealth and grandeur. He trod in the footsteps of Wykeham and Waynflete as a patron of true learning, and he provided for the foundation of Cardinal College (now called Christ Church) on a sumptuous scale at Oxford. Thus in 1524 he secured a papal bull to suppress monasteries which had less than seven inmates and to use their wealth to found the College. On July 15th, 1525, the foundation stone was laid on

---

[1] The first edition in 1516 was called the *Novum Instrumentum*.
[2] Foxe, Vol. V, p. 415.   [3] Ibid., p. 4.
[4] Mozley, p. 20 f.n.   [5] Ibid., p. 20.

the land of the dissolved priory of St. Frideswide; by the end of 1526, the first lodgings on the west and south sides of the great quadrangle were ready for occupation. Pollard says that "parental affection was stamped" all over the College,[1] and his arms were blazoned on almost every stone.[2] He was anxious to place in the College men who excelled in all kinds of learning, and he was less concerned with their spiritual affinities than their academic reputation. He sent agents to scour Cambridge for young men of ability during 1525. Cranmer and Parker were among others who were approached, but they declined to exchange Cambridge for Oxford. But the men who did go, at least ten in number, were largely from Bilney's circle: John Clark, Richard Cox, John Fryer, Henry Sumner, Godfrey Harman, Thomas Lawney, Bayly, Goodman, William Betts and John Frith.[3] They were chosen for learning and ability as the original members of the College, and they were meant to grace and bring honour to the Cardinal's foundation. Thus on December 7th, 1525, having taken his degree at Cambridge, John Frith was incorporated as a Junior Canon in this newly founded Oxford College.

The work of John Colet and his lectures on the Greek text of the Pauline Letters had left a deep imprint on the life of Oxford. He had urged the students to feed on Christ by the reading of the Bible, and this may well account for the fact that Tyndale had studied the Scriptures in his student days at Oxford.[4] But ten years had elapsed since he had left Oxford when Frith and the others came from Cambridge, and they felt that they had come to a place where God was not. They began to confer about means for the spread of the reformed theology, and the next step was that John Clark began to read St. Paul's Letters to young men in his rooms. The results were encouraging, and the Warden of New College wrote a bitter complaint to the Bishop of Lincoln in February 1528. "Would God," he said, "my lord's grace (Wolsey) had never been motioned to call him (John Clark) or any other Cambridge man unto his most towardly College. It were a gracious deed if they were tried and purged and restored unto their mother from whence they came if they be worthy to come thither again. We were clear without blot or suspicions till they

---

[1] Pollard, *Wolsey*, p. 326.   [2] Ibid., p. 217.   [3] Foxe, Vol. V, pp. 4–5.
[4] D. B. Knox, *The Doctrine of Faith in The Reign of Henry VIII*, p. 105.

came."[1] But there was difficulty as well as encouragement. In November 1527 Bilney had been seized and brought to trial on a charge of heresy. Two weeks later he was forced to recant and to bear a faggot through the streets to Paul's Cross in the heart of London. But facts brought to light at his trial revealed a clue to the distribution of Tyndale's New Testament. Dr. Forman of Honey Lane was examined as a witness on behalf of Bilney, and his evidence made it clear that his curate, Thomas Garret, had sold a large number of these New Testaments to "divers scholars in Oxford".[2] Thus early in 1528, a fresh search for copies of the forbidden Testament and a sustained attack on its readers was launched in the Diocese of London and in the University of Oxford.

Thus in February 1528, Thomas Garret who had within the last few months brought no less than 350 suspected books into the University, was apprehended, and his friends in Oxford were exposed to trouble.[3] Fryer, Harman and Drumme forsook both friends and faith, but the other Cambridge men were steadfast. John Clark, Frith and others who were known as friends of Garret, were thrown into prison. They were shut up in a deep cave beneath the ground level of the College where the salt fish was stored. The stench and the diet took its toll of their health; they had nothing but salt fish to eat from February to mid-August. Goodman fell ill and was removed from the prison, but he soon died in the city. Sumner, Bayly and Clark also succumbed and "died all three together within the compass of one week" in August.[4] News of their death induced Wolsey to write to the local authorities and to insist that the others should not be so straitly handled. Frith and Lawney and the others were then released, but were required not to travel more than ten miles out of Oxford. Garret and Dalaber were brought before the Warden of New College and the Dean of Cardinal College. They were forced to abjure and to carry faggots in a religious procession through the streets of Oxford.[5] There were others in the procession who were stamped with heresy; they were required as an act of penance to cast a book into a fire kindled at the top of Carfax.[6] Frith seems to have escaped this fate,

---

[1] D. B. Knox, op. cit., p. 43 fn.   [2] *Foxe*, Vol. V, p. 421.
[3] Ibid., pp. 421–427.   [4] Ibid., p. 5.   [5] Ibid., p. 427.   [6] Ibid., p. 428.

but he undoubtedly knew all about the trials of his brethren.[1] He may have been in the crowd that looked on when the two men passed by with their faggots or when the books were cast into the fire. It was humbling; perhaps it was terrifying. He could see no future for himself in Oxford, and he made up his mind to go abroad. Thus probably in December 1528, he slipped across the Channel to join Tyndale in Flanders. He was only twenty-five years old, but he had begun to taste persecution; he had been in prison where four of his friends had sickened and died, and he had been driven into exile because there was now no place for him in England.

Hard as it is to trace Tyndale's movements, it is harder still to trace those of Frith. Wolsey was anxious to secure Tyndale's arrest and extradition from 1527 onwards, and this compelled Tyndale to move with much greater caution. He seems to have left Worms during 1527 and to have spent a few months in Marburg, where the Landgrave of Hesse had just founded a University to promote the teaching of the Reformation. The first list of students in May 1527 includes the name of a young Scot, Patrick Hamilton, whose shining intellect and blameless character would appeal to Tyndale in the same way as Frith's had done. He was the same age as John Frith, for they were both born in 1503; but he belonged to one of the greatest houses in Scotland. He was a grandson of the first Lord Hamilton and his mother was a grand-daughter of James II. At the age of thirteen he had become the lay abbot of Ferne in Ross-shire, and the revenue from this abbacy had met all his expense as a student in Paris and Louvain and St. Andrews. He was well versed in the classics and was drawn to Erasmian philosophy. Then in 1526 trading vessels began to bring Tyndale's New Testament to Aberdeen, Montrose, Leith and St. Andrews, and James Beaton began to take severe measures against the spread of heresy. But this only fortified Hamilton in his Evangelical sympathies, and in 1527 he was cited before Beaton, the Archbishop of St. Andrews, as one who was daring "to propound his own false doctrines as well as the foreign opinions of Martin Luther".[2] He escaped across the Channel to hold converse with those who

---

[1] John Foxe, Vol. V, p. 5.
[2] Alexander Smellie, *The Reformation in Its Literature*, p. 227.

could help him to define and defend his faith, and thus enrolled among the first students at Marburg. By the end of 1527 he was back in Scotland, preaching in and about his father's seat at Kincavel in the county of Linlithgow. But he was soon summoned before Beaton's Council in St. Andrews and was tried for various heresies. He was condemned to death and the sentence was carried out on the same day. Thus on February 29th, 1528, at the age of twenty-four, this high-born Scot was burned to death and became the proto-martyr of the Scottish Reformation.

It was perhaps early in 1528 that Tyndale left Marburg for Antwerp, and there can be little doubt that Frith made straight for Antwerp when he fled from England at the end of that year. Tyndale would learn at first hand from Frith the course of events back in England; Frith would hear from Tyndale about his New Testament and the death of Patrick Hamilton. Frith had been thrown into prison in the very month in which Hamilton had died at St. Andrews. This may have touched a chord in his thinking which would vibrate with a perceptive sympathy, and he may have gone to Marburg, where he would find Hamilton's memory still fresh and green. One fact at least is clear. While at Marburg the young Scot had prepared a short series of terse, epigrammatic theological statements. These theses were academic, and were not meant for the ordinary reader; they did not claim to be original, and were largely borrowed from Tyndale and Luther. Nevertheless Francis Lambert said that they were "conceived in the most Evangelical spirit and were maintained with the greatest learning".[1] They are closely argued and abound in opposite quotations from the Scriptures; and they breathe a spirit of single-minded devotion and enthusiasm for truth and the Gospel. These theses came into Frith's hands and it fell to him to translate them from Latin into simple pungent English. "If ye list," he said, "ye may call it Patrick's Places; for it treateth exactly of certain common places, which known, ye have the pith of all divinity."[2] Thus it owed its title as well as its publication to Frith, and it was to become the first clear doctrinal manifesto of the Scottish Reformation. Hugh Watt declared that "no work of equal length known to me is more packed . . . with the

[1] Smellie, op. cit., p. 234. [2] Ibid., p. 235.

great positive discoveries at the heart of the Reformation Gospel"[1] It affirmed that "sola fides justificat" in a way that had no equal in Scotland and was scarcely surpassed in the immediate circle of Luther himself,[2] and it helped to decide the true character of the Scottish Reformation in its primary stage of development.

Frith was out of England from the end of 1528 until July 1532, except perhaps for a flying visit in Lent 1531;[3] but his movements are shrouded in uncertainty. These were years which saw the fall from office first of Wolsey and then of Sir Thomas More; they were also years which saw a growing severity on the part of Churchmen such as Nix and Stokesley. The fires were stoked for fresh martyrs, and the first to suffer were Bilney and Bayfield, who were friends of Frith and Tyndale. Hitherto the chief material in the trials for heresy had been supplied by the Lollards, but the death of Bilney marked a new stage in the course of persecution.[4] Even so mild a man as Sir Thomas More wrote in his Confutation of Tyndale: "There should have been more burned by a great many than there have been within this seven year last passed; the lack whereof I fear me will make more burned within this seven year next coming than else should have needed to have been burned in seven score."[5] Meanwhile Tyndale was a wanted man who had to live in hiding in or around Antwerp. Frith's name was linked with his, and the seizure of the one might have led to the arrest of the other. Tyndale went on with his writing, and Frith brought him welcome encouragement. Tyndale's books were in such demand that no condemnation by Church or Crown could "cast them out of some fond folk's hands, and that, folk of every sort".[6] Frith was his favourite disciple, and would serve with him as a son with his father. His learning and virtue were both exceptional, and it is hard to judge which was the more commendable. He was well read in both Latin and Greek, "ready and ripe in all kind of learning", at home in the Scriptures as well as the Fathers.[7] Added to this, his clear insight and grasp of truth in the school of adversity made him truly one with Tyndale in purpose and courage.

[1] Alexander Cameron, *Patrick Hamilton*, p. 28.　　[2] Ibid., p. 34.
[3] Mozley, p. 190.　　[4] Rupp, op. cit., p. 30.
[5] Tyndale, *Works*, Vol. III, p. 97 fn.　　[6] Knox, op. cit., p. 121.
[7] *Writings of John Frith and Dr. Robert Barnes* (R.T.S.), p. 4.

They were indeed to prove themselves the Mr. Standfast and Mr. Valiant-for-Truth in the first years of the English Reformation.[1]

It is almost certain that Frith's books, like Tyndale's, were published in Antwerp, though they professed to have come from the press of Hans Lufft at Marburg. Foxe tells us that Michael Lobley was in difficulties in London in 1531 because he had acquired three of these Lufft-Marburg books in Antwerp: two by Tyndale and one by Frith.[2] Frith seems to have published *Patrick's Places* during 1529, and the notes which appear in Foxe provide the true reformed answer to a subtle question: how can it be said that "sola fides justificat" if faith is one virtue among others which may all be present? Frith abandoned the argument that faith draws its value from the merit that God accords to it, and went on to reason that faith is the faculty by means of which alone we can apprehend the truth of God's promise in Christ.[3] Patrick's Places was in fact a succinct attempt at true systematic theology, and it is an open question whether Roye's Dialogue or any other British work followed its example. Then on July 12th, 1529, Frith brought out his next work with the title: *A Pistle to The Christian Reader: The Revelation of Anti-Christ; An Antithesis between Christ and the Pope*. This was another translation, and it appeared under the pseudonym of Richarde Brightwell.[4] It is not known whether Frith worked from a book or a manuscript, for the original work in German has not been traced. It was one of the first anti-Papal works to be put out in English, and there were seventy-eight antitheses in all. The first will serve as an illustration: "Christ was poor, saying 'The foxes have holes and the birds of the air have nests, but the Son of Man hath not whereon to lay His head'. The Pope and his adherents are rich, for the Pope saith, 'Rome is mine, Sicily is mine, Corsica is mine, etc'. And his adherents have also fruitful possessions; this every man knoweth."[5] But Frith did not restrict himself to a negative attitude. This book makes it clear that faith is personal in character; the Gospel is not only for the whole world, but for each hearer. "It is not sufficient to believe that He is a Saviour and Redeemer; but that He is a Saviour and Redeemer unto thee."[6] This was a

[1] Rupp, op. cit., p. 30. [2] Mozley, p. 124. [3] Knox, op. cit., pp. 134-135.
[4] D.N.B.   [5] Frith, *Works*, p. 98. [6] Knox, op. cit., p. 45.

clear message of personal salvation and Christian assurance, and
it lies at the heart of the Gospel.

The next glimpse of Frith is derived from a curious inter-
change of letters between Cromwell in England and his agent
Stephen Vaughan in Antwerp. On May 18th, 1531, Vaughan
received a letter while he was at Bergen, and it contained explicit
instructions about John Frith: "As touching Frith mentioned in
your letter" (now lost), the King "hearing tell of his towardness
in good letters and learning doth much lament" that he should
misuse it to further "the venomous and pestiferous works,
erroneous and seditious opinions of Tyndale". But he hoped that
he was not "so far as yet inrooted" in such evil doctrines that he
might not now be recalled to the right way. Therefore Vaughan
was to speak with Frith if he could and to counsel him by the
King's desire "to return unto his native country where he assuredly shall find the king's highness most merciful, and benignly,
upon his conversion, disposed to accept him to his grace and
mercy". This means that the King would provide for him if he
were to renounce error and return to England. Vaughan himself
was advised "for the love of God utterly to forsake, leave and
withdraw (his) affection from the said Tyndale and all his sort".[1]
Vaughan's reply was written on May 30th from Bergen: "As to
Frith, I will do my utmost, as soon as I meet him, to persuade
him to return. Howbeit I am informed that he is very lately
married in Holland, and there dwelleth, but in what place I can
not tell. This marriage may by chance hinder my persuasions. I
suppose him to have been thereunto driven through poverty
which is to be pitied."[2] We know no more, except that he refused;
but this letter affords the first explicit reference to his marriage.
Tyndale was never to marry, but he wrote of marriage with
tender insight and wistful beauty: "The preciousest gift that a
man hath of God in this world is the true heart of his wife, to
abide by him in wealth and woe, and to bear all fortunes with
him. . . . And all that ye suffer together, the one with the other,
is blessed also, and made the very cross of Christ, and pleasant
in the sight of God."[3]

There were other activities in which Frith was engaged during

[1] Tyndale, *Works*, Vol. I, p. xlviii; Mozley, p. 197.
[2] Mozley, pp. 197–198.   [3] Tyndale, *Works*, Vol. II, pp. 50–51.

these months. Vaughan had apparently seen a copy of Tyndale's *Answer to Sir Thomas More's Dialogue* in manuscript and had tried to persuade Tyndale to defer its publication on the ground that it would only exacerbate opposition.[1] But George Joye said that Frith saw it through the press at Amsterdam in July 1531. This fits in with Tyndale's statement to Vaughan on May 19th that "one that had his copy" would shortly print it, and with Vaughan's report on May 20th that Frith was in Holland. The book itself shows no signs of Dutch publication and is ascribed by experts to Antwerp.[2] It seems likely that Frith arrived back in Antwerp towards the end of July with the unprinted manuscript in hand and put it through the press in that city. It is clear from Stokesley's sentence on Richard Bayfield some months later that copies of Tyndale's *Answer* were by then in circulation. It was at the same time that Frith put through the press his own *Disputation of Purgatory divided into Three Books*. This bore the Lufft-Marburg impress of 1531, and a reprint appeared in London in 1533; it was prohibited by proclamation in 1534 after his death. It was slender in comparison with Tyndale's Answer to More, but it was a shrewd and significant piece of controversy. Simon Fish had attacked the doctrine of purgatory in a book called *The Supplication of Beggars* which was published and strewn about in the streets of London during the year 1529. This had evoked replies from Sir Thomas More in the form of *The Supplication of Souls*, and John Rastell who wrote *A New Book of Purgatory*. Frith's book was meant as an answer to More and to Rastell, and it went on as well to examine the arguments of the Bishop of Rochester. He wrote with a sure touch, drawing from the Fathers as well as the Scriptures, demonstrating the fallacious character of teaching about purgatory from the doctrines of Atonement and Forgiveness, and all with a restraining charity that was no less remarkable than its luminous argument.

The short Preface begins with a disarming reference to his want of age and learning. "As touching my learning," he wrote, "I must needs acknowledge, as the truth, is very small; nevertheless that little, as I am bound, have I determined by God's grace to bestow to the edifying of Christ's congregation which I pray God to increase in the knowledge of His Word. I would not that

[1] Tyndale, op. cit., Vol. I, p. l.   [2] Mozley, pp. 200–201.

any man should admit my words of learning except they will stand with the Scripture and be approved thereby. Lay them to the touchstone, and try them with God's Word."[1] But he held that God has yet more light to break from His Word: "The old Fathers and holy Doctors have not seen all the truth, but somewhat is also left through the high provision of God to be discussed of their successors."[2] Then he explains how the book came to be written: "I wrote a letter unto a certain friend in England desiring him instantly to send me certain books which I thought necessary for my use and were not to be gotten in these parts, as the Chronicles, Sir Thomas More's book against the Supplication of Beggars, and certain other. These books I received upon S. Thomas' Day before Christmas, the year of our Saviour MCCCCCXXX with a letter written in this form: Sir, I have sent you such books as you wrote for, and one more of Rastell's making wherein he goeth about to prove purgatory by natural philosophy."[3]

He began with Rastell and was emphatic in his conviction that sinners shall "enter into heaven and never come in purgatory".[4] This led him to discuss the ground on which God can forgive man's sin, for he held that "all sin by the justice of God must needs be punished".[5] It was for this reason that men had thought of a purgatory where sin could be purged and punished, but Frith declared that Christ has purged our sins by His death on the Cross. "Behold the true purgatory and consuming fire which hath fully burnt up and consumed our sins and hath for ever pacified the Father's wrath towards us."[6] God is glad to forgive, and love is "not greedy to be avenged";[7] but the demands of God's justice had to be met before God could forgive. All those demands were met and His wrath was appeased by the death of the Cross.

Then Frith continued with his argument: "If we believe that of merciful favour God gave His most dear Son to redeem us from our sin; if we believe that He imputeth not our sins unto us but that His wrath is pacified in Christ and His blood, ... then are we righteous in His sight and our conscience at peace with God, not through ourselves but through our Lord Jesus

[1] Frith, *Works*, p. 3. [2] Ibid., p. 3. [3] Ibid., p. 4.
[4] Ibid., p. 9. [5] Ibid., p. 9. [6] Ibid., p. 10. [7] Ibid., p. 8.

Christ. So mayest thou perceive that thou art a sinner in thyself and yet art thou righteous in Christ."[1] This was forceful logic. "What say you now? Shall they yet go into purgatory?"[2] Such a doctrine was in hopeless conflict with the mercy of God: "For the nature of mercy is to forgive, but purgatory will have all paid and satisfied; so that they twain be desperate, and can in no wise agree."[3] Frith summed up the whole case against Rastell in the crisp and telling alternatives: "You must grant that we have a Christ or no Christ; a Redeemer or no Redeemer; a Justifier or no Justifier. If there be none such, then all the repentance in the world could not satisfy for one sin."[4]

In his Answer to More, he went from text to text with a clear and faithful exposition. He reaffirmed that "the Scripture knoweth no other satisfaction to be made for sin towards God but only the blood of His Son Jesus Christ; for if there were another satisfaction, then died Christ in vain."[5] The non-imputation of sin is the corollary of the imputation of the righteousness of Christ, and this is taught from the analogy between Christ and Adam: "We have all sinned in Adam without our consent and work, and we are loosed from sin through Christ without our works or deservings. . . . Through Adam, Adam's sin was counted our own; through Christ, Christ's righteousness is reputed unto us for our own."[6] Thus the doctrine that the death of Christ on the Cross was an effective atonement for sin was of primary importance in his theology: "And to say that the Pope can give any pardon to redeem sins except he preach me that Christ's blood hath pardoned me is . . . vanity."[7] Frith was the first English writer to stress this great concept which was fundamental to the English Reformation. And it had by-products of far-reaching value as he strove to make clear: "Let them that pray for the dead examine themselves well with what faith they do it, for faith leaneth only on the Word of God, so that where His Word is not, there can be no good faith: and if their prayer proceed not of faith, surely it can not please God."[8]

The Third Book was written in reply to the Bishop of Rochester and set out to declare the mind of the Fathers. He argued that Rastell leant on More, and More on Fisher, and that Fisher tried

---

[1] Frith, op. cit., p. 10.   [2] Ibid., p. 10.   [3] Ibid., p. 29.   [4] Ibid., p. 16.
[5] Ibid., p. 47.   [6] Ibid., pp. 48–49.   [7] Ibid., p. 59.   [8] Ibid., p. 49.

to draw his authority from the Fathers. But Frith asked where men ought to look for their authority, and went on to say that it could only be found in the Scriptures. "No man is bound to believe the Doctors except they can be proved true either by Scripture or good reason not repugnant to Scripture."[1] More and Fisher had both argued that the Church cannot err and was therefore the true authority in all matters of faith; but Frith referred them to Tyndale's Answer to More and went on with his main thesis.[2] Fisher saw clearly that other doctrines of the mediaeval Church, like pardons, would be threatened if purgatory were denied. "If a man take away purgatory," he asked, "for what intent shall we need any pardons?... For all the estimation of pardons hangeth thereof, so that we shall have no need of them if there be no purgatory." But Frith replied: "I care not though I grant him that too. And I think that money was the mother of them both. For out of the Scripture shall he be able to prove neither. But Mammon is a great god, even of power enough to invent such knacks, yea, and to make them articles of the faith, and to burn those that can not believe them."[3] Then he added: "If the Pope may deliver any man from the crime that he hath committed and also from the pain due unto it, then may he by the same authority deliver an hundred, a thousand, yea, and all the world; for I am sure you can show me no reason why he may deliver some and not all. If he can do it, then let him deliver every man that is in the point of death both from the crime and from the pain, and so shall never man more neither enter into hell nor yet into purgatory; which were the best deed and most charitablest that ever he did; yea, and this ought he to do if he could. . . . Now, if he can do it as you say, and will not, then is he the most wretched and cruel tyrant that ever lived."[4] That was the real knub of the whole matter.

There is only one other fleeting glimpse of Frith during those years and it has a curious history. On October 10th, 1530, William Tracy, a squire of Toddington in the county of Gloucester, drew up his will shortly before his death. Tracy believed "without any doubt or mistrust" that he would have pardon for all his sins by the grace of God and through the merits of Christ

[1] Frith, op. cit., p. 54. [2] Ibid., pp. 46, 56. [3] Ibid., p. 58. [4] Ibid., p. 59.

and His Passion. "Therefore", he said, "will I bestow no part
of my goods for that intent that any man should say or do to
help my soul; for therein I trust only to the promises of Christ."[1]
He would have no pomp when he was buried and no masses
said for his soul. After his death, his son Richard Tracy applied
to the Archbishop of Canterbury to prove the will. Warham
brought the matter before Convocation, and the result was that
the dead man was condemned for heresy. In March 1532, his
body was exhumed and burned. News of this must have reached
Tyndale and Frith very quickly, and each of them wrote an
exposition of the will which had led to his condemnation. It is
almost certain that Frith wrote his exposition before he left
Antwerp in July; Tyndale no doubt wrote his exposition at the
same time. Neither Tyndale nor Frith published what had thus
been written, and their work was unknown until after Tyndale's
arrest in May 1535. Tyndale's Exposition was then found bound
up with Frith's work in his own handwriting,[2] and they were
both published in the same year, perhaps by John Rogers and
Hoochstraten. Tracy's will is short and simple, but it affords a
clear statement of trust in Christ alone. It was this that prompted
Convocation to order his body to be exhumed and burned, and
it was this that led Tyndale and Frith to write in its defence. It
may seem hardly more than a trifle, but, like the will of Humphrey
Monmouth in 1537, it points to great issues. It shows how great
was the darkness and how much need there was for true enlight-
tenment. And it also proves how closely Frith and Tyndale were
linked both in friendship and in common effort for the spread of
the truth.

In July 1532, Frith left Antwerp, crossed the Channel, and
made his way towards Reading, where he had some business
with the Prior of the Abbey. The whole journey was one of great
hazard and its motives are still obscure. Stephen Vaughan had
spoken of his "poverty", and it has been surmised that he risked
this visit because of some expectation of help in his material
necessities. But Frith must have known the Prior while he was
at Oxford, for his Lutheran sympathies had brought trouble on
his head in 1528. The arrest of Garret had led to the discovery of
a list of books which revealed that upwards of sixty had gone to

[1] *John Foxe*, Vol. V, p. 31.   [2] Tyndale, *Works*, Vol. III, p. 271.

the Prior of Reading.[1] Thus the Prior had been put in prison as Frith himself had been, and was only released at the King's wish twelve months later. He had since then kept the candle of truth alight in his house at Reading just as it was kindled by Barnes in the Abbey of Bury St. Edmunds. Frith must have kept in touch with him and may have come in the hope that he could guide him into safety across the sea. It is at least certain that the Prior was to go with him and share his fortunes both in hiding and in imprisonment.[2] But when Frith reached Reading, he fell into the hands of the local authorities. He would not give his name, and was placed in the stocks as a rogue and vagrant. There he remained until he was almost starving; then in desperation he asked to see the schoolmaster. This was Leonard Cox, a man of learning who enjoyed the friendship of Erasmus and Melancthon and who was to translate the Epistle to Titus from the Paraphrase of the New Testament by Erasmus in 1535. Cox was amazed to find that this vagrant in stocks was a scholar who could converse as freely in Latin as in English; then he turned from Latin to Greek, and Cox was charmed with his recitations from the first book of the Iliad. The man who knew Homer was no ordinary stranger, and Cox applied to the magistrates for his release.[3]

It is not known whether Frith had any further conversation with Cox, but news that he was in England soon reached the ears of the authorities. Perhaps it was Cox who helped him on his release from the stocks to join the Prior, and the two men then set out for London and the coastal counties. Frith was hoping to find a ship and to cross the Channel; but a warrant had been issued for his arrest, and a reward had been offered for his discovery. Frith found himself hunted and in hiding, and he knew not which way to turn. A watch was kept on the roads and harbours, and he was in constant difficulty. He was compelled often to change his clothes and to travel from house to house; "yet could he be in safety in no place; no, not long amongst his friends".[4] At last, early in October, both Frith and the Prior were seized near Southend at Milton Shore in Essex and were confined in the Tower of London. Sir Thomas More said that he was "taken by the Bishop's servants, by the aid of the King's

[1] Rupp, op. cit., p. 21.   [2] Mozley, pp. 245–246.
[3] *Foxe*, Vol. V, pp. 5–6.   [4] Ibid., p. 6.

officers, at commandment of His Grace and his Council".[1] It is
clear that Stokesley hoped that Frith would be placed in his
determined custody, and More thought that it was just a matter
of time before he was handed over to the doubtful mercies of the
Bishop. But he was spared from this when the servants of the
Crown marched him off to the Tower of London. This was
Cromwell's doing, and it had Cranmer's backing; Cromwell
and Cranmer were both anxious to avoid extremities. Cromwell
had been impressed the year before with Vaughan's report of
Frith's learning, and a report on Frith's arrest was in his hands
on October 21st, 1532. He seems to have paid a visit to the
Tower in person within the next few days and to have left
orders that his treatment should be governed by a lenient attitude.
Thus while others were placed in irons, Frith was allowed to
remain unshackled.[2]

Frith was now to remain for five months in the Tower while
no action against him was taken. Cromwell wanted to let
persecution subside, and Stokesley was helpless while he was a
prisoner of the Crown. Frith was allowed a good deal of freedom
at Cromwell's behest and obtained more still as a result of his
own winningness. Sir Edmund Walsingham, the Lieutenant of
the Tower, was deeply impressed with his pleasant conversation
as well as his remarkable learning, and said that he was a man
whom it were a great pity to lose if only he could be reconciled.[3]
His friends seem to have had access to him, and they relieved his
wants. They would supply writing materials and circulate his
manuscripts. "What can be more trial of a faithful heart", he
wrote, "than . . . to visit the poor oppressed and see that nothing
be lacking unto them, but that they have both ghostly comfort
and bodily sustenance, notwithstanding the strait inhibition and
terrible menacing of these wordly rulers."[4] There were times
when even greater freedom seems to have been allowed, though
it was not without danger. Thus in due course Strype was to
print a manuscript which had belonged to Foxe and which shows
how Frith had won the goodwill of an under-keeper. This man,
Thomas Philips by name, had been imprisoned in the Tower for
heresy some time before and had been made under-keeper of

[1] More, *Apology*, p. 100.
[2] Mozley, p. 246.
[3] Pollard, *Henry VIII*, p. 219.
[4] Frith, *Works*, p. 81.

those who were confined on the same charge. Stokesley would scarcely have approved, but all doubt is dispelled by Hall's reference to "one Thomas Phelips, then keeper of that prison", who procured "the Bible in English" for Sir Nicholas Carew during his imprisonment in February 1539.[1] Philips would sometimes open the prison doors at night so that Frith could go out and consult with the "godly" in the home of a friend. This friend was John Petit, a grocer and burgess, who had been in the Tower some time before. The same Philips had allowed Petit to remove a board in the ceiling so that he could dine with Bilney who was in the room just above.[2] Petit was a sick man and died within three months of Frith's arrest; the date of his death is not known, but his will was proved on January 24th, 1533.

Perhaps leniency of this kind was intermittent, for Frith himself made it clear that much of his work was done under difficulty. He was like a tennis player who is chained to a post and cannot place himself for the game so well as if he were free. "For", he wrote, "I may not have such books as are necessary for me, neither yet pen, ink nor paper, but only secretly; so that I am in continual fear, both of the Lieutenant and of my keeper, lest they should espy any such thing by me. . . . For whensoever I hear the keys ring at the door, straight all must be conveyed out of the way; and then if any notable thing had been in my mind, it was clean lost."[3] Neither the Lieutenant of the Tower nor the keeper could risk too much; they might lose all. They may have been drawn to him on account of his learning and charm; they may have been willing to stretch regulations in his favour to the utmost. But they did not dare to let him go on writing, for it might be said that they had encouraged heresy. Thus he had to carry on his work in secret, and he expressed his thoughts in a letter written from the Tower before the end of 1532. "I ever thought, and yet do think," he wrote, "that to walk after God's Word would cost me my life at one time or another. And albeit that the King's Grace should take me into his favour . . . yet will I not think that I am escaped, but that God hath only deferred it for a season to the intent that I should work somewhat that He hath appointed

[1] More, *Apology*, see Note, p. 322.
[2] Ibid., see Note, pp. 319–320; Mozley, p. 254.
[3] Frith, *Works*, p. 76.

me to do, and so to use me unto His glory."[1] Thus he composed himself to taste the loneliness and frustration of his imprisonment, and to brace the faith of his friends. "And I beseech all the faithful followers of the Lord to arm themselves with the same supposition, marking themselves with the sign of the cross ... in token that they be ever ready willingly to receive the cross when it shall please God to lay it upon them. The day that it cometh not, count it clear won, giving thanks to the Lord which hath kept it from you. And then when it cometh, it shall nothing dismay you: for it is no new thing, but even that which ye have continually looked for."[2] And the letter concludes with the valiant signature: "John Frith, the prisoner of Jesus Christ, at all times abiding His pleasure."[3]

Frith had voiced a protest against persecution as a means of forcing men to believe in his criticism of Fisher's doctrine of purgatory. "My Lord", he wrote, "saith that it is profitable and well done to compel men to believe such things whether they will or will not."[4] But Frith's reply was emphatic: "But with violence will God have no man compelled unto His law."[5] He based this claim on the fact that faith is a gift which God bestows at His own free pleasure. "If He give it not this day, He may give it tomorrow. And if thou perceive by any exterior work that thy neighbour have it not, instruct him with God's Word and pray God to give him grace to believe."[6] This is the right Christian attitude rather than to try to compel him by acts of external violence. Thus he drew the practical inference that to punish a man for his errors in faith is all in vain; persecution as a means to secure right belief will always fail in its end. Compulsion and violence will make no man a believer; they can only produce "a stark hypocrite: for no man can compel the heart to believe a thing except it see evidence and sufficient proof".[7] Outward assent is all that persecution can achieve; true faith can come from God alone. Severe measures might force some to recant, but this would only serve for their condemnation. "If I should believe thus fully in mine heart and yet for fear of persecution should deny it when I were examined openly of my faith, then shall I be condemned of God (except I repent), and also mine own heart

[1] Frith, op. cit., p. 82.   [2] Ibid., p. 82.   [3] Ibid., p. 82.
[4] Ibid., p. 57.   [5] Ibid., p. 57.   [6] Ibid., p. 57.   [7] Ibid., p. 57.

shall be a witness to condemn me."[1] Frith was beyond the thought of his own age on this subject; his clear insight into the real nature of faith and the folly of all persecution buoyed him up in spirit as he faced the unknown perils of the future. "I certify you", he told Rastell, "that I am Christ's, conclude what ye will, and the day shall come that ye shall surely know that so it is . . . for I know in Whom I trust, and He can not deceive me."[2]

Frith's main occupation during those months was in writing, and two or three little works were written before 1532 came to an end. There was *A Letter unto the Faithful Followers of Christ's Gospel* which was meant to strengthen the hands of his brethren in the day of adversity. There was *A Mirror or Glass To Know Thyself* which was written at the request of a friend so that in knowing himself he might give thanks to God for all that He had wrought. And there was *A Bulwark Against Rastell*. This John Rastell was a true son of the Renaissance, a product of Oxford, the friend and brother-in-law of Sir Thomas More: a lawyer, a printer, a dramatist, a venturer to New Found Land. He was a keen as well as an entertaining controversialist, and his *Book of Purgatory* had been written for the support of his brother-in-law. Frith had replied to this book in his *Disputation of Purgatory* and had ended that work with the sentence: "If any man feel himself grieved and not yet fully satisfied in this matter, let him write his mind, and by God's grace I shall make him an answer, and that with speed."[3] More and Fisher, men of great wit and learning, ignored this fresh challenge; but not Rastell. He wrote again, and his reply was soon placed in Frith's hands. Frith at once took pen in hand to reply, and his *Bulwark Against Rastell* was the final exchange in the controversy. "Brother Rastell," he wrote, "I thank you that it has pleased you to be so favourable to me a poor prisoner as to show me a copy of your book which you have written to confute my reasons and Scripture that I have alleged against purgatory."[4] Rastell had always been unorthodox in his approach to such questions and his mind was not closed against the appeal of reason. Frith's wit and good humour at a time when his life was in danger may have impressed Rastell as much as his actual argument. At all events, John Bale later declared that he was won over to the Reformed faith and was in

[1] Frith, op. cit., p. 58.   [2] Ibid., p. 65.   [3] Ibid., p. 60.   [4] Ibid., p. 62.

Tyndale's camp by the time when Sir Thomas More was executed.[1] "He was well content", said Foxe, to become "a child again" and to suck "the wisdom which cometh from above . . . in the which he continued to his life's end."[2]

Frith's reply to Rastell, taken with his *Disputation*, was a valuable contribution to the literature of the Reformation, for it covered a much wider field than that of purgatory. He had his say on the commercial character of that doctrine in plain enough language, and dealt with the kindred teaching on pardons and penance as well. But his work was far from negative; its main emphasis was on the positive character of all that God has wrought for us in Christ. Man in himself is ever a sinner, but God gave His most dear Son to redeem him from all sin. Thus "Christ's elect are sinners and no sinners";[3] "they are both sinners and righteous".[4] They are righteous because their sins are not reckoned against them, and the non-imputation of sin means that God will never thrust them into purgatory. Did that also mean, as Rastell alleged, that men may dwell in sin? "Nay, God forbid, saith Paul; and even so say I again."[5]

Frith turned Rastell's image of the tennis player against Rastell himself: "And whereas you write and protest that you will bring no Scripture against me but only rehearse my Scripture again . . . and will but even do as one that playeth at tennis with another tossing the ball again, I do very well admit your similitude. Notwithstanding you know right well it is not enough for a man playing at tennis to toss the ball again, but he must so toss it that the other take it not. For if the other smite it over again, then is the game in as great jeopardy as it was before, besides that he must take heed that he neither smite so short of the line nor yet under, for then it is a loss and he had been better to let it go. And finally sometime a man smiteth over and thinketh all won, and yet an ungracious post standeth in the way, and maketh the ball to rebound over the cord and so loseth the game. And . . . I ascertain you that ye have tossed never a ball but ye offend in one of these points."[6] Frith liked Rastell's image and took it up

---

[1] Knox, op. cit., p. 120.
[2] *Writings of John Frith and Dr. Robert Barnes* (R.T.S.), p. 47 fn.
[3] Frith, *Works*, p. 72. [4] Ibid., p. 10. [5] Ibid., p. 70.
[6] Ibid., p. 62.

again at the end of his book. He had not been free to play on equal terms with Rastell; he was like a player tied to a post. Nevertheless Rastell had been driven right off the court; he had "clean lost the game".[1]

There was another manuscript which he prepared while in prison and which was to increase all his troubles. His writings on purgatory were a part cause of his imprisonment; what then could save him if he were to write against transubstantiation? Yet this is what he did, and it produced a new factor in the English Reformation. All the Continental Divines who had severed their link with the theology of Rome were in opposition to the mediaeval doctrine of the presence of Christ in the sacramental emblems of bread and wine; but Lutherans and Zwinglians were sharply divided in their ultimate attitudes. Luther denied transubstantiation but taught consubstantiation; this meant that there is a local presence of the glorified Body of Christ in the bread and wine and that those who receive the bread and wine are in direct contact with the living Saviour. Zwingli turned the Sacrifice of the Mass into the Communion of the Lord's Supper; he held that the bread and wine are signs of the Body and Blood of Christ who died once for all on the Cross and that the means of appropriation is faith alone. But the separation caused by doctrinal difference was a source of weakness which led Philip of Hesse to make earnest efforts to bridge it with understanding, and he arranged for the famous Colloquy of Marburg from October 30th to November 5th, 1529. Luther, Melancthon, Justus Jonas and other German Divines came to Marburg Castle to confer with Zwingli, Oecolampadius, Martin Bucer, and other theologians. The Marburg Articles were drawn up and fourteen of them were signed both by Luther and by Zwingli. The only article on which they could not reach agreement was the relation of the Body of Christ to the sacramental bread and wine. Luther chalked out on the table the words "Hoc est Corpus Meum", and would not budge from a literal explanation; Zwingli argued that the Body of Christ is now at God's right hand and that the bread and wine are signs of what is now absent. The long debate circled round these two points of view, and the final breach was complete. Luther argued

[1] Frith, op. cit., p. 76.

that this primary difference would not permit them to unite in one visible brotherhood.[1]

The doctrine of transubstantiation had been firmly denied by John Wycliffe, and this had cost him the friendship of John of Gaunt as well as his place in Oxford. He had developed his views on this heresy in 1379 and 1380, but the little tract which became known as Wycliffe's Wicket was the only guide in the hands of the Lollards on this subject. Men like William Sawtrey and John Badby went to death at the stake because they held Wycliffe's doctrine that there was no change in the bread and wine after consecration. But this doctrine only won its way by degrees after the dawn of the English Reformation. Bilney never denied the Mass and was never involved in heresy concerning the Sacrament of the Altar.[2] Robert Barnes was strong in Lutheran sympathies and would have no truck with Zwingli's teaching.[3] Tyndale was grieved by the divisive influence of the quarrel between the Lutherans and Zwinglians, and tried to keep aloof from the growing controversy. Frith was the first English author to stand boldly forward as an advocate of the position held by Zwingli, and the Lollards were at length to follow his lead. He had formulated his views on this Sacrament with a clarity which no other leader of the English Reformation had yet equalled. Those views were summed up with hostile intent by Sir Thomas More, who declared that it is heresy to say that "in the blessed Sacrament of the Altar were not the very body and very blood of Christ, but AS FRITH TEACHETH, nothing but wine and bread".[4] Rupp points out that it is not yet clear how far Frith popularised the massive theology of Oecolampadius and how far his work was original.[5] He may have read Wycliffe's Wicket, and he must have known of the Marburg Colloquy; his book was to refer both to Wycliffe and to Oecolampadius in a noble tribute.[6] He was to prove himself so well versed in Patristic argument that opponents like Gardiner could not fault him, and he had thought out the problems with such thorough finality that his views could not be shaken when at last he stood quite alone, without friends at his side, without books for his help, and with nothing

---

[1] T. M. Lindsay, *History of the Reformation*, Vol. I, pp. 352–359.
[2] *Foxe*, Vol. IV, p. 649.   [3] More, *Apology*, see Note, p. 286.
[4] Ibid., p. 114.   [5] Rupp, op. cit., p. 10.   [6] Frith, *Works*, pp. 117–118.

but the prospect of death as the reward for fearless and steadfast courage.

Frith's first foray into this great field of controversy was the result of a conversation with a friend who for his godly life might well have been a bishop before many that wore mitres. He was asked by this good man to expound his views on "the Sacrament of the Body and Blood of Christ",[1] and he summed them up in four points which Foxe records: that the doctrine of the Sacrament is not an article of faith which must be held upon pain of damnation; that Christ's natural body, having all the properties of our body except for sin, cannot be in more than one place at the one time; that it is not necessary to impose a literal construction on the words of institution in the Gospel; and that the Sacrament ought to be received according to the original institution of Christ, and not according to the corrupt order which then prevailed.[2] Frith's friend then begged him to put these views in writing on the ground that all his reasons were overlong for memory at a single hearing to grasp and to retain. "And albeit I was loath to take the matter in hand," wrote Frith, "yet to fulfil his instant intercession, I ... wrote a treatise which . . is like to purchase me most cruel death."[3] This first "little treatise", as he called it,[4] was not printed; indeed he was anxious that it should be closely guarded as a secret.[5] But it seems that copies were made contrary to his intention, and it was passed from hand to hand among known friends. At length William Holt, a city tailor and an agent of Sir Thomas More, was able to secure a copy, and More himself was to write in mocking fashion: "I have been offered a couple of copies more in the meanwhile: whereby men may see how greatly these new named brethren write it out and secretly spread it abroad."[6] When Frith read this statement, he could only say in reply: "If it be so that his mastership received one copy and had a couple of copies more offered in the meanwhile, then may ye be sure that there are many false brethren."[7] Frith was left to reflect on the fact that he was betrayed and that it was freely said that his book would cost him the best blood in his body: "which", he wrote, "I would gladly were shed tomorrow if so be it might open the

[1] Frith, op. cit., p. 107.   [2] *Foxe*, Vol. V, p. 6.   [3] Frith, op. cit., p. 107.
[4] Ibid., p. 108.   [5] Ibid., p. 115.   [6] Ibid., pp. 113–114.   [7] Ibid., p. 114.

king's grace's eyes".[1] Was this saying the true inspiration of the famous prayer of Tyndale at the stake in 1536?

Sir Thomas More had become Lord Chancellor in succession to Wolsey on October 25th, 1529, and he held the seals of office until he tendered his resignation on May 16th, 1532. The old Lollard statutes made him responsible while in office for the issue of writs for the arrest of heretics and for the execution of the law "de heretico comburendo"; but the traditional allegation of cruelty to heretics is not sustained by the records of his term of office. He thought that the law should prevent the spread of all "seditious heresies" and should punish even with death those who obstinately defied such a prohibition; but the trial and condemnation was in the hands of the bishops and no layman could share in that prerogative.[2] When John Stokesley became Bishop of London in 1530 on the translation of Cuthbert Tunstall to Durham, a more rigorous policy with regard to heretics was soon enforced in the Diocese of London. It was during the last six months of More's Chancellorship that Richard Bayfield, Tewkesbury and Bainham were burned, and his own words show that he was present at some stage in each trial. But Stokesley was responsible for their condemnation and death. When More referred to them in his *Apology* which was written about one year later, it was as a layman who was trying to defend the clergy from the charge of unmerciful severity.[3] Foxe was misled in his statement that More was the author of Frith's arrest; More had retired from his tenure of power on May 16th, 1532, and Frith did not land in England until late in July. More was succeeded as Lord Chancellor by Sir Thomas Audeley, who was supposed to be favourable to the cause of Reformation; yet in less than three years while he was in office, fifteen men were burned at the stake. But it is true that More was a vigorous opponent of the Reformation and his eminent position made him a most formidable antagonist. He had been commissioned by Tunstall in 1528 to refute the heretical works abroad in England, and he gave all the time and skill in his command to this supreme service in the cause of his Church.

More was often violent in argument and controversy, and this

---

[1] Frith, op. cit., p. 115.   [2] R. W. Chambers, *Thomas More*, p. 274.
[3] Ibid., p. 280.

has lent colour to his image as an implacable persecutor. He wrote the first part of his *Confutation of Tyndale* while he still held office. Then he retired to his home at Chelsea in such straitened circumstances that he had to burn a little bracken for a brief fire in the winter evenings. But he finished his *Confutation of Tyndale*, and the Preface referred to Frith's *Disputation of Purgatory*. "After that I have so clearly confuted Tyndale concerning that point," he wrote, "and shall have plainly proved you the sure and stead-fast authority of Christ's catholic known Church against all Tyndale's trifling sophistications, . . . after this done I say, before I go farther with Tyndale, I purpose to answer good young father Frith."[1] This made it clear that he meant to answer Frith's *Disputation of Purgatory*, but he refused to let himself be drawn aside from more fundamental issues at the moment; meanwhile he was convinced that what he had written on the authority of the Church in matters of faith was an appropriate reply to Frith as well as to Tyndale. By the end of that year, 1532, he had time to reply to Frith in more detail; but the manuscript on the Sacra-ment had come into his hands. He could afford to postpone an answer to the book on purgatory, but he felt that he must reply at once to this attack on the doctrines of the Mass and transub-stantiation. It took the form of a supposed letter to the friend who had sent him Frith's treatise: this was perhaps because Frith's own treatise had been written out at a friend's request. It stands out in contrast with his other works of controversy in two respects: it is very short, and it is pleasantly moderate in tone.[2] This was partly because More was impressed with Frith's sweet and reasonable spirit; perhaps it was also partly because he was perplexed. This "young man", he wrote, "I hear say hath lately made divers other things that yet run . . . so close among the brethren that there cometh no copies abroad".[3]

Thus Frith's "little treatise", though not in print, was soon well known to the authorities, and More's *Reply* was finished on December 7th, 1532. He glanced at it in a revealing paragraph in his *Apology* which was written early in the new year. "After that Frith had written a false foolish treatise against the blessed Sacrament of the Altar," he said, "I, having a copy thereof sent

[1] See More, *Apology*, p. 195. [2] Ibid., pp. xxxiii–xxxiv.
[3] Frith, *Works*, pp. 114–115.

unto me, made shortly an answer thereto. And for because that his book was not put abroad in print, I would not therefore let mine run abroad in men's hands. For . . . I would wish that the common people should of such heresies never hear so much as the name."[1] Thus he had his *Reply* printed under his own name for private circulation among those who had seen copies of Frith's defenceless manuscript. If Frith had been anxious that his work should not fall into More's hands, More was no less anxious that his *Reply* should not reach Frith. Each of them sought to guard his own work as a secret, but their reasons had nothing in common. Frith knew that his treatise was loaded with danger; More knew that his *Reply* was inadequate and vulnerable. More had begun as though he meant to treat Frith as a young man who had been misled by bad counsel. But he found it hard to keep up the role of a kindly mentor, and his feelings were not disguised by an apparent gentleness. Thus he declared that the devil himself could not make a worse book than this; that it even outdid Luther. He had avowed his hatred of heresy in connection with the Sacrament in his Dialogue in 1528: "Zwinglius and Oecolampadius, scholars of Luther," had gone beyond him in teaching "that the Sacrament of the Altar is not the very body nor blood of our Lord at all".[2] He now returned to this charge and declared that Frith had heaped up in a few pages all the poison found in Wycliffe, Oecolampadius, Tyndale and Zwingli: for he not only said that the sacramental bread is very bread still, as did Luther; but he also affirmed, "as these other beasts do", that it is nothing else but bread.[3]

Frith knew nothing of More's *Reply* when on December 26th, 1532, he was summoned before Stephen Gardiner, the Bishop of Winchester, for an informal interview. This is described in a picturesque paragraph in More's *Apology*. "Now happed it that upon a time", he wrote, "the . . . Bishop of Winchester sent for Frith unto his own place, of very fatherly favour toward the young man's amendment which he sore desired."[4] The Bishop reproached his erstwhile pupil for having written against the Sacrament. "Your books of this matter have been seen abroad in many men's hands," he said, "and that so long that lo, here

---

[1] More, *Apology*, p. 139. [2] More, *English Works*, Vol. II, pp. 260–261.
[3] Frith, *Works*, p. 116. [4] More, *Apology*, pp. 139–140.

is an answer already made unto it."[1] He showed him a printed copy of More's *Reply*, but would not place it in his hands. We know little more of this strange conversation other than the fact that More spoke of "a disputation between the boy and the Bishop".[2] But More's *Reply* was a surprise for Frith: More had been at such pains to keep the book secret that he had not so much as heard of it. Frith had great trouble to get a copy at all, and he has left his own account of the affair. "Some may think that (More) is ashamed of his part and for that cause doth so diligently suppress the work which he printed. For I myself saw the work in print in my Lord of Winchester's house upon S. Stephen's day last past. But neither I neither all the friends I could make might attain any copy, but only one written copy which as it seemed was drawn out in great haste."[3] Frith at once set to work on an *Answer* to More, and More somehow was made aware of it. Thus he remarked in his *Apology*: "Howbeit soon after (his visit to the Bishop of Winchester) he got mine answer, I can not tell of whom, and since have I heard of late that he . . . hath begun and gone on a great way in a new book against the Sacrament."[4] Frith was emphatic in his rejoinder: "This I am right sure of, that he never touched the foundation that my treatise was builded upon," namely, "that it is no article of our faith necessary to be believed under pain of damnation that the Sacrament should be the natural body of Christ".[5]

Before Frith could complete this book he had received a letter from Tyndale. It was written in January 1533 and was addressed to him under the pen-name of Jacob. Tyndale had heard of his imprisonment and wrote to him as his "dearly beloved brother" to arm him with patience and strength.[6] Tyndale did not know that he had written his first "little treatise" on the Sacrament, but he foresaw that the subject would come into dispute and he advised him to say as little about it as he could. "Sacraments without signification refuse. If they put significations to them, receive them if you see it may help, though it be not necessary."[7] He should content himself with a plea for toleration of his own views and should refrain from mere debate. "Of the presence of

---

[1] More, op. cit., p. 140. [2] Ibid., p. 141. [3] Frith, *Works*, p. 108.
[4] More, *Apology*, pp. 140–141. [5] Frith, op. cit., p. 108.
[6] *Foxe*, Vol. V, p. 133. [7] Ibid.

Christ's body in the Sacrament, meddle as little as you can."[1] Tyndale and Frith could not side with Luther and Barnes in their concept of the presence of Christ's body, but it would be wise to avoid the appearance of division as far as the case would permit. George Joye wanted to put out a treatise on the question, but he had stopped him for the time being. "My mind is that nothing be put forth till we hear how you shall have sped. I would have the right use preached and the presence to be an indifferent thing, till the matter might be reasoned in peace, at leisure, of both parties. If you be required, show the phrases of the Scripture, and let them talk what they will: for . . . to believe that the body of Christ is everywhere, though it can not be proved, hurteth no man that worshippeth Him nowhere save in the faith of His Gospel. You perceive my mind: howbeit if God show you otherwise, it is free for you to do as He moveth you."[2] He was ever to urge "that the Scripture may be in the mother tongue, and learning set up in the Universities".[3] So this moving, tender, fatherly, sagacious letter goes on, a true model of courage and friendship, with its penetrating counsel and its affectionate promise: "Finally, if there were in me any gift that could help at hand and aid you if need required, I promise you I would not be far off, and commit the end to God.[4]

Tyndale's letter was too late to prevent the first "little treatise", but it came in time to guide Frith in his *Answer* to More. This is clear from Frith's own remark in the Answer: "I received a letter from him which was written since Christmas."[5] And Frith repaid Tyndale's trust and friendship with a tribute in the finest spirit. Thus in 1531 Tyndale had informed Stephen Vaughan that he would desist from all controversy if the King would only grant his licence for an English version of the Scriptures.[6] Frith now renewed this promise and challenge in his own name and in that of Tyndale; he did so by way of answer to More's complaint that he would not refrain from his literary activity even though in prison. "I answer", he wrote, "that . . . I think no man more hateth to be idle than I do. Wherefore, in such things as I am able to do, I shall be diligent as long as God lendeth me my life. . . . And therefore until we see some means found by

[1] Foxe, op. cit.   [2] Ibid.   [3] Ibid.
[4] Ibid., p. 134.   [5] Frith, *Works*, p. 118.   [6] Mozley, p. 252.

the which a reasonable reformation may be had on the one part, and sufficient instruction for the poor commons, I insure you I neither will nor can cease to speak, for the Word of God boileth in my body like a fervent fire, and will needs have an issue, and breaketh out when occasion is given. But this hath been offered you, is offered, and shall be offered. Grant that the Word of God, I mean the text of Scripture, may go abroad in our English tongue as other nations have it in their tongues, and my brother William Tyndale and I have done and will promise you to write no more. If you will not grant this condition, then will we be doing while we have breath and show in few words that the Scripture doth in many; and so at the least save some."[1] And his heart warmed when he came to write of Tyndale in his reply to More's strictures: "And Tyndale I trust liveth, well content with such a poor Apostle's life as God gave His Son Christ . . .; which is not sure of so many mites as ye be yearly of pounds, although I am sure that for his learning and judgment in Scripture, he were more worthy to be promoted than all the bishops in England."[2] Tyndale's letter to Frith and Frith's *Answer* to More both at length fell into More's hands, and their drift was not lost on him. "All the brethren", he wrote, "look what shall become of him, and upon his speed hangeth all their hope."[3]

Frith not only denied the doctrine of transubstantiation; he went further. He argued that even if it were true, such a doctrine was not to be maintained as an essential article of faith. "It is not His presence in the bread that can save me," he wrote, "but His presence in my heart through faith in His blood which hath washed out my sins. . . . And if I do not believe His bodily presence in the bread and wine, that shall not damn me, but the absence out of my heart through unbelief."[4] But he would not condemn other views as to the nature of Christ's presence, and he argued that the theory of the Sacrament is in itself indifferent if there be no idolatry attached to it. "Luther is not the prick that I run at," he wrote, "but the Scripture of God. I do neither affirm nor deny anything because Luther so saith, but because the Scripture of God doth so conclude and determine. I take not

---

[1] Frith, *Works*, p. 115. [2] Ibid., p. 118.
[3] More, *Apology*, p. 102. [4] Frith, *Works*, p. 108.

Luther for such an author that I think he can not err.... And where you say that I affirm it to be bread still as Luther doth, the same I say again, not because Luther so saith, but because I can prove my words true by Scripture, reason, nature and doctors."[1] So too he did not hold this thing as truth because Wycliffe, Oecolampadius, Tyndale or Zwingli taught it, but because he saw that they were "more purely" taught by Scripture. "And where ye say that it is well known what manner of folk they be, ... I answer that Master Wycliffe was noted while he was living to be a man not only of most famous doctrine, but also of a very sincere life and conversation.... And as for Oecolampadius, ... his most adversaries have ever commended his conversation and godly life.... And Zwinglius was a man of such learning and gravity beside eloquence that I think no man in Christendom might have compared with him.."[2] Frith was explicit in his assertion that the saying, Hoc est Corpus Meum, must be understood, not in a literal, but in a spiritual sense,[3] and he went on to say: "For as verily as that bread is broken among them, so verily was Christ's body broken for their sins; and as verily as they receive that bread into their belly through eating it, so verily do they receive the fruit of His death into their souls by believing in Him."[4]

Frith then proceeds to show "the mind of the faithful Fathers",[5] and to quote and comment on at least a dozen ancient writers. He quotes Augustine seventeen times, Ambrose and Chrysostom five times, Jerome and Fulgentius three times, Tertullian twice, and others once like Cyprian and Origen and Athanasius. This was a fine accomplishment for a man in prison cut off from all his books; we know that this was so from his reply to More's demand that he should be precise about a quotation from Augustine: "Which thing, although it were hard for me to tell since I have not his books to look for it, yet I thank God my memory is not so bad but I can show him where he shall find it."[6] He had observed at the outset: "I think" that More "hath not one of the old Fathers for him, but certain new fellows ... which ... have made men believe what they list and made articles of the faith at their pleasure. One article must be that

---

[1] Frith, op. cit., pp. 116–117.   [2] Ibid., pp. 117–118.   [3] Ibid., p. 120.
[4] Ibid., p. 121.   [5] Ibid., p. 123.   [6] Ibid., p. 137.

they be the Church and can not err; and this is the ground of all their doctrine. But the truth of this article is now sufficiently known. For if Queen Katherine be King Henry's wife, then they do err, and if she be not, then they have erred, to speak no more cruelly."[1] He came back to this point in his comment on the novelty of More's doctrine of the Sacrament: "Peradventure he may allege me certain new fellows for his purpose as Duns, Dorbell, Durand . . .; but I speak of the old holy Fathers and Doctors as S. Austin, Ambrose, Jerome, Cyprian, Cyril, Chrysostom, Fulgentius, and such other: these I say do not teach me to worship it, and by that I dare abide."[2] But the belief that the sacramental bread is Christ's own body had led to "plain idolatry",[3] and this was the real ground of his protest.[4] "If you will grant and publish but this one proposition, that it ought not to be worshipped," he wrote, "I promise you I will never write against it. . . . But in the mean season I must think that you fill the world with damnable idolatry."[5] He was equally emphatic in his protest against those who "shame not to say that we affirm it to be only bread and nothing else. And we say not so: but we say that beside the substance of bread it is the Sacrament of Christ's body and blood. . . . And this Sacrament signifieth unto us . . . that as verily as that bread is broken, so verily was Christ's body broken for our sins; and as that bread is distributed unto us, so is His body and fruit of His Passion distributed unto all His faithful."[6]

This book ran to sixty-three pages with double columns of print in the folio edition of 1573, and Frith said that "necessity" compelled him to write it because his "first treatise . . . was too slender to instruct all them which have since seen it, albeit it were sufficient for their use to whom it was first delivered".[7] That first treatise contained a form of prayer for use at the reception of the Sacrament and this had led More to inveigh against him for trying "as a new Christ" to teach men how to pray.[8] "Frith is an unmeet master to teach us what we should pray at the receiving of the blessed Sacrament when he will not knowledge it as it is, but take Christ's blessed body for nothing

[1] Frith, op. cit., p. 126.   [2] Ibid., p. 151.   [3] Ibid., p. 151.
[4] Ibid., p. 151.   [5] Ibid., p. 152.   [6] Ibid., p. 168.
[7] Ibid., p. 167.   [8] Ibid., p. 156.

but bare bread."[1] But this prayer was Frith's true alternative to More's idolatry and he resolved to conclude his *Answer* by printing it again so that readers might judge between himself and More. This prayer is an address to each Person in the Triune Godhead and it reflects the true devotional application of his doctrine. "Blessed be Thou, most dear and merciful Father," he wrote, "which of Thy tender favour and benignity (notwithstanding our grievous enormities committed against Thee) vouchsafedst to send Thine own and only dear Son to suffer most vile death for our redemption. Blessed be Thou, Christ Jesu our Lord and Saviour, which of Thine abundant pity considering our miserable estate, willingly tookedst upon Thee to have Thy most innocent body broken and blood shed to purge us and wash us which are laden with iniquity; and to certify us thereof hast left us not only Thy Word which may instruct our hearts, but also a visible token to certify even our outward selves of this great benefit, that we should not doubt but that the body and fruit of Thy Passion are ours through faith as surely as the bread which by our senses we know that we have within us. Blessed be also that Spirit of verity which is sent from God our Father through our Saviour Christ Jesu to light our dark ignorance and lead us through faith into the knowledge of Him which is all verity: Strength we beseech Thee our frail nature and increase our faith that we may praise God our most merciful Father and Christ His Son our Saviour and Redeemer. Amen."[2]

Frith's *Answer* was smuggled out of the Tower and across the Channel to Antwerp for printing; but it did not appear until after his death and time had to elapse before it could make its proper impact on the minds of English churchmen. He was the first English theologian to expound the doctrine which would lie at the heart of the Reformation in the reign of Edward VI, and his teaching was then enshrined in the Communion Office in the Book of Common Prayer in 1552. John Lambert in 1538 and Anne Askew in 1545 were to die for holding Frith's views,[3] and the martyrs of the second generation were all condemned on the same grounds. Foxe says that when Cranmer wrote his famous volume on the Sacrament in reply to Gardiner, he was helped by

[1] Frith, op. cit., p. 156. [2] Ibid., p. 157.
[3] Foxe, Vol. V, pp. 227–236; 538–550.

Frith's use of the Fathers, "gathering the principal and chiefest helps from thence that he leaned unto".[1] But Strype observes that while "he might peruse Frith as he did almost all other authors that wrote of this controversy, yet he was too well versed in the ecclesiastical writers that he needed to go a borrowing to the readings of any others".[2] Strype is no doubt correct, but Foxe may be nearer the truth in his further remark: "I doubt much whether the Archbishop ever gave any more credit unto any author of that doctrine than unto ... Frith."[3] But while Frith's use of the Fathers may have sowed the seed which was to bear fruit in the mind of Cranmer, there was a more remarkable point of contact between Frith and Cranmer in Frith's discovery of the treatise by Bertram, or Ratramnus, *De Corpore et Sanguine Domini*.[4] Frith quotes Bertram with strong approval: "Whereupon at the instance of great Charles the Emperor, he made a book professing even the same thing that I do, and proveth by the old Doctors and faithful Fathers that the Sacrament is Christ's body in a mystery, that is to say, a sign, figure or memorial of His body which was broken for us, and not His natural body. And therefore that doctrine is new which otherwise teacheth, and not mine, which is not mine, but the doctrine of Christ and of the old Fathers of Christ's Church."[5] In 1545 Bertram's book came into Ridley's hands and convinced him that the Mass was neither primitive nor Scriptural. Ridley at once went to Cranmer, who in 1546 was won over by the weight of Bertram's work and Ridley's learning. Cranmer's debt to Ridley is clear; who can say what Ridley may have owed to John Frith as well as to Bertram?

But what manner of man was Frith? He was only in his twenties, yet his worth was measured by the first men in the kingdom. There was singular attraction for them in his youth and his rare ability, and all who knew him spoke of his unaffected simplicity, goodness and charm. His life and work belong to the last long night of winter before the dawn of the Reformation, and he was once described as "a primrose in the new spring of

[1] Foxe, op. cit., Vol. V, p. 9.
[2] John Strype, *Memorials of Thomas Cranmer,* Vol. II., p. 326.
[3] Foxe, Vol. V, p. 9.
[4] M. L. Loane, *Masters of the English Reformation,* pp. 143–146.
[5] Frith, *Works,* p. 136.

the Gospel".[1] Perhaps no one among early English leaders of the Reformation possessed such an attractive character or such outstanding qualities. His gentleness and scholarship won the respect even of those who were opposed to him. Wolsey, who had chosen him for his new College at Oxford, procured his release from prison in 1528; Henry, who could roar like a lion against those who wished for reform, hoped that he would renounce his errors and return home in 1531. Walsingham, who was Lieutenant of the Tower in 1532, was well disposed to him; Gardiner, who had been his tutor at Cambridge, was to treat him with "fatherly favour" in 1533. More matched his own glorious intellect with his and wrote against him more than once; he could not overlook the fact that he was a heretic, but he faced it with "a regret that was far from impersonal".[2] "So help me God and none otherwise," he wrote in his Apology which was published about Easter 1533, "but as I would be glad to take more labour, loss, and bodily pain also, than peradventure many a man would ween to win that young man to Christ and His true faith again."[3] Both Cromwell and Cranmer strove to save him, and George Joye was to write of him in his *Apology* in February 1535: "The man was gentle and quiet and well learned, and better should have been if he had lived."[4] And for Tyndale, he was the most dearly loved friend of all. One who exercised such an attraction for men who were in high authority and who were so diverse in sympathy and interest must have possessed a most lovable character. We could wish that we knew more of the wife whom he left in Antwerp; were there little children as well? Young and brilliant in learning, gay and winning in nature, cool and steadfast in courage, he was like the proto-martyr Stephen in his firm and unfaltering testimony both in life and in death.

Frith was a fine controversialist, with a lighter touch than More and Tyndale and a surer hold on the point which was being argued.[5] He wrote, said Foxe, with "prudent and godly moderation, . . . no less godly than learnedly".[6] He had gifts for sustained and lucid and logical argument beyond any of his

---

[1] *Vox Piscis or The Fish Book* (London, 1627), p. 33.
[2] More, *Apology*, p. xxxiv.   [3] Ibid., pp. 137–138.
[4] Butterworth and Chester, *George Joye*, p. 178.
[5] Mozley, p. 251.   [6] *Foxe*, Vol. V, p. 9.

contemporaries in England. Rupp points out that he drove even a man like Sir Thomas More to fall back on the desperate remedy of an argument from seniority and a spate of references to "this young man".[1] He was never cynical or negative in criticism, for his great aim was to expound and commend the Gospel. He did attack doctrines like purgatory and transubstantiation, but he was one of the clearest expositors of the Scriptures in the reign of Henry VIII. He taught the non-imputation of sin and the imputation of Christ's righteousness with a refreshing clarity. More might say that "your sect scorneth and blameth the Church because the Church saith that faith will not suffice but if it have charity and good works";[2] Frith would reply that faith which is the gift of God alone can save, and that charity and good works are the fruit of such a faith. He was implacable in his opposition to the mediaeval Schoolmen and their view of the Mass because he saw that it led to idolatry; but he would not quarrel with the German Divines and their teaching on the presence of Christ's body because he knew that they did not worship the bread and wine.[3] He held strongly that the body of Christ could not be in more than one place at the one time, but he denied that the bread and wine were bare signs with no value except as signs; thus he rebuked those who said that they "did only receive the Sacrament, and not also the thing which the Sacrament doth signify".[4] He was the first English writer to insist that only what is taught in Scripture may be required as an essential article of faith; and he went still further. There are many doctrines taught in Scripture, but it is not necessary to hold them all under pain of damnation; the Creed contains all that men must believe, and the Church must not make still more rigid demands.[5] He was willing to die at the stake in order to establish this distinction.[6]

The monotony of imprisonment was relieved by writing, and a series of small pamphlets flowed from his pen. They were smuggled out of the Tower and were published by friends after his death. Perhaps only one was written in the way of direct controversy: *A Mirror or Looking Glass wherein you may behold the Sacrament of Baptism described*. It refutes the doctrine of the

---

[1] Rupp, op. cit., p. 199.
[2] More, *English Works*, Vol. II, p. 284.
[3] Frith, *Works*, pp. 151-152.
[4] Ibid., p. 168.
[5] Ibid., p. 172.
[6] Knox, op. cit., p. 49.

Schoolmen and the Anabaptists alike, and it reiterates his own teaching on faith: "Thou must be surely persuaded that... thy sins are not imputed to thee, but forgiven through the blood and passion of Christ according unto the promise of God."[1] He gave much thought to the application of his doctrine of faith to the circumstances of life, as the titles of his other books show: there were *The Treasury of Knowledge* and *Vox Piscis*, which was only brought to light in 1616; there were *A Brief Instruction to teach a person willingly to die* and *The Preparation to The Cross and to Death*. These books, written while he was in prison, had a special message for those who faced adversity and were widely read during the Marian troubles. "Good brother," he wrote of the words of institution in *The Preparation to The Cross and to Death*, "think that these words be spoken to thee. Print them most deeply in thy mind, for when He speaketh to all, He speaketh also to thee, to thee, to thee I say they profit. All things that Christ hath suffered shall profit thee no less than they do help Peter and Paul."[2] There is one more book which must be mentioned, although Frith was not the author. On April 5th, 1533, this work, named *The Supper of The Lord*, was published ostensibly in Nurnberg but probably in Antwerp. It reinforced Frith's arguments and replied with vigour to More's strictures. But who wrote it? Was it Tyndale, or Joye, or someone else? Foxe and More both leave the question open, but More replied to it in the autumn. It is clear that he thought that the author could only be Tyndale, and he may have been right; Tyndale would spring to Frith's defence, but would withhold his name for Frith's own sake. But so trenchant was the teaching and the language of this book that it may well have hardened the authorities in England in their final treatment of Frith himself.[3]

Frith spent some six months in the Tower before matters came to a head. "Pray Christian reader," so ran the last sentence in his *Answer* to More, "that the Word of God may increase and that God may be glorified through my bonds. Amen."[4] Cromwell had kept him out of the hands of men like Stokesley as a prisoner of the Crown, and no one could proceed against him without the King's warrant. But the Bishop of Winchester was not

---

[1] Frith, *Works*, p. 94.
[2] See Knox, p. 47.
[3] Mozley, pp. 252–253.
[4] Frith, *Works*, p. 169.

content to let things drift, and he contrived to use one of the royal chaplains to stir the King into action. When this chaplain was called upon to preach before Henry during Lent in 1533, he said that it was no wonder that error was current with regard to the Sacrament: there was at that moment one in the Tower who had been "so bold as to write in the defence of that heresy, and yet no man goeth about his reformation".[1] Henry at once required Cromwell and Cranmer to arrange Frith's trial and he was examined in the presence of six Bishops and Peers: the Lord Chancellor, the Duke of Suffolk, the Earl of Wiltshire, the Archbishop of Canterbury, the Bishop of Winchester and the Bishop of London.[2] He held his ground in spite of the Archbishop's persuasion, and the Archbishop determined to defer the hearing and to arrange for an informal discussion in his home at Croydon. Cranmer had only returned to England in the month of January, and his Consecration had only been performed on March 30th. This must have been the first time that he was required to deal with a charge of heresy, and it was for him a task of supreme distaste. He still adhered to the mediaeval doctrine of the Sacrament, but he abhorred the prospect of persecution. Thus his plan to see Frith away from the Court in London was meant in true kindness; but it was to involve Frith in a new predicament. More had once asked what the Ordinary ought to do in Frith's case: "Should he let him walk abroad upon his promise to appear again, which Frith were likely to break and get him over sea?"[3] This was a jibe at his escape from England in 1528; but what would Frith do now? He was in far greater peril than in 1528; it was more than doubtful whether Cranmer himself could save him now if he would not recant.

Cranmer sent one of his gentry and a porter from his household with a warrant to bring Frith to Croydon. They left the Tower in a wherry and rowed down to Lambeth, where they paused for a meal. It is possible that it was a result of the Archbishop's instructions that the gentleman seized the chance to give Frith some plain advice: let him act with prudence for the sake of wife and children as well as truth; he would live to

---

[1] *Foxe*, Vol. VIII, p. 695.
[2] Cranmer, *Miscellaneous Writings and Letters*, p. 246.
[3] More, *Apology*, p. 100.

promote his cause yet more widely if he would yield for the moment; Cromwell and Cranmer would favour him, but he had foes who sought his ruin. Frith thanked him, but went on to say that come what might, he could and would only declare the truth. "But this I will say to you," he said as he took his friend by the hand, "that if you live but twenty years more, whatsoever become of me, you shall see this whole realm of mine opinion concerning this Sacrament of the Altar."[1] They left Lambeth and went on by foot to Croydon. Presently this gentleman with the porter's assent proposed that Frith should slip away into the woods on the left side of the road near Brixton and make for his native county of Kent; they would wait a while and then raise a hue and cry on the right hand towards Wandsworth. But Frith only smiled and declined. "If you should both leave me here and go to Croydon declaring to the Bishops that you had lost Frith," he said, "I would surely follow after as fast as I might and bring them news that I had found and brought Frith again. Do you think that I am afraid to declare my opinion unto the bishops of England in a manifest truth?"[2] Why did he turn his back on the chance of escape now, when six months before he was straining every nerve to keep his freedom? It was because he was then a free man and had no need to give himself away; but now he had been put on trial and was under special obligation to stand his ground. He knew that his hour had now come, and that he must declare his faith once and for all. "And so with a cheerful and merry countenance, he went with them, spending the time in pleasant and godly communications until they came to Croydon."[3]

Frith spent the night in the porter's lodge at Croydon and was summoned before Cranmer and Gardiner in the morning. He still adhered firmly to the Zwinglian doctrine of the Sacrament and cited the Fathers in its support; but he added that he would not condemn transubstantiation if it were held without idolatry. Gardiner thought that he made "the Sacraments acts indifferent, to be used and not to be used as it pleaseth man", and condemned this teaching as "detestable" when he came to write the book he called *The Detection of The Devil's Sophistry*. Hooper replied that "there was a sort of heretics called Enthusiastae that were

[1] *Foxe*, Vol. VIII, p. 697.   [2] Ibid., p. 698.   [3] Ibid., p. 699.

of that ill opinion; but not Tyndale, Frith, nor none other that writeth or hath written in our days except the ungodly Anabaptists".[1] But how did it affect Cranmer? He sent for Frith three or four times and saw him quite alone, but he could not persuade him to change his mind or to yield his faith. Who can tell what effect that quiet steadfast witness had on Cranmer? It was Cranmer himself who was at last to change and in 1546 was to embrace the views which Frith had held. Cranmer has not left on record what his debt to Frith may have been, but there is a letter which he wrote from Croydon on June 17th, 1533, to Nicholas Hawkyns, who had succeeded him as ambassador in the court of Charles V. "Other news have we none notable," he wrote, "but that one Frith which was in the Tower in prison was appointed by the King's Grace to be examined before me, my Lord of London, my Lord of Winchester, my Lord of Suffolk, my Lord Chancellor, and my Lord of Wiltshire; whose opinion was so notably erroneous that we could not despatch him, but was fain to leave him to the determination of his Ordinary which is the Bishop of London. His said opinion is of such nature that he thought it not necessary to be believed as an article of our faith that there is the very corporal presence of Christ within the host and Sacrament of the altar, and holdeth of this point most after the opinion of Oecolampadius. And surely I myself sent for him three or four times to persuade him to leave that his imagination; but for all that we could do therein, he would not apply to any counsel."[2] Frith, like Standfast, had survived the Enchanted ground, for he was "a right good pilgrim".[3]

Cranmer's letter makes it clear that, having failed to persuade Frith to recant, he had to leave the case in the hands of Stokesley. So things came to pass at length as More had foreseen and he was tried by his Ordinary. On Friday, June 20th, 1533, he appeared before Stokesley, Longland and Gardiner in St. Paul's Cathedral. He summed up the points at issue in a paper which was dated on June 23rd and which bears the title *The Articles wherefore John Frith died*. This paper is preserved in more detail in *John Foxe*

[1] Hooper, *Early Writings*, pp. 245–246.
[2] Cranmer, *Miscellaneous Writings and Letters*, p. 246.
[3] John Bunyan, *The Pilgrim's Progress* (Everyman's Edition), p. 362.

than in the folio edition of John Frith's *Works*, though there is no essential difference.[1] "The whole matter of this my examination", he wrote, "was comprehended in two special articles, that is to say, of purgatory and of the substance of the Sacrament."[2] He was asked first if he believed that there was a place "to purge the spots and filth of the soul after this life".[3] He said that he thought not, and his answer was summed up in one phrase: "The soul is purged with the Word of God which we receive through faith to the salvation both of body and soul."[4] But he would not reckon it a necessary article of faith, to be believed under pain of damnation, whether there be such a purgatory or no. He was then asked if he believed that the Sacramental bread and wine were "the very body of Christ or no", and he answered that it was His body "in that it is received"; "As verily as the outward man receiveth the Sacrament with his teeth and mouth, so verily doth the inward man through faith receive Christ's body and the fruit of His Passion, and is as sure of it as of the bread which he eateth."[5] Then he denied transubstantiation, but he refused to think that to affirm or to deny was in itself essential to our salvation. "The cause why I die is this," he wrote, "for that I can not agree with the divines and other head prelates that it should be necessarily determined to be an article of faith, and that we should believe under pain of damnation, the substance of the bread and wine to be changed into the body and blood of our Saviour Jesus Christ."[6] He was emphatic in his denial both of purgatory and of transubstantiation, but he would bind nothing on the conscience of Christ's congregation that went beyond the Creed.[7] Thus he was to die not only in the cause of truth but also for an enlightened tolerance which was rare in that age.

Frith subscribed his answers with his own hand: "I, Frith, thus do think; and as I think, so have I said, written, taught, and affirmed, and in my books have published."[8] He was condemned and was sent to Newgate instead of the Tower to await the end. He knew that he would die, and that the eyes of all were on him to see how he sped. Cranmer had told Hawkyns in his letter on June 17th: "Now he is at a final end with all examinations, for

---

[1] *Writings of John Frith and Dr. Robert Barnes*, p. 10 fn.
[2] *Foxe*, Vol. V, p. 11. [3] Ibid., p. 11. [4] Ibid., p. 12.
[5] Ibid., p. 12. [6] Ibid., p. 13. [7] Ibid., p. 14. [8] Ibid., p. 14.

my Lord of London hath given sentence and delivered him to the secular power where he looketh everyday to go unto the fire."[1] Meanwhile Tyndale had lost hope that he would be saved and had written again towards the end of May. He wrote to him under his own name and as his "dearly beloved brother John" to strengthen his hands for the ordeal.[2] Did Frith ever read it? We do not know. It has the ring of a profound simplicity and it reveals the fine understanding and trust of true friendship. "However the matter be," he wrote, "commit yourself wholly and only unto your most loving Father and most kind Lord. Fear not men that threat, nor trust men that speak fair; but trust Him that is true of promise and able to make His word good."[3]

Tyndale knew that there was truth in the taunt that men were ready to abjure rather than to suffer extremity, and he would have Frith keep his conscience pure and blameless. "The death of them that come again after they have once denied, though it be accepted with God and all that believe, yet it is not glorious. . . . If you give yourself, cast yourself, yield yourself, commit yourself wholly and only to your loving Father, then shall His power be in you and make you strong; and that so strong that you shall feel no pain. . . . Let Bilney be a warning to you; let not their visor beguile your eyes. . . . If the pain be above your strength, remember, Whatsoever ye shall ask in My Name, I will give it you. And pray to your Father in that Name, and He shall ease your pain or shorten it."[4] There was one more word of tender counsel and true comfort: "Sir, if you may write, how short soever it be, forget it not, that we may know how it goeth with you for our heart's ease. . . . Sir, your wife is well content with the will of God, and would not, for her sake, have the glory of God hindered."[5]

Frith was poised and steadfast, and he was not to die alone. Cranmer's letter concludes with a significant sentence: "And there is also condemned with him one Andrew, a tailor of London, for the said self-same opinion."[6] In his *Answer* to More, Frith had spoken of the companionship of a friend who "for his

---

[1] Cranmer, *Miscellaneous Writings and Letters*, p. 246.
[2] *Foxe*, Vol. V, p. 131.   [3] Ibid.   [4] Ibid., p. 132.   [5] Ibid., p. 132.
[6] Cranmer, op. cit., p. 246.

commendable conversation ... might better be a bishop than many that wear mitres if the rule of S. Paul were regarded in their election".[1] This may have been Andrew Hewet in view of More's reply: "Suppose me now that a tinker or a tailor which could ... read English ... and that were such a one as Frith writeth resorted to him, which though he was but Frith's disciple and scholar, was yet (he saith) more meet to be bishop than many that wear the mitre."[2] Andrew Hewet, born in Kent like Frith and only twenty-four years old, was a tailor's apprentice in Watling Street and was betrayed by Holt; this was the man who betrayed the book which Frith wrote at Hewet's request into the hands of More. He was placed in irons in the Bishops' house, but was able to file them off and to escape. He was betrayed again, and was sent to the Lollards' Tower. "After long and cruel imprisonment", he was, like Frith, brought up for trial before Stokesley, Longland and Gardiner.[3] They asked him what he thought about the Sacrament of the Altar, and he replied: "Even as John Frith doth." Then one of them asked him: "Dost thou not believe that it is really the body of Christ, born of the Virgin Mary?" But he answered: "So do not I believe." And he gave his reason when they asked why: "Because Christ commanded me not to give credit rashly unto all men who say, Behold, here is Christ, and there is Christ." The Bishops smiled, but Stokesley said: "Why, Frith is a heretic and already judged to be burned; and except thou revoke thine opinion, thou shalt be burned also with him." But he only said in reply: "Truly I am content therewith." He was asked if he would renounce his faith, but he said that he would do as Frith did. Therefore he was condemned and sent to join Frith at Newgate.[4]

Frith was sent to Newgate on June 20th; fourteen days were all that remained. He was loaded with irons so that he could neither stand up nor yet stoop down, and a collar of iron round his neck bound him to a post so that he could not move. He tried to write in the faint gleam of a candle both day and night, "for there came no other light into that place".[5] But his last known work was dated on June 23rd and it drew to an end with the

---

[1] Frith, *Works*, p. 107.   [2] More, *Apology*, p. 186.
[3] *Foxe*, Vol. V, p. 17.   [4] Ibid., pp. 17–18.
[5] *Writings of John Frith and Dr. Robert Barnes* (R.T.S.), p. 9.

remark: "It is true that I lay in irons when I wrote this."[1] The clarity and tolerance of that paper is all the more enhanced in view of the circumstances in which it was written. Gardiner sent two or three messengers to persuade Frith and Hewet to recant, but they showed no sign of weakness. On July 4th, 1533, the Lord Mayor, Sir Stephen Peacock, and the Sheriff of the city led them out to Smithfield where they were bound back to back at the stake. Dr. Cook, the parson of All Hallows in Honey Lane, Cheapside, openly admonished the crowd that they should pray for them no more than they would for a dog. Frith smiled and asked the Lord to forgive him. Every reference at the time bears witness to his exceptional courage as he faced the ordeal of death. When the faggots were heaped round the stake and the flames leaped up round his body, he put out his arms to embrace them as if to declare that he was glad to die in such a cause. "The wind made his death somewhat the longer," Foxe explained, "which bare away the flame from him unto his fellow that was tied to his back; but he had established his mind with such patience, God giving him strength, that even as though he had felt no pain in that long torment, he seemed rather to rejoice for his fellow than to be careful for himself."[2] Bale was to write of his courage in death as a fact well known to all that generation: "John Frith never showed himself once grieved in countenance."[3] Tyndale's counsel and prayer for him was thus fulfilled; he stood unmoved as though he felt no pain until death came. Frith was scarcely thirty years old; Andrew Hewet was only twenty-four. But God gave them great grace and crowned them with triumph: "And they overcame by the blood of the Lamb and by the word of their testimony: and they loved not their lives unto the death" (Rev. 12:11).

[1] Frith, *Works*, p. 172.   [2] *Foxe*, Vol. V, p. 15.
[3] Bale, *Select Works*, p. 586.

BIBLIOGRAPHY

JOHN FRITH, *The Works of The Excellent Martyr of Christ, John Frith, and the Works of Doctor Barnes*, 1573

JOHN FRITH, *Writings of John Frith and of Dr. Robert Barnes* (R.T.S.)

JOHN FOXE, *The Acts and Monuments of John Foxe* (Edited by Stephen Cattley) (8 Vols.), 1841

Dictionary of National Biography, John Frith (Vol. VII), 1950

A. I. TAFT, *The Apologye of Sir Thomas More, Knyght* (Edited with Introduction and Notes by A. I. Taft), 1930

W. E. CAMPBELL, *The English Works of Sir Thomas More* (Reproduced in facsimile from William Rastell's edition of 1557 and edited with a modern version of the same by W. E. Campbell, with Introduction and Philological Notes by A. W. Reed), 1931

E. G. RUPP, *Studies in the Making of the English Protestant Tradition*, 1949

D. B. KNOX, *The Doctrine of Faith in the Reign of Henry VIII*, 1961

M. L. LOANE, *Masters of The English Reformation*, 1954

T. M. LINDSAY, *A History of The Reformation* (2 Vols.), 1933

ALEXANDER SMELLIE, *The Reformation in Its Literature*, 1925

ALEXANDER CAMERON, *Patrick Hamilton: First Scottish Martyr of the Reformation, by Several Authors* (Edited by Alexander Cameron), 1928

A. F. POLLARD, *Henry VIII* (New Edition), 1951

A. F. POLLARD, *Wolsey* (Second Impression), 1929

R. W. CHAMBERS, *Thomas More* (Reprint), 1953

J. F. MOZLEY, *William Tyndale*, 1937

C. C. BUTTERWORTH AND A. G. CHESTER, *George Joye, 1495–1553*, 1962

JOHN STRYPE, *Memorials of Thomas Cranmer* (3 Vols.), 1848

WILLIAM TYNDALE, Doctrinal Treatises (Parker Society Edition, *Works*, Vol. I), 1848

WILLIAM TYNDALE, Expositions (Parker Society Edition, *Works*, Vol. II), 1849

WILLIAM TYNDALE, Answer to Sir Thomas More's Dialogue (Parker Society Edition, *Works*, Vol. III), 1850

THOMAS CRANMER, *Miscellaneous Writings and Letters* (Parker Society Edition), 1846

JOHN HOOPER, *Early Writings of Bishop Hooper* (Parker Society Edition), 1843

JOHN BALE, *Select Works* (Parker Society Edition), 1849

THE BURNING OF ROBERT BARNES
(with Garratt and Jerome)

ROBERT BARNES

1495–1540

"I think within this realm of England . . . the spirit of Elias was not at all asleep in good William Tyndale, Robert Barnes, and such other more whom Anti-christ's violence hath sent hence in fire to heaven, as Elias went afore in the fiery chariot."—JOHN BALE, *Select Works*, p. 138.

Robert Barnes, like Thomas
Bilney, and John Lambert, was a child of Norfolk, where he was
born in the sea-port of Lynn about the year 1495. Foxe says that
he was "from a child in the University of Cambridge",[1] and this
refers to the fact that he was enrolled as a novice in the local
house of Austin Friars. John Bale was one of his fellow students
during the year 1514, and he was to recall how he had been
outstripped by the "peculiar genius" and the academic abilities
of Barnes.[2] Indeed Barnes showed such marked signs of promise
that his friends sent him to the University of Louvain in Brabant,
where he read the Latin Classics with great profit. It is hard to
resist the thought that Barnes must have felt the inspiration of the
Prince of Letters who had been in Cambridge from 1511 until
1514 and in Louvain from 1517 until 1521; but not a word about
the influence of Erasmus occurs in all the works of Barnes, and
not a word about Barnes is found in all the correspondence of
Erasmus. It is also tempting to think that while he was still at
Louvain he must at least have heard something of the thunder of
a fellow Augustinian at Wittenberg; but there is no indication
that the name of Luther at this stage made any impact at all on
the mind of this young English student. It is not known how long
he remained at Louvain or when he returned to Cambridge; but
he took back with him a young friend named Thomas Parnell
and he was made Prior of the house in which he had served as a
novice. Foxe says that he took his degree as a Doctor of Divinity
at Louvain,[3] and in 1523 he received the same degree at Cambridge
by incorporation.[4] He had at once begun with the help of Parnell
to make his house a home for the study of the Classics, and he
read the works of Terence, Plautus and Cicero in a circle of
young men among whom were Field and Miles Coverdale. His

---

[1] *Writings of John Frith and Dr. Robert Barnes* (R.T.S.), p. 77.
[2] Rupp, op. cit., p. 31.
[3] *Writings of John Frith and Dr. Robert Barnes*, (R.T.S.), p. 77.
[4] Rupp, op. cit., p. 32.

house soon began "to flourish with good letters",[1] and he became
known as a rising figure in the life of Cambridge.

There is nothing to show at what point his love of letters
turned to concern for the Gospel, but it appears to have been a
gradual transition between 1523 and 1525. Stephen Gardiner,
who knew him at Cambridge, described him as being "a trim
minion friar Augustine, one of a merry scoffing wit, friarlike,
and as a good fellow in company was beloved by many".[2] But
he began to turn away from Duns Scotus and the Schoolmen
and to read the Pauline Letters; and what he was reading himself,
he read also with the young men like Coverdale who were in his
house. He was still "a questionary",[3] not yet aware of the saving
strength and comfort of the Gospel; but he strove to "have
Christ there taught",[4] and to school both himself and his pupils
in the Scriptures. He was making a name for his skill in disputation in the schools and his force as a preacher in the University,
and in 1524 he was called upon to preside when Master George
Stafford had to engage in a public disputation for his degree as
a Bachelor of Divinity. Stafford argued from the Scriptures with
such convincing eloquence that it was a marvel in the eyes of the
"blind doctors" and a source of great joy to the "godly spirited".[5]
But the turning point for Barnes as for Latimer was when he
came to know Thomas Bilney. Latimer's conversion had a
dramatic element which was absent from the experience of
Barnes, but it was through "that good Master Bilney" that both
men were "converted wholly unto Christ".[6] We know little
of this experience as to detail, but the change could not be concealed. Barnes had found the secret of full personal acceptance
with God by means of faith and was soon made welcome among
those who met in the White Horse Inn. This band of friends
was then comprised of such men as Bilney and Stafford, Arthur
and Thixtill, Fooke and Soud of Benet,[7] Parker and Powry,
Lambert and Latimer:[8] a goodly fellowship in what Barnes was
to call "the most glorious and heavenly Word of God".[9]

It was not long before Barnes found himself in sharp conflict

---

[1] *Foxe*, Vol. V, p. 415.   [2] Rupp, op. cit., p. 32.   [3] *Foxe*, Vol. V, p. 415.
[4] Ibid., p. 415.   [5] Ibid., p. 415.   [6] Ibid., p. 415.
[7] William Soud or Sowode was Master of Benet Hall (Corpus Christi College)
from 1523 to 1544, when he was succeeded by Matthew Parker.
[8] *Foxe*, Vol. IV, p. 620.   [9] Barnes, *Works*, p. 184.

with the authorities as a result of his peremptory criticism from the pulpit. During 1525, the Bishop of Ely tried to discipline Latimer by suspending his licence to preach in the diocese. This shut him out of his pulpit in St. Edward's Church in Cambridge, but it did not apply to the house of Austin Friars of which Barnes was the head. Thus on Christmas Eve, Barnes invited Latimer to preach in his Chapel while he took the pulpit in St. Edward's. Foxe hints that Barnes was encouraged by Bilney and Stafford in the course of action which he pursued;[1] but Barnes always loved the drama of a popular occasion and would need small encouragement. His text was drawn from the Epistle of the Day: Gaudete in Domino; but the sermon covered a wide field in topical allusion. He spoke against the abuse of litigation, the observance of festivals, and what Gardiner was to summarise as the "cardinal affections";[2] a play on words which hides the fact that this item was a risky glance at Wolsey's love of pomp and splendour. Perhaps it was hardly tactful to preach against litigation in St. Edward's of all places, for this church was in the gift of Trinity Hall, where the study of civil and canon law was pre-eminent. But Barnes had a particular abuse in mind, and the person concerned had been impervious to his private remonstrations. When Barnes saw this man, still impenitent, sitting in the congregation, he made a veiled appeal to his conscience. Rupp points out that this is the clue to the course of events which followed the sermon;[3] it was the real basis of the accusation that Barnes held the Anabaptist doctine that lawsuits were sinful. Barnes would say in reply that he did not condemn the law itself or the makers of law, but only "the uncharitableness of some men which rather seek vengeance of their brethren than any right or help of the law".[4] But that as yet belonged to the future.

Barnes may have been blind to the risks of a sermon which flicked the raw surface of so many vested evils, but it played right into the hands of those who were hostile to the Reform party. They drew up a list of twenty-five articles which were based on the text of his sermon and which furnished the ground for their accusation.[5] Barnes then offered to preach again the next Sunday and to declare his meaning more plainly; but the

---

[1] *Foxe*, Vol. IV, pp. 620–621.   [2] More, *Apology*, see Note, p. 285.
[3] Rupp, op. cit., p. 33 fn.   [4] Barnes, *Works*, p. 207.   [5] Ibid., pp. 205–217.

Vice-Chancellor inhibited him on the ground that it would be safer for him to hold his peace. He was summoned to appear before the Vice-Chancellor behind the closed doors of the schools, and he found four doctors and two masters there as well while he stood alone. He was confronted with the articles and asked what he had to say in reply; but he answered that in that form they were not his at all because they had left out certain statements which were vital to his meaning. "He said that I should take heed what I denied," wrote Barnes, "for if they brought witness against me, then must I needs die".[1] Master Tyrell then stood forward and said that some of the articles were "contentious, some were seditious, some were slanderous, and some were heretical".[2] Barnes asked him if he meant to charge him with heresy, but the Vice-Chancellor would not let him press the question. He was asked if he would submit himself and he replied: "Wheresoever I have spoken against God's Word or against the exposition of holy doctors, I will be content to be reformed and to submit myself."[3] He was urged to submit if he were found guilty of an offence against the laws of the Church; but this was too large a claim and he declined. Thus the inquiry continued until a crowd began to knock at the school doors with a demand for a public hearing. They would not be put off with less than this, and the Vice-Chancellor was forced to break off the inquiry on the ground that the University was in an uproar.

Two or three days later Barnes was summoned before the same men, who had now convened in the Vice-Chancellor's rooms at Clare Hall. They urged him "with good words" to be content to accept the Vice-Chancellor's ruling, while he argued that the Vice-Chancellor ought to provide for an impartial inquiry into the whole dispute. They said that they were all his friends and would be loath for the matter to come before a court: for if any witness was brought against him, as they were sure there would be, he was as good as lost. "Then said I", wrote Barnes, ". . . I would abide the danger and let mine adversaries do their uttermost. If I shall thus die, I must be content, said I; I am no better than our Master Christ."[4] He was then sent out of the room while they consulted together. In the end the Vice-

[1] Barnes, op. cit., p. 218.   [2] Ibid., p. 219.
[3] Ibid., p. 219.   [4] Ibid., pp. 219–220.

Chancellor saw him alone and seems to have prevailed with him. He was brought back to face them and give his assent to their demands. "I trust you be all my friends", he said, "and have so much charity in you that you will not cast me away, . . . for I did never intend to speak nor yet to do against Christ's holy doctrine. Notwithstanding seeing that the Law is so dangerous as Master Vice-Chancellor and you have told me: therefore I had rather put myself unto your charity than to stand to the danger of the Law."[1] He still refused to swear that he would stand by the Vice-Chancellor's judgment, but at length he agreed so long as it were not "against learning and charity".[2] He did not know that a notary had been recording the whole conversation; he did not discover this until the notary's document was produced as evidence against him in London. Meanwhile friends had become aware of the situation, and a crowd had arrived outside Clare Hall. Certain Masters and Bachelors of Divinity asked the Vice-Chancellor to admit them to the inquiry on the ground that they had heard the sermon, and the result was that conversation was once again discontinued.

Barnes was always bold and even reckless when he had the ear of a crowd; he was at his weakest when he was left alone in the hands of antagonists who could play on his fears and misgivings. There was no sign of his imperious spirit when he became exposed to the subtle pressure of the Vice-Chancellor and his colleagues in their semi-private examination. He did not seem to know how grave were the issues at stake, nor to see that his own career at Cambridge was ruined. He tried to hold his ground, but was forced to yield inch by inch. A month went by while two of the doctors drew up forms of revocation which would require him to grant what he had denied in the character of the articles. The man who was employed to write out the revocation was a good friend of Barnes, and gave him a copy at the same time as he gave the original to the Doctors. Barnes at once asked some of "the best learned men that were in Cambridge" to meet him in his room: there were Bilney, and George Stafford, and six or eight others, no doubt all from the White Horse Inn fraternity.[3] They all declared that he could not in good conscience agree to this revocation, and he drew strength from their encouragement.

[1] Barnes, op. cit., p. 220.   [2] Ibid., p. 220.   [3] Ibid., p. 221.

Thus when he was again summoned by the Vice-Chancellor, he was prepared. He found that three of the Doctors and Master Tyrell were present, and that he was asked to read the recantation, "neither more nor less than was therein written", in St. Edward's Church the next Sunday.[1] But he firmly refused, and after some debate, they all adjourned while he was told to take eight days in which to think it all over. Meanwhile Tyrell had lost patience; he rode down to London and placed the whole matter before Wolsey, who sent Doctor Capon and a serjeant-at-arms to effect his arrest. On Monday, February 5th, 1526, Barnes was surprised and placed under arrest "in the Convocation House to make all others afraid".[2]

There were about thirty others whom the authorities had begun to suspect, and the Vice-Chancellor with the serjeant-at-arms and the proctors set out to search their rooms for works of a Lutheran tendency. They went straight to the place where the books as a rule were kept, and this was proof that there must have been one or more who had betrayed their friends. But they had been warned by Doctor Forman and the books had all been safely concealed. That night they took counsel with each other and gave Barnes their advice before he set out for London. He reached London on the Tuesday evening, "and lay at Master Parnell's house by the stocks".[3] The next morning he was taken under escort to Westminster, where he was kept waiting all day. At last, through the goodwill of two old friends, Gardiner, now secretary to the Cardinal, and Edward Foxe, now Master of the Wards, he was allowed to kneel before Wolsey in an informal interview that night. Wolsey asked them: "Is this Dr. Barnes your man that is accused of heresy?" And they replied: "Yea, and it please Your Grace; and we trust you shall find him reformable, for he is both well learned and wise."[4] Wolsey was more than once to prove himself willing to wink at mild heresy, and he showed a genuine reluctance to start the wheels of law. He began to peruse the catalogue of articles, and read quietly down to the sixth. "I will never believe," so it ran, "... that any one man may be by the law of God a bishop of two or three cities."[5] He stopped and said that this touched him: and he would

---

[1] Barnes, op. cit., p. 221.　　　[2] *Foxe*, Vol. V, p. 416.
[3] Ibid., p. 416.　　[4] Ibid., p. 416.　　[5] Barnes, *Works*, p. 210.

know if a bishop might have under him more cities than one. Barnes held that such terms as bishop and presbyter were synonymous, and that St. Paul ordained elders for the church in every city; but he answered that a bishop might have under him as many cities as he could teach.[1] "He would hear me no more", wrote Barnes; he resumed his reading of the articles.[2]

At last Wolsey read the twenty-second article which summed up the sallies of Barnes at the pillars and pole-axes, the red gloves and golden shoes, and all the other marks of pomp and pageantry so dear to the Cardinal. "I pray you," Barnes had said, "what is the cause that you call your staff a shepherd's staff? You help no man with it; you comfort no man; you lift up no man with it. But you have stricken down kings and kingdoms with it."[3] Wolsey stopped at this point and in a good-tempered vein tried to make him see reason. "What! Master Doctor," he said, "had you not a sufficient scope in the Scriptures to teach the people but that my golden shoes, my pole axes, my pillars, my golden cushions, my crosses did so sore offend you that you must make us 'ridiculum caput' amongst the people? We were jollily that that day laughed to scorn. Verily it was a sermon more fit to be preached on a stage than in a pulpit." But Barnes was incorrigible. "I spake nothing", he said, "but the truth out of the Scriptures according to my conscience and according to the old doctors."[4] Barnes then handed him six sheets of paper written in self-defence. Wolsey received them with a smile and said: "We perceive then that you intend to stand to your articles and to show your learning." And Barnes replied: "Yea, that I do intend, by God's grace, with your Lordship's favour."[5] Wolsey asked him if he thought it were good that he should lay down his pillars and pole-axes, and Barnes answered that it would be well done. Wolsey then asked if Barnes thought that he should sell them and give to the poor, or if he thought that he should keep them for the good of the realm. "To this I did answer", wrote Barnes, "that I reckoned it more to the honour of God and to the salvation of his soul and also to the comfort of his poor brethren that they were coined and given in alms. . . . For as His Grace knew, the common wealth was afore His Grace and must

[1] Barnes, op. cit., pp. 210, 221.   [2] Ibid., p. 222.
[3] Ibid., p. 214.   [4] *Foxe*, Vol. V, p. 416.   [5] Ibid., p. 416.

be when His Grace is gone, and the pillars and pole axes came with him and should also go away with him."[1]

Barnes could not see that his attack on a man like Wolsey was a mistake, and he would not apologise. At last Wolsey told him that he had been defamed for heresy, and that to stand his ground only meant that the Law would have to take its course. Barnes said that no good man who knew him would believe such a report, and that it had only been spread by those who bore him some malice. Wolsey replied: "I believe that to be true, but how will you purge yourself?"[2] It would not be enough for him to call any honest man as witness; he would have to bring as many as ten Doctors who would all swear on his behalf. But only two Doctors had been present at his sermon, and they were the very men who had brought him before the Vice-Chancellor. Therefore Barnes said that this would be impossible. Wolsey then voiced words of warning which must have sent a chill through his inmost being: "Then you must be burned."[3] Wolsey went on to say that he should choose whether he would appear before the court of law or would submit himself to the Legate's authority. But Barnes replied: "I thank Your Grace for your good-will; I will stick to the Holy Scripture and to God's Book according to the simple talent that God hath lent me." "Well," said Wolsey, "thou shalt have thy learning tried to the uttermost, and thou shalt have the law."[4] Barnes asked that he might have justice with equity, but Wolsey terminated the conversation. "He ... said how that I was but a fool," so Barnes recalled, "and could not perceive how good he was unto me."[5] He would have been sent to the Tower had not Gardiner and Foxe offered to act as his sureties. "And so he came home to Master Parnell's house again, and that night fell to writing and slept not."[6] Coverdale, Goodwin and Field were his secretaries, helping him to prepare for his defence, and their presence in his time of trouble is a splendid testimony to the best side of Barnes.

The next morning, Thursday, February 8th, he was taken by the serjeant-at-arms to the Chapter House at Westminster, where the Bishop of Bath was to preside over a court of which Bishops,

[1] Barnes, *Works*, p. 215.   [2] Ibid., p. 222.   [3] Ibid., p. 222.
[4] *Foxe*, Vol. V, p. 417.   [5] Barnes, *Works*, p. 222.
[6] *Foxe*, Vol. V, p. 417.

Abbots, and Doctors, including Gardiner, were members. This was a formal trial for heresy on the ground of twenty-five articles of which not one had the remotest connection with the central doctrines of the Gospel. Barnes came before this court, handed in the statement of his defence, and then was told to stand aside while five German merchants of the steel-yard were examined for Lutheran books and Lollardry. At length he was called in again, subscribed the articles, and was committed with "young Master Parnell" and the German merchants to the Fleet, whose Warden was charged to let no man converse with them.[1] Barnes was now caught in the formal process of a long and gruelling examination which was to last for two more days. He would first be asked some question to which he would reply; then he would be required to stand apart while his judges conferred; then he would be recalled and asked a fresh question; then the course of events would follow the same sequence as before. They used his ignorance of the law to drive him into one last corner where the alternatives were to revoke all or to die. Thus on Saturday afternoon "about four of the clock", he was offered another document as a form of submission.[2] He asked to see what it contained before he would accede. But he was told that if he read it as it stood, all would be well; if not, he would stand in peril. He then asked if they had condemned the articles for heresy, and was told that they had; but they would not tell him what was condemned, nor offer him any information except what he would find in the submission. Once more they pressed him to say if he would accept this document or not. "This is the third time and the last",[3] so he was told. "Then said I, I will not grant to it except I may first see it. Do as it shall please you."[4]

They all sat still at this unexpected reverse; then he was thrust aside while a whispered consultation took place. He was recalled and told that a notary would read the document to him in private. But this man could not tell him what was the heresy in his articles, and he applied to the judges again. "So went I again before the bishops," he wrote, "and fell down on my knees, and desired them for the bitter passion of Christ that they would show unto me which article they condemned for heresy."[5] But the

[1] *Foxe*, op. cit., p. 417.
[2] Barnes, *Works*, p. 223.
[3] Ibid., p. 224. [4] Ibid. [5] Ibid.

Bishop of Bath had lost patience and was seriously annoyed; and his only reply was an angry demand. He asked "whether I would read the roll or else be burned: the one of both I should do. Then said I, Jesus, have mercy on me, I will surely not read it."[1] This caused minor consternation. "Then the other Doctors cried upon me, the one here, the other there, that I should remember myself and not to cast myself away after this manner. For to read the roll, said they, was but a small thing, and I was never the worse man. And I should see that my Lord Cardinal should be good and gracious unto me, and they would all speak for me."[2] The agony of decision found Barnes torn in two quite different directions: his first thought was to burn rather than to abjure, but he could not hold to that high resolve. He gave in at last and agreed to read the document of submission. The doors were thrown open and for the first time the crowd was brought in while he read the form of abjuration, "adding nothing to it, nor saying one word that might make for mine excuse".[3] Then he subscribed it with his name as well as with a cross and knelt down to receive absolution from the Bishop of Bath. But there was no word of absolution until he had first sworn to fulfil the penance which would then be enjoined. "So did I swear," he wrote, "not yet suspecting but these men had had some crumb of charity within them."[4] He was then sent back to the Fleet, having been told that he must make public penance the next day at St. Paul's.

Thus on Sunday morning, February 11th, at eight o'clock, Barnes and four of the five German merchants, each with a faggot in his hand, were brought out of the Fleet by the Warden and Knight-Marshall with their bills and glaives and tip-staves.[5] They were marched to St. Paul's, which was "so full that no man could get in",[6] and made to stand before Wolsey, who sat on a throne in purple splendour on a dais at the head of the stairs. There were "six and thirty abbots, mitred priors, and bishops", as well as "chaplains and spiritual doctors in gowns of damask and satin".[7] The Bishop of Rochester preached a sermon against Luther while large baskets filled with Luther's works

---

[1] Barnes, op. cit. [2] Ibid. [3] Ibid., pp. 224–225.
[4] Ibid., p. 225. [5] A glaive was a broad-sword, a kind of halberd.
[6] *Foxe*, Vol. V, p. 418. [7] Ibid., p. 418.

stood within the rails ready for "the great fire".[1] Barnes and the four steel-yard merchants had to kneel down and "ask forgiveness of God, of the Catholic Church, and of the Cardinal's grace."[2] Wolsey retired after Barnes had declared that he had been better handled than he deserved; he walked with a canopy overhead and an escort of robed and mitred prelates as far as the second gate of St. Paul's and then withdrew in state. It was as though he had arranged the whole pageant, golden shoes, red gloves, crosses and all, to mock the man who had dared to mock him; he left the rest of that day's work to the other bishops. Thus they sat down again while the Warden of the Fleet and the Knight-Marshall led Barnes and the merchants to the rood at the north door of St. Paul's. There the fire was kindled, the books were burned, and they went round three times while their faggots were thrown into the flames. The Bishop of Rochester then absolved them and declared that they had been received into the Church again. But if Barnes had hoped to return to Cambridge in freedom, he was disappointed. They were sent back to the Fleet to await Wolsey's "farther pleasure";[3] but they had the freedom of the prison, and their friends were allowed access to them.

Six months later, that is about August 1526, Barnes was transferred from the Fleet to the house of the Austin Friars in London, where he was "a free prisoner".[4] He was not inactive. It was during that year that John Tyball and Thomas Hilles, two Lollards from Steeple Bumpstead, found Barnes and a small group of friends reading Tyndale's New Testament. This was the first and, as yet, the only Reformation book to have been printed in the English language. They showed Barnes their copy of John Wycliffe's Bible, but he declared that Tyndale's New Testament was "of much cleaner English".[5] The two Lollards secured copies of Tyndale's New Testament from Barnes: Hilles said that they cost three shillings each and that they were bought "about Whitsun"; Tyball declared that they were three shillings and two pence each and that they were purchased at Michaelmas.[6] There was also another incident in his London

[1] *Foxe*, op. cit., p. 418. [2] Ibid.
[3] Barnes, *Works*, p. 225. [4] *Foxe*, Vol. V, p. 419.
[5] Strype, *Ecclesiastical Memorials*, i, ii, p. 55.
[6] Mozley, *Tyndale*, pp. 348–349.

imprisonment which reveals his activity in the spread of Tyndale's writings. Richard Bayfield, a Benedictine monk in Bury St. Edmunds, was one of his early converts. Barnes had rescued him from duress in the Abbey prison and sent him to Cambridge where he became a member of Corpus Christi. Bayfield came to London during 1528 and two godly laymen named Stacy and Maxwell hid him until he could cross the Channel. Barnes had given him a copy of the New Testament in Latin, and the others now gave him a copy of Tyndale's New Testament in English. Foxe says that they also gave him Tyndale's *Wicked Mammon* and *The Obedience of A Christian Man*.[1] Both these books were published during 1528, and this bears out Foxe's claim that Bayfield was in contact with Barnes before he left London. At last, "two years and three quarters" after his trial,[2] that is, about October 1528, Barnes sent Parnell and some other laymen to speak on his behalf to the Bishop of London. Tunstall dismissed them so coldly, "that when they came home there was not one of them that durst give me so much bread and meat as he durst give his dog, nor yet speak one word to me."[3] Instead of the hoped-for release, he was transferred to the Northampton Friary "there to remain as in a perpetual prison".[4]

Foxe goes on to say that "Master Horne who had brought him up and was his special friend" warned him that a writ would soon be sent down to have him burned.[5] This meant that he was now to be treated as a relapsed heretic, and it may have been a result of the information which had been gleaned from the trial of Tyball and Hilles on April 28th that year. On Horne's advice, Barnes made up his mind to escape. He wrote letters to say that he proposed to drown himself, and he left a note with his clothes to say where they should search for his body; then he vanished. For a week they dragged the river while he fled in poor man's guise to London. Then he crossed the Channel, and by Christmas 1528 he was safe in Antwerp. Barnes knew that the suicide of a heretic was the kind of material which lent itself to strong propaganda, but not all the authorities were so quickly deceived. "The Bishop of London," wrote Barnes, ". . . said . . . that I was not dead, (for I dare say his conscience did not reckon me such a heretic

[1] *Foxe*, Vol. IV, p. 681.   [2] Barnes, *Works*, p. 225.
[3] Ibid.   [4] Ibid.   [5] *Foxe*, Vol. V, p. 419.

that I would have killed myself . . .), but I was, said he, in Amsterdam, where I had never been in my life."[1] Tunstall was said to have sworn that "my Lord Cardinal would have me again, or it should cost him a great sum of money".[2] Tunstall was at least right when he declared that Barnes would yet be found alive, for it was Barnes who had the last retort on this question: "I am a simple poor wretch and worth no man's money in the world", he said; ". . . And to burn me or to destroy me can not so greatly profit them. For when I am dead, the sun and the moon, the stars and the element, water and fire, yea, and also stones, shall defend this cause against them rather than the verity should perish".[3] Those words are not without true dignity and eloquence; but the threat of burning was to haunt him from then on to the end.

Barnes had proved a stormy petrel ever since he had first adhered to the new faith, and "his ill-starred attempt" at swift reform had ended in ignominy.[4] His trial had stirred into action all the latent hostility of the authorities, and a fresh hunt was on. In the early months of 1526, Bilney, Arthur and Latimer were compromised and brought before Wolsey, and in 1527 Bilney was thrown into prison, put on trial and forced to abjure and carry a faggot to the Cross at St. Paul's. Then in February 1528, John Clark, Frith and other men in Oxford were thrown into prison, and by August, four of them had succumbed and died as a result of its rigours. Bayfield and Frith crossed the Channel and threw in their lot with Tyndale; and now Barnes had broken penance and there was no room for him in England. He must have reached Antwerp at much the same time as Frith did, and it is clear that he was in touch with Tyndale. Nothing more can be traced of his movements until the summer of 1530, but by then he had crossed the Low Countries and was in the home of Bugenhagen (Pomeranus) at Wittenberg in Saxony.[5] Foxe says that here he was "made strong in Christ and got favour with the learned in Christ" such as Luther, Pomeranus, Justus Jonas and Melancthon.[6] There was a bond between Barnes and Luther in the fact that they had both once belonged to the Augustinian

---

[1] Barnes, *Works*, p. 215.
[2] Ibid.
[3] Ibid.
[4] Darby, *Latimer*, p. 34.
[5] Mozley, *Tyndale*, p. 150 fn.
[6] *Foxe*, Vol. V, p. 419.

Order, and Barnes was to provide the main personal connection between the English and Lutheran Reformers. He was received by them with much kindness, and the spirit of that friendship was to survive his death. He now took the name of Antonius Anglus and gave himself up to writing. His first work in Latin was a useful book of patristic quotations with the title *Sententiae ex doctoribus collectae quas papistae valde hodie damnant*. His next work was published in German by Bugenhagen late in 1531; it was a short treatment of nineteen Principal Articles of Faith, and it clearly shows how much he had learned through his intercourse with the Lutheran theologians.

He had another manuscript which was ready by the month of September 1531; this was his *Supplication to King Henry VIII*, an attempt to rehabilitate himself in the eyes of the King. He left Wittenberg and travelled to Magdeburg; then he went to Lubeck and at length to Antwerp, where the *Supplication* was put through the press at the same time as Tyndale's *Answer* to More and Frith's work on Purgatory.[1] This book by Barnes was a vehement indictment of the proceedings which had been brought against him for heresy and it contains "an interesting but prolix account" of his treatment at the hands of Wolsey and the Bishops.[2] Wolsey was now dead and Barnes knew that he could write without too much restraint. He knew that his attack on the temporal claims of the Pope would have its own appeal, and he hotly argued that the Scriptures teach true obedience to the Prince as to the head of the State. "We poor men must be accused of insurrection and treason", he wrote, "we must bear all the blame, we must be driven out of the realm, we must be burned for it, and as God knoweth, there is no people under heaven that . . . more diligently doth preach against disobedience than we do."[3] Barnes felt the keen edge of this charge in his own case. "The very truth is", he said, "I can suffer through God's grace all manner of wrongs, injuries and slanders; but to be called an heretic against God or a traitor against my prince, he liveth not but I will say, he lieth."[4] He asked Henry to judge between himself and the Bishops as to who was the more faithful

[1] Mozley, *Tyndale*, p. 201 fn.
[2] *Writings of John Frith and Robert Barnes* (R.T.S.), p. 96.
[3] Barnes, *Works*, p. 190.   [4]Ibid., p. 201.

to God and the King's Grace,[1] and he finished with a peroration
of force and power: "And as for me, I do promise them here
by this present writing, and by the faith that I owe to Christ
Jesus, and by that fidelity that I owe to my prince that if they
will be bound to our noble Prince after the manner of his law
and after good conscience and right, that they shall do me no
violence nor wrong, but discuss and dispute these articles and all
other that I have written, after the holy Word of God and by
Christ's holy Scripture, with me, then will I, as soon as I may
know it, present myself unto our most noble prince . . . that I
will either prove these things by God's grace against you all or
else I will suffer at His Grace's pleasure."[2]

On November 14th, 1531, Stephen Vaughan sent Cromwell
two new books from Antwerp: they were Tyndale's *Exposition
of the First Epistle of St. John* and Barnes' *Supplication*. Vaughan
was disturbed by the latter and wrote strongly: "Such a piece
of work as I yet have not seen one like unto it; I think he shall
seal it with his blood."[3] He went on to urge his patron to bring
Barnes back into England so that he could speak for himself,
for "when men be secretly examined, the world murmureth and
hath thereby cause to deem wrongfully".[4] Cromwell knew that
Henry now had need of Protestant arguments in his struggle with
Rome, and the King was ready to use them as far as they served
his turn. A safe conduct had been proposed for Tyndale in
January and for John Frith in May that year, but each had been
refused. There were other reasons why both Tyndale and Frith
rejected the overture from England, but it was also true that
safe conducts might be broken again as they had been broken
before. John Huss had been burned at Constance in spite of such
a safe conduct; Luther had not been far from the same fate at
Worms. But in response to Vaughan's appeal, Barnes was
offered a safe conduct for six weeks and he set out at once for
England. He reached London before December 21st, 1531, and
seems to have received some kind of a hearing. He went about
among his friends dressed in the guise of a merchant so as not
to attract notice; but he could not hide his movements from
More's agents, and they tracked him down to his host's house

[1] Barnes, op. cit., p. 205. [2] Ibid., pp. 215–216.
[3] Mozley, *Tyndale*, p. 206. [4] Ibid.

at "the Sign of the Bottell in Botolf's wharf".[1] Barnes failed to win the King's goodwill, but he seized the chance to write one letter at least in self-defence; since he could not call on More in person, he wrote to say that he had been wrongly accused on the subject of his sacramental teaching.[2] This letter proved even more effective than Barnes could have foreseen and was to have its own special bearing on the controversy which was soon to break out. Meanwhile he could do no more and he left England in safety by January 22nd, 1532.

In the early months of 1532, the first three books of More's *Confutation of Tyndale* were published, and the Preface shows how grave a risk Barnes had run during his visit to England. "Then have we, now come forth, the book of Friar Barnes, sometime Doctor in Cambridge," wrote More, "which was for heresy before this time abjured and is at this day comen to the realm by safe conduct which at his humble suit the King's Highness of his blessed disposition condescended to grant him to the end that if there might yet any spark of grace be founden in him, it might be kept kindled and increased rather than the man to be cast away.... If God give him the grace to amend, every good man will be glad thereof.... But as for hence, he shall I am sure have leave to depart safe according to the King's safe conduct. And yet hath he so demeaned himself since his coming hither that he hath clearly broken and forfeited his safe-conduct, and lawfully might be burned for his heresies, if we would lay his heresies and his demeanour sith his coming hither, both twain, unto his charge. But let him go this once, for God shall find his time full well."[3] More seems to have thought that he had violated the terms of safe conduct and that he had out-stayed the time limit. But there is an interesting sidelight on these facts in two other works of the time. In 1532 More published his Reply to Frith's *Treatise on The Sacrament* and referred to the letter which he had received from Barnes "at his last being here".[4] In 1533 Frith finished his *Answer* to More and he observed with some asperity: "I think it was more wisdom for him twice to have written to you than once to have come and tell you of it. For it was plainly told him that you had conspired his death, and

---

[1] Rupp, op. cit., p. 40.
[2] More, *Apology*, see Note, p. 286.
[3] Ibid., see Note, p. 258.
[4] Frith, *Works*, p. 155.

that notwithstanding his safe conduct, . . . and for that cause, he was compelled both being here to keep himself secretly, and also privily to depart the realm."[1] Did More claim that he had violated the terms of safe conduct? Frith would reply to that as well. "I myself read the safe conduct that came unto him which had but only this one condition annexed unto it, that if he came before the Feast of Christmas then next ensueing, he should have free liberty to depart at his pleasure. And this condition I know was fulfilled. How should he then forfeit his safe conduct?"[2]

Barnes had made his one great venture into print in English with his *Supplication*; but that work did not end with its account of his Disputation with the Bishops. This was followed by a kind of doctrinal appendix in which he dealt with ten propositions and drew support from the writings of the Fathers as well as the text of Scripture. Eight of the ten dealt with subjects which had appeared in his German volume on the Principal Articles of Faith, and they furnish the best commentary on his contribution to the theology of the English Reformation. The first chapter was called "Only Faith justifieth before God", and this is the finest piece of writing in all his works. It was the most able exposition of the doctrine on the part of any early English writer, and it reflects clearly how much he had learned from Luther. Broughton Knox points out that Catholic opponents of the Reformation were willing to allow faith a place, but not sole place, in their doctrine of justification; but the Reformation Divines held that the word "only" was an essential addition to the word "faith". Luther had introduced this word into the text of the German Bible (Romans 3:28), and had argued that it was an essential addition in order to preserve the plain meaning of the Greek text. But those who were opposed to his teaching fastened upon this word as a wilful innovation; they gazed at it, so Luther said, as a cow at a new barn door.[5] Barnes summed up their outlook in one graphic sentence: "You were wont to cry for Sola, sola, sola, only, only, only."[4] He was anxious to show that the word was not an innovation, but that it had both Scriptural and Patristic authority. Thus he quoted the comments of Ambrose and Origen on the text in dispute (Romans 3:28), and then de-

[1] Frith, op. cit., p. 155.   [2] Ibid., p. 156.
[3] Knox, op. cit., p. 64.   [4] Barnes, *Works*, p. 230.

clared: "Here have you Sola, sola, sola, so that you need not
cry no more for sola."[1] Barnes used this word "only" to show
the place of faith in justification, and it occurs many times in the
course of his writings. Thus he declared that "the Scripture doth
say that faith alonely justifieth, because that it is that thing alonely
whereby I do hang of Christ. And by my faith only am I partaker
of the merits and mercy purchased by Christ's blood, and faith
it is alonely that receives the promises made in Christ."[2]

Barnes valued this doctrine of *sola fide* because it ascribed pre-
eminence to Christ as the Saviour, and he preserved the balance
between the subjective character of faith and the objective
character of Christ's merits.[3] "You grant", he wrote, "that He
is a Saviour, but you deny that He is alonely the Saviour. I pray
you, wherefore was He born? To justify us in part? To redeem
us in part? To do satisfaction for part of our sins?... Say what
you will, if you give not all and fully and alonely to one Christ,
then deny you Christ.... The Lamb hath alonely died for us.
The Lamb hath alonely shed His blood for us. The Lamb hath
alonely redeemed us. These things hath He alone done. Now if
these be sufficient, then hath He alone made satisfaction, and is
alonely worthy to be our Redeemer and Justifier."[4] St. Paul
took more pains to prove this than he took with any other
doctrine; those who deny it are described as "the crooked enemies
of Christ's blood".[5] It is not that there is any merit in faith
itself; it is altogether the gift of God. "First cometh God for the
love of Christ Jesus, alonely of His mere mercy, and giveth us
freely the gift of faith whereby we do believe God and His holy
Word and stick fast unto the promises of God."[6] Such faith is
more than mere assent to a creed, "for it must come from heaven,
and not from the strength of reason; it must also make me
believe that God the Maker of heaven and earth is not alonely
a Father, but also my Father."[7] This strong note of personal
assurance was in pointed contrast with the mediaeval uncertainties.
"To this stick I fast," he wrote, "that He is not alonely my
Father, but also a merciful Father, yea, and that unto me merciful,
and so merciful that He will not impute my sins unto me, though

[1] Barnes, op. cit., p. 230.
[2] Ibid., pp. 241–242.
[3] Rupp, op. cit., p. 167.
[4] Barnes, *Works*, p. 227.
[5] Ibid., p. 227.
[6] Ibid., p. 235.
[7] Ibid., p. 235.

they be never so great, so long as I hang on the blessed blood of Christ."[1] Our righteousness means nothing less than remission of sins and is totally different from that of the Schoolmen: "Our justice is not, as the school men teacheth, a formal justice which is by fulfilling of the Law, deserved of us, for then our justification were not of grace and of mercy; but of deserving and of duty. But it is a justice that is reckoned and imputed unto us for the faith in Christ Jesus, and it is not of our deserving, but clearly and fully of mercy imputed unto us."[2]

The next treatise bore the title: *What the Church is, and who be thereof, and whereby men may know her.* This tract seems to have been inspired by the recollection of the troubles he had incurred at the hands of Bishops, and it was marred by the intemperance of its attacks on Wolsey and Fisher. Signs and tokens were not enough to make the Church. "Nay, nay, my Lords, it will not be," he wrote; "but they that believe that Christ hath washed them from their sins and stick fast unto His merits and to the promise made to them in Him only, they be the Church of God."[3] The true Church is invisible just as faith is invisible, and "all the whole rabble" of bishops and friars could not alter this fact.[4] He called up the image of Wolsey in words that were reminiscent of his sermon at St. Edward's Church in Cambridge: "It is plain that all your exterior signs with all your holy ornaments as your holy mitres, your holy cross staves, your holy pillars, pole axes, your holy red gloves, your holy ouches and your holy rings, your holy anointed fingers, your holy vestments, your holy chalices and your holy golden shoes, yea, and take also to help you S. Thomas of Canterbury's holy shoe, with all the holy boots of holy monks, and all these together can not make one crumb of holiness in you, nor help you one prick forward that you may be within this Church."[5] He proved that Church Councils may err, and he argued that "a private person, having Scriptures for him, is to be heard before the Pope and also the Council, having no Scriptures for them".[6] But he also argued that the Church of God is indefectible: "The very true Church . . . can not err."[7] This true Church may be known by sure signs of God's grace: "Where the Word of God is truly and

---

[1] Barnes, op. cit., p. 235.   [2] Ibid., p. 242.   [3] Ibid., p. 244.
[4] Ibid., p. 244.   [5] Ibid., p. 246.   [6] Ibid., p. 248.   [7] Ibid., p. 248.

perfectly preached without the damnable dreams of men, and where it is well of the hearers received, and where we see good works that do openly agree with the doctrine of the Gospel, these be good and sure tokens whereby we may judge that there be some men of holy Church."[1] And he summed up with a phrase which has its echo in the Prayer Book: "Now have I declared unto you what is holy Church, that is, the congregation of faithful men throughout all the world, and whereby she is holy, that is, by Christ's holiness and by Christ's blood, and also what is the cause that she can not err, because that she keepeth herself so fast to the Word of God."[2]

This tract provoked the special indignation of Sir Thomas More because of its violent diatribe against his friend Bishop Fisher, and he denounced Barnes both in the eighth book of his *Confutation of Tyndale* and in his *Apology*. He wrote fiercely against the "false blasphemous heresies by Tyndale and Barons",[3] but he recognised a marked distinction between them in ability. "As for Friar Barons," he wrote, "I perceive by sundry ways that the brotherhood speak much less of him (than of Tyndale), either for that they find him in their own minds well and fully answered, or else that they take him in respect of Tyndale but for a man of a second sort."[4] More glanced at his academic standing when he spoke of him as "sometime Doctor in Cambridge", and once or twice he called him "Doctor Barnes" without comment.[5] But his normal designation was just "Friar Barons", and he argued that this was all that Barnes deserved: for Barnes had been declared unfit to teach and was "by the Church for false teaching forbidden to teach".[6] This must refer to his trial in 1526, and the prohibition was still in force.

The point which had hurt most of all was the accusation by Barnes that the lives of the clergy were a reproach to the Gospel, and More's sorrowful admissions make it painfully evident that this was all too true. More said in reply that he would condemn evildoers in every class, but he would not impute their sins to the whole class from which they came: he had ever held it as his duty to refrain from accusations against the two consecrated orders of princes and priests. "And over this," he wrote, "I can

---

[1] Barnes, op. cit., p. 249.   [2] Ibid., p. 249.   [3] More, *Apology*, p. 2.
[4] Ibid., p. 4.   [5] Ibid., see Note, p. 258.   [6] Ibid., p. 46.

not see what need there were that I should rail upon the clergy and reckon up all their faults. For that part hath Tyndale played, and Friar Barnes, both already, and left nothing for me to say therein, not though my mind were sore set theron. They have with truth and lies together laid the living of bad, to bad and good both."[1] Barnes then wrote *Another Declaration wherein he answereth M. More*. "After that cometh M. More," he wrote, "and he layeth to my charge that I counted all the spirituality to be naught because he would make my name somewhat odious unto them. But verily he doth me great wrong; for it was never my meaning, nor yet my saying. But mine intent was to declare that neither the Pope nor his College of Cardinals nor yet all the Bishops in the world ... did make holy Church because of their names, or else for their long gowns or for their shaven crowns, or else anointed fingers, nor yet for any other exterior things.... But yet I did grant and also do now confess many good men to have shaven crowns and also long gowns. But yet for these things, they were never the more of the Church. ... The Church which I did speak of ... is a fellowship specially gathered in the unity of faith."[2]

This was followed by *What the keys of the Church be, and to whom they were given*. Barnes was better versed in the great Schoolmen than most of the early English Reformation Divines, and this tract was a strong refutation of the teaching of Duns Scotus. "Duns and all his scholars", wrote Barnes, "say that these keys be nothing else but an authority given to priests whereby they give sentence that heaven must be opened to this man and shut unto the other: so that heaven is opened and shut at the sentence of the priest.... Who could have invented such a doctrine but the devil himself? Who can speak greater heresy than this is?"[3] The true key is "nothing else but the holy Word of God whereby that we receive faith into our hearts.... This is the thing only whereby that our conscience is loosed and made free from sin."[4] This is all that men have; there is no other kind of key: "In that is all the might and power to loose our sins, and man is but a minister and a servant unto this Word."[5] But did not the Lord give men power to bind and loose? He did indeed.

[1] More, op. cit., p. 55.   [2] Barnes, *Works*, pp. 252–253.
[3] Ibid., p. 257.   [4] Ibid., p. 258.   [5] Ibid., p. 259.

"They did bind with the Word when it was not believed; they did loose by the Word when it was believed: thus did they by one Word preach both salvation and damnation; but unto divers men."[1] But were not the keys of heaven meant for one man only? No; he did but receive them for the whole Church of Christ: "And they be the common treasure of the Church, and belong no more to one man than to another."[2] But this pure and wholesome doctrine had been abused for the sake of money. "For money you sell man, wife, maid and child. . . . If you did not these shameful deeds, I should have none occasion to make this shameful writing. Take you away the cause, and I will take away the writing. Yea, you are not so content but you sell Christ, you sell the blessed Sacrament of His flesh and blood, . . . you sell all other Sacraments. Briefly you sell all manner of thing that ever He left on earth to the comfort of man's soul, and all for money. Yea, and not so content, but you make also more laws and more statutes, and dispense with them for money, and all these things do you by the authority of the keys."[3] The tract concludes with a damning sentence: "Wherefore I can no more say unto you but the words of our Master Christ, Woe be unto you, hypocrites, the which shut heaven gates . . . you have taken away the key of science and neither enter in yourself nor yet suffer other that come to enter in. Now let me see how all your keys and all your power can assoyle you from this same woe that our Master Christ doth here lay unto you. This Word of God bindeth you to everlasting damnation: let us see if your picklock can open this lock. Then will I say that you have the keys of heaven, or else not."[4]

Then came *Free Will of Man after the fall of Adam of his natural strength can do nothing but sin before God*. Barnes, like all the early English Reformation Divines, held the doctrine of absolute predestination; and this was before the rise of Calvin. And he did so because the fact of God's choice goes hand in hand with the fact of *sola fide*. Barnes shows that the error of Duns Scotus was in fact the Pelagian error, and that it lacked all true understanding of the function of grace. "Here is also to be noted that the Pelagians and our Duns men agree all in one," he wrote, "for they both

---

[1] Barnes, op. cit., p. 260.   [2] Ibid., pp. 261–262.
[3] Ibid., p. 265.   [4] Ibid., p. 266.

say that the grace of God doth help man's good purpose. . . . But the truth is contrary, for there is no good purpose in man, no good disposition nor good intent, but all is against goodness . . . until that God of His mere mercy cometh, and giveth grace, . . . and giveth him will to will goodness, yea, and that when he thought nothing of goodness."[1] Pelagius had argued that God would command nothing that is impossible; and this led him to the view that man's own efforts rather than God's mercy are the essentials in our salvation. But Barnes claimed that he had "proved by invincible Scriptures and by Doctors of great authority that free will of his natural strength, without a special grace, can do nothing but abide in sin".[2] Grace had come to hold an ambiguous place in mediaeval theology. It was said that merit did not attach to works unless they sprang from grace; thus the need of grace was prior to the thought of merit. But the Schoolmen taught that merit caused an increase of grace, and their emphasis fell on the thought that the possession of grace was the result of the merit-earning efforts of man's own will.[3] Barnes held that Duns could not decide whether God's choice was an act of His own goodwill or a result of man's merit, and he appealed to the text of St. Paul to prove that the cause lies only in God's goodwill. It is true that we need faith to believe that He is "most wise, most righteous, and most merciful; and that He is so in all His dealings with men".[4] But such faith is the means of great comfort: "If you did believe that He were good, righteous and merciful, it were a great comfort for you that the election stood all only by His will. . . . But you have no faith, and therefore must you needs mistrust God, and of that fall you to invent causes of election of your own strength."[5]

One more treatise must be mentioned: *That by God's Word it is lawful for priests that hath not the gift of chastity to marry wives.* Luther's marriage had made this a burning question and had evoked Sir Thomas More's special anger. Barnes seems to have written this tract partly in defence of Luther and partly to deny what people were saying about himself. He made it clear that "heaven is neither the price of virginity nor yet of marriage. . . . Virginity is no nearer way to heaven than marriage is."[6] He went

---

[1] Barnes, op. cit., p. 272.   [2] Ibid., p. 274.   [3] Knox, op. cit., p. 80.
[4] Barnes, op. cit., p. 277.   [5] Ibid., p. 279.   [6] Ibid., p. 313.

on to argue that "virginity is a thing alonely that ought to be counselled, but not to be commanded; it is rather a thing of voluntary will than of a precept".[1] Then he referred to a current rumour with some indignation: "There runneth a great voice of me that I have married a wife, and for that cause men doth reckon that I will something prove my wit and also stretch my learning to maintain that priests might have wives. But the very truth is before God and man that I have no wife nor never went about to marry: I thank God of His grace. And of this I have as noble princes as be in Germany to bear me witness, and also many other worshipful and honest men that doth know me and my conversation ... Yea, I dare boldly say, that mine adversaries have not so good testimony that they keep their vow of chastity as I have that I am not married. But all is done to bring me in defamation. Let God provide. Nevertheless, what if I had a wife? Is that so great a crime? ... Will men make more articles of salvation for me than for princes or for other Christian men? ... I do not abstain from a wife because that is evil and unclean to marry; but I have other lawful considerations."[2] So he goes on: "Therefore have I taken this labour on me to write my meaning, and so much the more boldly, because that men have no cause to suspect me that I speak to defend mine own cause, but all only to set out the verity, so God help me. Amen."[3] And the tract ends with a final testimony to the honourable estate of true marriage: "I trust there is no Christian man but he will grant me that matrimony is of God's ordaining and setting: wherefore it must needs be pure and clean."[4]

The one doctrine about which Barnes radically differed from such men as Frith and Tyndale was that of the sacramental presence of Christ. Barnes was a Lutheran as they were Zwinglians. He had stated as one of his Principal Articles that all men should receive the Sacrament in both kinds, but in another Article he had argued that the Body of Christ is truly present in the Sacrament of the Altar. It is little wonder that Sir Thomas More was at first confused by the Lutheran and the Zwinglian doctrines with the result that he said that Zwingli was "the first that brought Barnes' heresy" concerning the Sacrament into Switzer-

[1] Barnes, op. cit., p. 319.   [2] Ibid., p. 330.
[3] Ibid., p. 331.   [4] Ibid., p. 335.

land.[1] When Barnes was in England at the end of 1531, he wrote to More to say that he had been wrongly informed. In 1532, More published his *Reply to Frith's Treatise on the Sacrament* and referred to this letter from Barnes. He then went on to jibe at Frith: "It well contenteth me that Friar Barnes, being a man of more age and of more ripe discretion and a Doctor of Divinity, and in those things better learned than this young man is, abhorreth this young man's heresy in this point as well as he liketh him in many another."[2] But Frith replied that while Barnes might differ from him as to the real nature of the Sacramental Presence, they both agreed on one main point: "In this we both agree, that it ought not to be worshipped; yea, and blessed be God, all the other whom you call heretics. And so both of us do avoid idolatry which you with so great danger do daily commit."[3] Sir Thomas More returned to the subject in the *Apology*; he was anxious to drive this wedge between the Reformers if possible. Thus he declared that Barnes "leaveth out somewhat that Tyndale taketh in, that is to wit, the making of mocks . . . against the Mass and the blessed Sacrament of the Altar".[4] Tyndale had once conferred with Barnes in the hope that they could avoid a breach, but Barnes was as much in Luther's camp on this vexed doctrine as on that of *sola fide*. Tyndale's letter to John Frith in January 1533 shows that he had failed to persuade Barnes not to make it an issue and that he was more than ever anxious that there should be no rift. "Of the presence of Christ's body in the Sacrament," he wrote, "meddle as little as you can that there appear no division among us. Barnes will be hot against you. The Saxons be sore on the affirmative; whether constant or obstinate, I commit it to God."[5]

Barnes left England in January 1532 before his safe conduct expired and settled at Hamburg, where he lodged with Aepinus. In April 1533 he went on to visit Bugenhagen, and in June he enrolled in the Wittenberg register. He used the name Antonius Anglus, but his proper name was written in the margin by his friend Melancthon. Barnes had acquired the goodwill of John Frederick of Saxony and of Frederick I of Denmark, and this was now to stand him in good stead. Henry VIII had now begun

---

[1] More, *Apology*, see Note, p. 286. [2] Frith, *Works*, p. 155.
[3] Ibid., p. 155.   [4] More, *Apology*, p. 4.   [5] Foxe, Vol. V, p. 133.

to seek allies among German courts and cities against Francis I.
Thus in 1534, Christopher Mont and Nicholas Heath were sent
on a tour of the Courts while Thomas Legh was sent to the
cities of Hamburg and Lubeck. Legh was friendly to Barnes, and
on July 12th, 1534, Barnes wrote from Hamburg to urge Henry
to make an alliance with Christian III, the new King of Denmark.[1] Hamburg and Lubeck were induced to send ambassadors
to negotiate with Henry, and three from each city sailed for
London with their eighteen servants. Adam Paceus and Aepinus
were the two chief theologians in the party, and Barnes seems
to have sailed with the Hamburg mission. Rupp points out that
he would clearly have "some utility value" as the friend both of
the Hamburg doctors and the Lubeck merchants.[2] Thus in
August he was back in England, staying with the Lubeck merchants at the Steelyard, and it must have revived curious mem-
ories of the trouble he had shared with some of them in 1526.
Foxe tells us that "Cromwell was his great friend", and speaks of
him as in daily conversation with the Bishops.[3] Perhaps it was
the new doctrine of the Royal Supremacy which was now so
diligently canvassed. But the mission was hardly a success. Henry
showed a growing distaste for the discussions on *sola fide* and the
Sacrament, and Aepinus asked Cromwell to obtain the King's
leave for them to depart.[4] Barnes returned to Hamburg with
Aepinus in January 1535.

Barnes spent the next few months with his friends at Hamburg,
and his name was linked once more with that of Tyndale. There
had been an altercation between Tyndale and George Joye, who
had brought out a reprint of Tyndale's New Testament in August
1534, three months before Tyndale's own revision was published,
and had introduced amendments to the text which Tyndale could
not approve. On February 27th, 1535, Joye published his *Apology*
to defend himself against Tyndale's strictures. He said that he
had gone four times to see Tyndale without any satisfaction. But
on the fourth visit, Tyndale had offered "to submit the dispute
to Doctor Barnes and his fellow Aepinus, pastor of St. Nicholas
Hamburg".[5] But this quarrel broke out just at the time when the

[1] *Dictionary of National Biography*, Robert Barnes.
[2] Rupp, op. cit., p. 42.   [3] *Foxe*, Vol. V, p. 419.
[4] Rupp, op. cit., p. 42.   [5] Mozley, *Tyndale*, p. 279.

Netherlands Government had made its plans for the arrest of Barnes and Joye as well as of Tyndale. It seems that the procurer-general thought that they might visit the great fair at Bergen, which was open to the end of April, and he sent an order for their arrest; but the stad-holder gave a friendly hint to Flegge, who was one of the English merchants. This is disclosed in a letter which George Collins wrote from Antwerp to a merchant friend in London on May 1st. "Sir", he said, "it may please you to understand that the stad-holder of Barrow spake with Mr. Flegge in the church, and he said: Mr. Flegge, there is commission come down from the procurer-general of Brussels to take three Englishmen whereof one is Dr. Barnes. Notwithstanding the stad-holder said: we would be loath to do anything which were displeasure to the company (the merchant adventurers). Wherefore he willeth Mr. Flegge to give Mr. Doctor warning: so that Mr. Flegge took so great kindness withal that he forgot to know who the other two persons shall be. By my next letter I shall write you what be the names of the other two persons. I pray you, show Mr. Doctor hereof."[1] Tyndale suffered arrest at the hands of Henry Phillips on May 21st, but Barnes and Joye escaped. Barnes was back in London by May 27th, and Joye was in Calais on June 4th, trying to make peace through Cromwell so that he could return home to England.

It had been a near thing for Barnes and Joye, but the danger had not come from England. Thomas Tebold wrote to Cranmer during July with a little more news. He was sure that Tyndale would die, and he referred to the fact that Phillips had been employed by the Netherlands Government to take "Dr. Barnes and George Joye with the other".[2] Meanwhile Barnes was engaged in fresh efforts to rehabilitate himself at home. It was hard to avoid the fact that he had been condemned as a heretic and had abjured his own articles of faith; it was even harder to live down the fact that he had broken penance and escaped from lawful restraint. But his quarrel with Church authorities did not exclude him of necessity from the King's grace, and the circumstances in which Henry now found himself made Barnes useful to him as a foreign agent. His residence in Germany and his acceptance by the Lutherans gave him ideal advantages as an

[1] Mozley, op. cit., pp. 307–308.   [2] Ibid., p. 304.

intermediary with rulers and theologians. Cromwell felt free to treat him with "cautious favour"[1] and to employ him in certain delicate overtures. Thus he had left Hamburg in March 1535 to visit Melancthon at Wittenberg and to seek a favourable verdict about the King's divorce and re-marriage. This was not a very hopeful task, since Luther himself had been opposed to the divorce; but the visit was a success and Melancthon wrote a tactful letter to Henry in which he said: "Dr. Antonius disputed with us certain articles, showing the highest faith and diligence, and I have given him my judgment in writing."[2] As a result, Barnes was allowed to return to England and was back in London by May 27th. He had managed so well that the next step was the despatch of a formal mission to the Court of John Frederick of Saxony. Thus at last in July 1535, with the status of a "beloved and faithful chaplain",[3] Barnes was sent to prepare for the arrival of an embassy to be headed by Foxe and Heath; and he carried with him a safe conduct for Melancthon, who was earnestly invited to visit Henry in England.

Barnes had now won recognition at the hands of the King and was to prove himself a good and loyal servant. His arrival in Wittenberg coincided with the publication of his *Vitae Romanorum Pontificum*. This was his main work in Latin and was written in the same bold spirit which marked Luther himself. It was in the cause of diplomacy that the preface was written by Luther and the dedication was inscribed to Henry. On September 6th, 1535, Luther referred to his coming, and he assumed that it was in connection with the proposals about Melancthon's projected journey. But it became clear that Barnes had other matters about which to speak as well. On September 12th, Luther, Justus Jonas, Cruciger and Bugenhagen wrote to ask John Frederick to grant him a "private or close audience, for there is good reason why what he has to say should not be made public before we know where we stand".[4] This no doubt means that Barnes had not only referred to the hope that they would express themselves favourably about the King's divorce, but had informed them of Henry's desire to become a member of the Schmalkaldic League of Protestant Princes. Luther was so sanguine that he wrote that "the King is ready to receive the

[1] Rupp, op. cit., p. 42.　　[2] Ibid., p. 93.　　[3] Ibid., p. 95.　　[4] Ibid., p. 95.

Gospel, and to enter the alliance with the Princes, and to set forth our Apology (the Augsburg Confession) in his Kingdom".[1] On September 13th, John Frederick arranged that Barnes should be received and asked for the presence of Spalatin or Melancthon as the conversation would take place in Latin. It was perhaps September 20th when the meeting was held, and a paper in the Weimar archives records the main points of conversation. Henry was willing to become a member of the Schmalkaldic League and to discuss terms for doctrinal agreement; he was sending further envoys to pursue the matter, and he urged that Melancthon should be sent to England.[2] John Frederick gave a cautious but favourable reply: conversations on issues of theology were to proceed, but the political matters would be deferred until Henry's other envoys arrived.

Weeks of delay ensued, partly as a result of the outbreak of plague, partly because of the shifting currents in Henry's policy. Barnes was deeply concerned until his mind was set at rest by the arrival of the English delegation at Erfurt late in November. Luther himself wrote of their arrival with a sense of relief: "I rejoice that Dr. Antonius has been freed from his anxieties . . . for I too had begun to fear the worst since the other envoys have been so slow".[3] Barnes now gave way to Edward Foxe and Nicholas Heath as the senior members of the delegation, and a series of articles on political issues was exchanged on Christmas Day. Foxe, Heath and Barnes on the one side and John Frederick and Philip of Hesse on the other signed these articles, and the envoys then turned to the need for doctrinal agreement. But Henry was only interested in a favourable verdict on the divorce question, while the German theologians were lured on by the hope that the Augsburg Confession would become the basis for Reformation in England. The death of Catherine on January 7th, 1536, put an end to the need for the King to argue the case of the divorce, and the arguments on the subject of the Augsburg Confession were quite unrelated to the realities of the situation. But the discussions were continued for another three months during which the growing hostility between Charles V and Francis I began to make Henry indifferent to the Schmalkaldic League. It seems that Barnes left for

[1] Rupp, op. cit., p. 96.   [2] Ibid., pp. 96–97.   [3] Ibid., p. 98.

England towards the end of March with a statement which set out the progress of the debate up to that point. On April 1st, Chapuys told Charles V that the English prelates were daily engaged in drawing up an answer to the Lutheran arguments,[1] and on April 9th Luther wrote to Cromwell with a complaint about Barnes who had left without saying farewell.[2] But the abrupt return of Barnes was not his own doing, and it did not disturb his friendship with Luther. Foxe and Heath brought the whole mission to a close in April and returned to England in May.

Thus there was an interruption in the conversations between the English and German theologians after 1536, but Barnes was now allowed to remain in England. He was therefore available to take part in renewed conversations when at last in 1538 a small German delegation came to England. It was led by Francis Burchardt and Frederick Myconius, and the conduct of the debate on the English side was left in the hands of three Bishops and four Doctors, including Heath and Barnes. The most able theologians in these debates were the Germans, but Barnes was the only member of the English party to speak in their support. Conversation was based on the Augsburg Confession and the Wittenberg Articles of 1536: these comprised seventeen articles which had been drawn up by Melancthon, approved by Luther, and accepted by Foxe, Heath and Barnes subject to the King's approval. The English and German theologians soon reached agreement on the doctrine of Original Sin, but there was a vehement argument on the doctrine of Justification by Faith Only. Myconius declared that the Reformed doctrine would have melted in the heat of debate had it not been pure gold. By the month of August, they had compiled thirteen Articles as a result of the discussions; but the conversations stuck fast and the German delegation began to sigh for home. They had been led on by a "bright mirage",[3] and on October 1st they left England. In June 1539, the Act of Six Articles was passed by the English Parliament with Henry's full support. This Act affirmed the doctrines of Transubstantiation, Communion in one kind, clerical celibacy, the absolute obligation of vows of chastity, private masses and auricular confession. This Act made it clear

[1] Rupp, op. cit., p. 109.   [2] Ibid., p. 106.   [3] Ibid., p. 117.

that Cromwell was now moving uncertainly towards his fall,
and it put an end to all hope of a Lutheran alliance. Luther, Justus
Jonas, Bugenhagen and Melancthon had lost all faith in the
spiritual sincerity of the King of England. They had heard Barnes
himself declare more than once that "our King really cares
nothing at all for religion and the Gospel".[1]

Barnes was slender enough in his literary output, but his work
left its mark on the theology of the Reformation. He was served
by no mean gifts of learning and an inborn love of controversy,
and he believed that all doctrine ought to derive support from
the writings of the Fathers as well as the teaching of the Scriptures.
He drew freely from Fathers and Schoolmen, from mediaeval
Canons and Papal Decrees, and he wrote with a verve which was
sure to attract readers. Indeed he wrote as he would preach, and
this accounts for the thrust and freshness of his thought and
language. Barnes and Latimer were both hard-hitting in their
sermons, full of trenchant criticism, outspoken, topical, popular,
vehement. There was always a measure of egotism in Barnes
which could not be concealed; he was theatrical, full of bombast,
always ready to play up to the crowd. He had all the impulsive
excitement which throws discretion overboard, and memory
was seldom to prevent him from making the same mistake
again. Nevertheless Coverdale was to testify in his reply to
John Standish: "I am one of them which have heard him
as oft as ever did ye: and yet as I hope to have my part
of God's mercy in Christ's blood, I never heard him preach
against (the ordinance of Christ's Church) since he was converted first from the wicked papistry."[2] Barnes must have
been free to resume his role as a preacher after his return to
England in March 1536. Thus on July 17th, 1537, Latimer
wrote to Cromwell: "Dr. Barnes, I hear say, preached in London
this day a very good sermon with great moderation and temper-
ance of himself. I pray God continue with him: for then I know
no one man shall do more good."[3] And when Humphrey Monmouth died in 1537, it was found that he had left a sum of money
to provide for the preaching of thirty sermons in All Hallows'
Church at Barking: this was to take the place of the customary

[1] Rupp, op. cit., p. 124.   [2] Coverdale, *Remains*, p. 336.
[3] Latimer, *Sermons and Remains*, p. 378.

trentals (thirty masses for the repose of the soul), and the four preachers were to be Latimer, Taylor, Crome and Barnes.[1] And on Christmas Day in 1537, Latimer wrote again to Cromwell: "Mr. Doctor Barnes hath preached here with me at Hartlebury, and at my request at Winchester, and also at Evesham. Surely he is alone in handling a piece of Scripture, and in setting forth of Christ he hath no fellow."[2] That was high praise indeed; praise from the prince of English preachers.

Barnes was a less likeable character but a much more complex person than some of the leaders in the Reformation. He was not so gentle in spirit as Bilney, nor so true in purpose as Frith, nor so steadfast in courage as Tyndale. But there must have been an attractive quality as well, for he made friends and won converts all through his life. Thomas Parnell and Miles Coverdale were his devoted disciples; Richard Bayfield and Hugh Latimer knew the value of his friendship. Luther and Melancthon received him into their circle; Bugenhagen and Aepinus made him welcome as a guest in their homes. Barnes had owed his soul to Bilney and he voiced a noble protest against his death: "And what fault could ye find in good Master Bilney whom ye have cast away so violently? I dare say there is not one among you that knew him but must commend and praise his virtuous living. And though you had found him with a little fault (the which I think, and he were now alive, should be no fault), alas would you cast away so cruelly so good a man and so true a man both to God and to his King?"[3] We are not told what he thought when he heard of the death of Bayfield in 1531, or John Frith in 1533, or Tyndale in 1536; but his life was haunted by the threat that he would die as they did, and their death at the stake must have left its deep burn on his spirit. It is all the sadder that he should have become involved in the death of Lambert who was also one of Bilney's converts. Some time during 1538 Lambert had a conversation with Taylor about the Lord's Supper. Taylor asked him for a written statement of his views and took it to Barnes. Tyndale's warning to Frith was still applicable: "Barnes will be hot against you."[4] He still adhered to the Lutheran view of the Sacrament, and he induced Taylor to lay the whole affair before

[1] Mozley, op. cit., p. 50. [2] Latimer, op. cit., p. 389.
[3] Barnes, *Works*, p. 193. [4] *Foxe*, Vol. V, p. 133.

Cranmer, who then sent for Lambert and forced him to defend his cause. Lambert is said to have appealed to the King and was brought before him in full court. Henry was ruthless in asking: "Dost thou say that it is the body of Christ, or wilt deny it?" Lambert answered: "I deny it to be the body of Christ".[1] He was condemned and was burned at the stake in November 1538. Thus what began as a private conversation turned into a public matter, and Barnes must share in the blame for his death. Would Barnes forget how he suffered beyond all the others who died as he lifted up "such hands as he had and his finger's ends flaming with fire", and cried aloud with his last strength: "None but Christ! None but Christ"?[2]

Barnes had re-established himself in England since 1536, "but neither his literary efforts nor his diplomatic service" had won him the reward of official church preferment.[3] On August 28th, 1538, Cranmer wrote to Cromwell and asked for a minor office for Barnes: "Your Lordship knoweth full well that hitherto he hath had very small preferment for such pains and travail as he most willingly hath sustained in the King's affairs from time to time."[4] But the future for Barnes was to be shaped by much wider issues. On October 24th, 1537, Queen Jane had died, and for more than two years Henry remained without a wife. Then, early in 1539, Cromwell began to hint at a marriage with Anne of Cleves; this would forge a link with the Duchy of Guelders which had always been a thorn in the side of Charles V. A strong overall alliance between England, Guelders, Denmark and the German Princes would be a threat to the security of Charles in his Netherlands Dominions. Thus the marriage with Anne and an attempt to constitute this alliance became Cromwell's great aim and it was to give Barnes his chance at last. Bugenhagen had been called in to help in the reform of the Church in Denmark, and Barnes and Saint Leger were sent with full diplomatic status on behalf of England. Gardiner objected in the Privy Council to this assignment for a man who was an abjured heretic; but his violent objection was set aside on the ground that Barnes was the best man to foster such a Lutheran alliance.[5] But his mission was a failure, and the news that Parliament had passed the Act

---

[1] *Foxe*, op. cit., p. 230.　　　　[2] Ibid., p. 236.　　　　[3] Rupp, op. cit., p. 43.
[4] Cranmer, *Miscellaneous Writings and Letters*, p. 381.　　[5] Rupp, op. cit., p. 44.

of Six Articles on June 28th filled him with keen apprehension. On July 1st, Latimer of Worcester and Shaxton of Salisbury resigned from their sees and were forbidden to preach. Barnes was afraid to go back to England; when he did go, he was coldly received. Constantine's narrative says that at last he went to Court one Sunday in August: "He was very sad and had licence to depart without speaking with the King."[1] Henry always had a dislike for Barnes with his variable mixture of defiance and submission, and he was to have no more use for him in the affairs of Church or State. Barnes was closely linked with Cromwell, and that statesman's downfall was now at hand.

Cromwell had now begun to stake his last throw on his plans for the marriage with Anne of Cleves. The treaty of marriage was signed on October 6th, 1539, and the marriage took place on January 6th, 1540. But it was a fatal blunder, and Cromwell found himself hemmed in on all sides by the friends of a Catholic reaction. Latimer and Shaxton were placed under restraint, and Cranmer was exposed to new difficulties. All this had dangerous repercussions for Barnes, who soon became involved in a course of events which moved to one "grim end".[2] Thomas Garret, William Jerome and Barnes, men with "a past" and all prone to indiscretion,[3] had been chosen to preach the Lent Sermons at Paul's Cross in 1540. Gardiner intervened the day before the first Sunday in Lent, and preached the first sermon instead of Barnes. Tunstall had preached before Henry on Palm Sunday the year before and had condemned the phrase "by faith alone".[4] This was just a foretaste of the battle which was now to take place, for the Bishop's sermon to mark the first Sunday in Lent 1540 was an angry attack on the doctrine of "faith only". Gardiner drew a parallel between the doctrine of pardons and the claims of *sola fide*, and he argued that they were both alike since they denied the necessity of moral effort to win heaven.[5] "And now that the devil perceiveth that it can no longer be borne to buy and sell heaven by the friars", he said, "he hath excogitated to offer heaven, without works for it, so freely that men shall not need for heaven to work at all, whatsoever opportunity they have to work: marry! if they will have any higher place in

---

[1] Rupp, op. cit., p. 44, fn. 2.   [2] Ibid., p. 44.   [3] Ibid., p. 44.
[4] Knox, op. cit., p. 221.   [5] Ibid., p. 222.

heaven, God will leave no work unrewarded; but as to be in heaven needs no work at all but only belief, only, only, and nothing else."[1] This made it plain that man's effort rather than God's promise was the central factor in his doctrine, and it was a deliberate attempt to gag Barnes in advance. But the Act of Six Articles had not condemned the doctrine of Justification by Faith Only, and Barnes sharpened his sword for the counter-attack.

The next Sunday Barnes took the same text and replied with a popular eloquence which pleased the crowd but which gave much offence to the Bishop. Thus on February 20th, 1540, Bartholomew Traheron wrote to Henry Bullinger: "I must not omit to tell you that the Bishop of Winchester preached a very popish sermon to the great discontent of the people on the first Sunday in Lent, and that he was ably answered by Dr. Barnes on the following Lord's Day with . . . all but universal applause."[2] "But", as Rupp points out, "it was one thing for a bishop to taunt an unfrocked friar with a past, and another for an abjured heretic under a cloud to poke fun at the Lord Bishop of Winchester."[3] Gardiner at once lodged a complaint with the King, who summoned Barnes into his presence the next Friday. When Barnes tried to submit himself, Henry would not let him. "Nay", said the King, "yield thee not to me; I am a mortal man." He stood up, turned to the host, put off his bonnet, and said: "Yonder is the Master of us all, the Author of truth; yield in truth to Him, and that truth will I defend; and otherwise yield thee not unto me."[4] Barnes was thoroughly overawed; he knew that once more as in 1526 he was dangerously close to condemnation and death. But the King did not go to that extreme; he only gave order that the debate between Barnes and Gardiner should be continued in the presence of two divines who would report to him. In the consequent discussion, Gardiner said that he forgave all that was personal and would confine himself to the points at issue. Both men agreed that the work of Christ was supreme, but they differed as to whether faith stands alone or needs love and obedience as well as the essential conditions before sinners can share in the merits of His Passion. Gardiner sketched his

[1] *Foxe*, Vol. V, p. 431.
[2] *Original Letters*, Vol. I, p. 317.
[3] Rupp, op. cit., p. 45.
[4] *Foxe*, Vol. V, p. 431.

argument and gave Barnes a night to think it over. The debate was resumed in the morning and went on for two hours. Gardiner overwhelmed Barnes by the claim that his argument meant that man is justified even before he believes, since faith itself is as much a work as love is. Barnes fell down on his knees, asked the Bishop's pity, praised his learning, and asked for instruction. Gardiner, touched as well as triumphant, offered him a pension if he would come and live with him as his scholar and friend.

The King approved of this plan, and on the Monday, Barnes went to the Bishop's house in London. Gardiner had prepared ten articles to the effect that faith and love are both essential for our acceptance with God. Barnes seems to have faltered for two more days; then he "clean gave over the Bishop".[1] But Henry was incensed at this report and sent for Barnes again. Jerome, Garret and Barnes were all ordered to preach during Easter at St. Mary's Spittal in order to revoke their doctrines in public. Gardiner unwisely chose to attend, and Barnes saw him as he began to make a mild recantation. As soon as this was done, Barnes addressed the Bishop. He called on him "in the face of all the audience" to hold up his hand as a sign that he forgave his past offence.[2] When the Bishop made no response, Barnes called on him again to lift up his hand as a sign of charity and forgiveness. Gardiner was embarrassed and angry; but he held up his hand. Barnes then offered prayer and entered on a sermon which was meant to restate in an ambiguous way all that he had just revoked. Jerome and Garret did likewise, and the Lord Mayor was so angry that he wanted to send them at once to prison. But they were left alone for the moment, and Barnes wrote a letter to Aepinus "from the house of Thomas Parnell" bearing a date as late as May 21st. "You will learn from the bearer of this letter", he wrote, "all the circumstances respecting myself more clearly than I can write them. . . . Write I entreat you to Philip (Melancthon) in my name, as soon as possible, that he come not hither before he receives a letter from me; for I would not have him exposed to danger by reason of any hopes he builds upon me. For I have been deceived myself. . . . A fierce controversy is going on between . . . Gardiner and myself respecting justi-

[1] *Foxe*, op. cit., Vol. V, p. 433.   [2] Ibid., Vol. V, p. 420.

fication by faith and purgatory. He holds that the blood of Christ cleanseth only from past sins previous to baptism, but that those committed since are blotted out partly by the merits of Christ and partly by our own satisfactions. . . . But I on the other hand, in opposition to all these things, vindicate the efficacy of the blood of Jesus Christ my Lord; but hitherto I stand alone in doing it. For although many persons approve my statements, yet no one stands forward except Latimer."[1]

But a report soon came before Henry, and by order of the Council, Jerome, Garret and Barnes were all sent to the Tower. This must have been before the end of May, for a letter during that month written by John Butler refers to their imprisonment.[2] Gardiner afterwards denied that he was a party to this action on the ground that at that time he had no access to the Council; but though he may never have meant to bring about their death, he had set things going which led to it, as Barnes himself had done in the case of Lambert. Cromwell could help no more, for his own hour had come; on June 10th he found himself under arrest and in the Tower. The King now had recourse to the terrible procedure known to history as an Act of Attainder: a procedure first developed during the Wars of the Roses as a means of putting a man to death by an Act of Parliament regardless of how his case might stand in law. Thus Cromwell was condemned unheard; so too Jerome, Garret and Barnes were all condemned without trial and without cause of death being shown. On July 7th, Convocation ruled that Henry's marriage with Anne of Cleves was null and void, and the last link with the German Princes and theologians was destroyed. Henry then announced a general amnesty for heresies and felonies which had occurred before July 1st, 1540; it went on to declare that "no further persecution should take place for religion, and that those in prison should be set at liberty".[3] Latimer and Shaxton probably owed their lives to the King's act of pardon; Cromwell, Garret, Jerome and Barnes were all denied its grace by name. "I could never ascertain, though I have made diligent inquiry," wrote Richard Hilles, "why these three Gospellers were excepted from the general pardon."[4] Luther supposed that it was on the ground

---

[1] *Original Letters*, Vol. II, pp. 616–617.   [2] Ibid., p. 632.
[3] Darby, *Hugh Latimer*, p. 162.   [4] *Original Letters*, Vol. I, p. 209.

of their opposition to the divorce from Anne of Cleves; and this may have been true.[1] Thus on July 28th, Cromwell went to the block and on July 30th, 1540, the three preachers were dragged on a hurdle through the streets of London from the Tower to Smithfield. "They were tied to one stake" and were burned as heretics.[2] At the same time and not far from the same place, three others, Featherstone, Abel and Powell, were hanged, drawn and quartered because they had denied the Royal Supremacy.

Barnes was allowed to speak while he prepared himself for the ordeal by fire and he never preached with more telling effect in St. Edward's Church at Cambridge or at St. Paul's Cross in London. "I am come hither to be burned as a heretic," he said, "and you shall hear my belief whereby you shall perceive what erroneous opinions I hold. God I take to record, I never, to my knowledge, taught any erroneous doctrine but only those things which Scripture led me unto. . . . With all diligence evermore did I study to set forth the glory of God, the obedience to our sovereign Lord the King, and the true and sincere religion of Christ. And now hearken to my faith."[3] The Protestation which followed summed up his faith and teaching with admirable simplicity. "I believe", he said in the course of this statement, "that this His death and passion was the sufficient ransom for the sin of all the world . . . and that there is none other satisfaction unto the Father but this His death and passion only; and that no work of man did deserve anything of God, but only His passion, as touching our justification: for I know the best work that ever I did is impure and unperfect."[4] And with this, he spread out his hands and asked God to forgive him all his sins. "Wherefore", he went on to say, "I trust in no good work that ever I did, but only in the death of Christ. I do not doubt but through him to inherit the kingdom of heaven."[5] This was Barnes at his best; it was the clear authentic utterance of his ultimate convictions at a time when he stood on the threshold of death. Here was a profound sense of sin, and the absence of all merit; here was a clear recognition of the merits of Christ's Passion, and a humble faith in Him as the one Saviour; here was forgiveness; here was

---

[1] *Dictionary of National Biography*, Robert Barnes.
[2] *Original Letters*, Vol. I, p. 209.   [3] *Foxe*, Vol. V, p. 434.
[4] Ibid., p. 434.   [5] Ibid., p. 435.

assurance. Such a Protestation was not to die; it was widely circulated after his death and was highly valued by the friends of Reformed teaching. As a result, it was answered line by line in a work written by John Standish. On December 7th, 1540, Miles Coverdale had a copy of this work in his hands and at once set out to reply in his *Confutation of the Treatise of John Standish*. This was the last service of a faithful convert and friend for the man whom he had known and revered since his days at Cambridge.

Barnes then asked the sheriff if he knew why he was to die, seeing that he had not been tried nor shown any cause of condemnation; but the sheriff could only answer "No". "Then said he, 'Is there here any man else that knoweth wherefore I die or that by my preaching hath taken any error? Let them now speak and I will make them answer.' And no man answered. Then said he, 'Well, I am condemned by the law to die, and as I understand by an Act of Parliament; but wherefore I can not tell, but belike for heresy, for we are like to burn. But they that have been the occasion of it, I pray God forgive them as I would be forgiven myself. And Dr. Stephen, Bishop of Winchester that now is, if he have sought or wrought this my death either by word or deed, I pray God forgive him, as heartily, as freely, as charitably, and without feigning, as ever Christ forgave them that put Him to death.'"[1] Then he took the sheriff by the hand and went on to say: "Bear me witness, and my brothers, that we die Christianly and charitably; and I pray you and all the people to pray for us."[2] Jerome and Garret spoke briefly in the same vein, and all three joined in prayer. Then they kissed each other, took each other by the hand, and prepared to die. Gentle, patient, unfaltering, they stood tied to one stake in the midst of the flames. "They remained in the fire without crying out," so it was affirmed, "but were as quiet and patient as though they had felt no pain."[3] John Bale testified that even his enemies agreed that "Barnes never moved".[4] Coverdale asserted in answer to Standish: "Yea, even by your own pen have ye brought it to pass that it shall not be forgotten till the world's end what a Christian testimony and last will Dr. Barnes made at his death,

---

[1] *Foxe*, op. cit., p. 435. [2] Ibid., p. 421.
[3] *Original Letters*, Vol. I, p. 209. [4] John Bale, *Select Works*, p. 586.

and how patiently he forsook this life."[1] We may safely believe that the three men who were in the midst of that fire were not alone: but did many have eyes to see the Son of Man at their side in the flames until they heard the call to come forth and stand before Him who is King of kings and Lord of lords?

[1] Coverdale, *Remains*, p. 328.

BIBLIOGRAPHY

ROBERT BARNES, *The Works of the Excellent Martyr of Christ, John Frith, and the Works of Doctor Barnes,* 1573

ROBERT BARNES, *Writings of John Frith and of Dr. Robert Barnes (R.T.S.)*

JOHN FOXE, *The Acts and Monuments of John Foxe;* edited by Stephen Cattley (8 Vols), 1841

Dictionary of National Biography, Robert Barnes (Vol. 1), 1950

A. I. TAFT, *The Apologye of Sir Thomas More, Knyght;* edited with Introduction and Notes by A. I. Taft, 1930

E. G. RUPP, *Studies in the Making of the English Protestant Tradition,* 1949

D. B. KNOX, *The Doctrine of Faith in the Reign of Henry VIII,* 1961

A. F. POLLARD, *Henry VIII* (New Edition), 1951

J. F. MOZLEY, *William Tyndale,* 1937.

H. S. DARBY, *Hugh Latimer,* 1953

JOHN STRYPE, *Ecclesiastical Memorials,* 1822

THOMAS CRANMER, *Miscellaneous Writings and Letters* (Parker Society Edition), 1846

HUGH LATIMER, *Sermons and Remains* (Parker Society Edition), 1845

JOHN BALE, *Select Works* (Parker Society Edition), 1849

MILES COVERDALE, *Remains* (Parker Society Edition), 1846

HASTINGS ROBINSON, *Original Letters relative to the English Reformation* (2 Vols.) (Parker Society Edition), 1846

JOHN ROGERS

JOHN ROGERS

1500–1555

"Upon his waye to the place where he sholde presentlye be burned dyd Master Rogers espye his wyfe with her eleven smal chyldren comyng to meete him, who never had beene suffred to come at him whileas he layd in pryson which was nowe more than a yere. So cruellie and with suche unkynde malyce dyd his ennemyes deale with this godlye man who whenas he was at the stake, and even then a pardon from the Quene helde before him, wolde in no wyse recant or thynk to possesse lyfe by the renouncyng of his constancye, and so endured unto the ende: and that with suche marvellous pacience and stedfast joye that all menne blessed God for the same and rejoysed beholdynge him."—R. FALKENBRIDGE, *Ephemeris—Leaves from the Journal of Marian Drayton* (1592).

J OHN ROGERS WAS BORN AT DERITEND
and was christened with his father's name in 1500. Deritend was
a hamlet in the parish of Aston, a quiet rural community of
green fields and small farms; but it is now in the heart of the
Black Country and has lost its identity in the city of Birmingham.
His father had married Margery Wyatt and was a bit and spur
maker. We do not know whether there were other children or
what schooling a loriner's son would receive in Deritend. There
is very little information at all about the first thirty years of his
life. John Foxe merely says that he was "brought up in the
University of Cambridge where he profitably travailed in good
learning".[1] He became a member of Pembroke Hall about the
year 1521, and he took his degree as a Bachelor of Arts in 1525.
Thus he was a contemporary of Nicholas Ridley, who took his
degree in 1522 and became a Fellow of Pembroke Hall in 1524.
Rogers' account of his trial in January 1555 has a remark about
"mine old master, Dr. Heath, now Bishop of Worcester".[2]
Heath had taken his degree in 1521, and may have been Rogers'
tutor while at Cambridge. It is sometimes said that he was
chosen as a Junior Canon for Wolsey's College at Oxford in
1525 and was ordained with this title.[3] If this were true, it would
prove that he had built up a good reputation for sound learning;
but there is no definite evidence to link his name with the
Cardinal's foundation, and such a claim must be viewed with
reserve. The first positive reference to John Rogers after 1525 is
in connection with his appointment as the Rector of Holy
Trinity or Trinity the Less in the City of London, a church which
was united with St. Michael's Queenhithe after the Great Fire
in 1666. A list of the Rectors compiled from "the original records
in the Bishop of London's registry" states that Rogers was
presented to that living by the Prior and Convent of St. Marye-
over-ye-waye in Southwark on December 26th, 1532, and he

[1] *Foxe*, Vol. VI, p. 591.   [2] Chester, *John Rogers*, p. 336.   [3] Ibid., p. 2.

must have resigned before October 1534 when Master John Darrell was appointed his successor.[1]

There is little variation in the account of John Rogers in the several English editions of John Foxe's Acts and Monuments; we are simply told that he was at length "chosen and called by the merchant adventurers to be their chaplain at Antwerp in Brabant".[2] But the original Latin edition of 1559 makes it clear that Rogers was an orthodox Catholic in good standing with the authorities of the Church when he left England. He had given up his living in the City in a voluntary spirit; it was "vacant by the free resignation of Dominus John Rogers".[3] He did not leave England for motives of safety as so many others had done: Tyndale and Frith, Lambert and Barnes, Coverdale and Constantine, Simon Fish, George Joye, and others had all crossed the Channel for the sake of spiritual freedom. Rogers must have had some leanings towards the New Learning, or he would not have found goodwill with the merchants; but he was as yet a stranger to the inner ferment of change which sprang from the faith and doctrines of the Reformation. There is nothing at all that would link his name with Bilney's band of converts in Cambridge or with John Clark's group of converts at Oxford. Both Rogers and Ridley had stood aloof from the spiritual movement which had grown up during the years while they were at Pembroke. Thus he did not know when he left England that he was on the eve of a discovery which would change the whole course of his life and make it unsafe to recross the Channel until 1548. Foxe says that "it chanced him to fall in company with William Tyndale"[4] who had found a lodging in the Merchant House at Antwerp as the guest of Thomas Poyntz in 1534. Rogers began to confer with Tyndale in the Scriptures and soon came to a clear knowledge of the Gospel; he turned his back on the doctrines of Rome and found himself in the full light of the message of grace. This was the great crisis of his spiritual experience and the time is confirmed by his statement to Gardiner on January 29th, 1555, that he had not been a member of his false church "these twenty years".[5]

Rogers had arrived in Antwerp at a time when Tyndale stood

[1] Chester, op. cit., p. 3.   [2] *Foxe*, Vol. VI, p. 591.
[3] Chester, p. 5.   [4] *Foxe*, Vol. VI, p. 591.   [5] Ibid., p. 602.

in special need of understanding friendship. The skies over England had grown dark with persecution, and the signs of the times were spelt out in letters of fire. Tyndale had read those signs across the Channel when Lambert, who had served as Chaplain to the Merchant House at Antwerp, had been betrayed, extradited, tried and sent to prison in March 1531; he read them in yet more vivid letters with the death of Bilney at Norwich and of Bayfield in London later that year. He was still more deeply moved in July 1533 when his dearest friend and convert, John Frith, was sent to the stake at Smithfield. He might dwell with comparative safety in the house of Thomas Poyntz at Antwerp, but the taste of sorrow was in his heart. He was lonely, and in exile, and with no clear prospect for the future; but he never lost the vision that had made him willing to leave England and he was still absorbed in the task of bringing out the Scriptures in the language of the people. Tyndale must have found in Rogers one whose faith and insight were more welcome than words could tell and whose trust and friendship would help in part to fill the gap caused by Frith's death. But the tide of freedom was fast running out for Tyndale, and their companionship must have been for less than nine months all told. Rogers may have arrived in Antwerp a little before October 1534; Tyndale was betrayed and immured in the Castle of Vilvorde in May 1535. Poyntz spared no pains in his efforts to save Tyndale, but in November he was seized and placed in custody. He was released three months later, but was forced to fly from Antwerp, leaving behind his wife, his goods and his merchant career. Rogers is not mentioned during these months, and there is no record of his feelings. He must have been aware of the troubles in which Poyntz was involved and of Tyndale's trial and condemnation; and he would hear at length how on October 6th, 1536, Tyndale was first strangled, and then burnt at the stake.[1]

John Foxe says that Rogers came to know Coverdale as well as Tyndale in Antwerp, "and joined himself with them two in that painful and most profitable labour of translating the Bible into the English tongue".[2] But this statement has been questioned

[1] See M. L. Loane, *William Tyndale* (Chapter Two in *Masters of The English Reformation*).
[2] *Foxe*, Vol. VI, p. 591.

and his connection with Miles Coverdale still needs to be cleared up. Chester asserts that Coverdale was in England at the time when Rogers was in Antwerp and that they could not have met each other in the final months of Tyndale's freedom. He points out that Coverdale lived until 1569, and yet that his published works and sayings tell us nothing at all about Rogers; and he claims that the best explanation for this unexpected silence is that Coverdale never knew Rogers.[1] One great weakness in this explanation lies in the fact that both Rogers and Coverdale were in England from 1548 to 1555, when Rogers was put to death and Coverdale went into exile: it seems impossible to think that two men who had so much in common would have remained unknown to each other in the reign of Edward VI. But Mozley goes further than this. He has proved that Coverdale's translation of the Bible was first taken in hand late in 1534 and was carried out in Antwerp; he earned his bread with the printer Martin de Keyser and he engaged in the translation at the request of Jacob van Meteren.[2] The connection of Coverdale with Tyndale had begun as early as 1529, and all the facts are in favour of the statement by Foxe that John Rogers must have been in touch with both men. Coverdale and Rogers were the "two disciples" of whom George Joye was so disparaging in his Apology: "And as for his two disciples that gaped so long for their master's morsel that they might have the advantage of the sale of his books, of which one said unto me, it were alms he were hanged that correcteth the Testament for the Dutch, and the tother harped on his master's untuned string, saying that because I english resurrection the life after this, men gathered that I denied the general resurrection: which error by their own saying was gathered long before this book was printed: unto which either of these disciples I seemed no honest man for correcting the copy —I will not now name them."[3]

Tyndale had begun to publish the first edition of his translation of the New Testament at Cologne in 1525. The type had been set up as far as the letter K in the signature of the sheets for the first Gospel when the secret leaked out; he had only enough time to snatch up the sheets and fly to Worms, where six thousand

[1] Chester, op. cit., pp. 20–23.   [2] Mozley, *Coverdale and his Bibles*, pp. 6, 72.
[3] Ibid., p. 6.

copies were struck off the press by spring in 1526. They were smuggled into England in bales of cloth and sacks of flour, and found willing buyers in the Eastern Counties and in London. Meanwhile Tyndale had made up his mind to translate the Old Testament from Hebrew, and he spent the latter half of 1529 in the translation of the Pentateuch with the help of Coverdale at Hamburg. This was published in 1530 at Antwerp, which now became the real headquarters of the contraband traffic in books. In May 1531 he produced his translation of Jonah as a tract for the times, and there were some detached fragments of Old Testament translation bound up with the second edition of the New Testament. This was published at Antwerp in November 1534 and sold with great rapidity. But he had told readers that if any faults came to light, he would shortly attend to them. As a result, almost at once he was at work again, and in December 1534, his third and last edition of the New Testament made its appearance. The text furnished high proof of his sustained care in detail, and showed that his skill in translation was matched by his strength in revision. All his alterations helped to draw the spirit of the text still closer to that of the original, and they gave a rhythm to its language which no English classic has yet excelled. The Word of God in the Pentateuch and in the New Testament had thus been turned in to English by one to whom that Word was life itself, and there is an unvaried tradition that he also left a manuscript translation of the historical books from Joshua to Chronicles in the hands of Rogers.[1]

Meanwhile in May 1532 John Campensis of Louvain had published a paraphrase on the Psalms in Latin and in 1534 Miles Coverdale published a translation in English. He had no thought at that stage of attempting a full translation of the Scriptures, for his knowledge of Greek and Hebrew was inadequate. However, late in 1534 Jacob van Meteren, a merchant of Antwerp, induced him to undertake such a translation and he agreed because the need for a complete English Bible was so great and Tyndale could not finish the work alone. "When I considered how great pity it was that we should want it so long," he wrote, "and called to my remembrance the adversity of them which were not only of ripe knowledge but would also with all their hearts

[1] See M. L. Loane, op. cit., pp. 56–78.

have performed that they began if they had not had impediment, ... these and other reasonable causes considered, I was the more bold to take it in hand. ... Therefore when I was instantly required, though I could not do so well as I would, I thought it yet my duty to do my best."[1] Coverdale was well aware that he lacked the scholarship to work direct from the text in Hebrew and Greek, but he was at home in Latin and in German. He made it clear in the Prologue that he had based his work on five other versions: the Vulgate and Pagninus in Latin, Luther and the Zurich Bible in German, and Tyndale in English. He placed least weight on the Latin versions, leant hard on the German versions, and borrowed freely from Tyndale; his New Testament translation relied most of all on Tyndale's editions in 1534, though he revised the text to some extent with help from the German versions which Jacob van Meteren commended. The whole task was finished within twelve months and the last page came off the press at Cologne on October 4th, 1535. It was the first complete Bible in the English Reformation and he had wrought better than he could tell. He returned to England at the end of 1535, hardly conscious that he had placed a mark on the English Bible second only to that of Tyndale himself.[2]

Rogers was therefore in Antwerp when the second and third editions of Tyndale's New Testament were published and while Coverdale's translation was in progress. It is impossible to say in what sense he may have "joined himself with them two in that painful and most profitable labour".[3] He may have helped Tyndale with the preparation of his text for the press and he may have assisted Coverdale both as a scribe and as a proof reader. At all events, Rogers served his apprenticeship with the greatest master of all such work; he had filled Frith's place in his heart and had become in effect his literary trustee. We know that the authorities came to Tyndale's rooms after his arrest and took away all the books and papers that they could find. But there was one important manuscript which escaped their knowledge; this was his still unpublished translation of the historical books of the Old Testament from Joshua to Chronicles. Rogers was in possession

---

[1] Mozley, *Coverdale and his Bibles*, p. 70.   [2] Ibid., pp. 65–109.
[3] *Foxe*, Vol. VI, p. 591.

of that manuscript and he would not let it perish. He may have been disappointed because Coverdale's translation did not incorporate Tyndale's work *in toto*. His friendship for Tyndale and anxiety to rescue Tyndale's work from oblivion led him therefore to set about a new version of the English Bible. Coverdale had nothing to do with this; he had left Antwerp and was in England. Rogers worked in secret throughout the year 1536 and the Bible was printed by Matthew Cron at Antwerp in the early part of 1537.[1] Rogers took his version of the Pentateuch and of the New Testament almost without change from Tyndale; he borrowed his version of the books from Ezra to Malachi as well as the Apocrypha with but minor changes from Coverdale. All this material had been in print before; what was new was Tyndale's hitherto unpublished translation of the section from Joshua to Chronicles. There was little that came from the pen of Rogers himself; he provided a translation of the Prayer of Manasses in the Apocrypha and a number of small changes in the texts which he used. But his great aim had been achieved; he had conserved all that Tyndale had done. The duties of friendship had been discharged.

This new English Bible did not refer to John Rogers at all, but the title-page and the end of the Dedication bore the name of Thomas Matthew in red and black letters. It claimed that the Scriptures had been "truly and purely translated into English by Thomas Matthew",[2] and the Dedication was signed by "your Grace's faithful and true subject, Thomas Matthew".[3] Who was Thomas Matthew? All the evidence goes to prove that this was just a pseudonym for John Rogers. Thus in 1548, John Bale said that Rogers had translated the whole Bible from Hebrew, Greek, Latin, German and English sources and had dedicated it to Henry VIII as the work of Thomas Matthew. Mozley points out that "this description is incomplete"; but if a loose meaning is attached to the word "translated", it is reasonably correct.[4] John Foxe in his earlier editions in Latin in 1559 and English in 1563 said that Rogers had helped Tyndale and Coverdale to translate the Bible into English, and that it had circulated with the name of Thomas Matthew. His second English edition in 1570 had a

---

[1] Mozley, *Coverdale and his Bibles*, pp. 129–130. [2] Ibid., p. 142.
[3] Ibid., p. 143. [4] Ibid., p. 136.

more detailed passage, though it was not without its own errors. It spoke of the Matthew Bible as the work of Tyndale and Coverdale, and it ascribed to Rogers the duty of having to correct the print: "But because the said William Tyndale was apprehended before this Bible was fully perfected, it was thought good to them which had the doing thereof to change the name of William Tyndale because that name then was odious and to father it by a strange name of Thomas Matthew."[1] Thus, as Mozley says, "both Bale and Foxe treat Thomas Matthew as a dummy name and father the book in some sense upon Rogers".[2] Both men lived through the times of which they wrote; they must have known Rogers when he was in London in the reign of Edward VI. They knew many others who must have known the facts, and it becomes very hard to believe that they were both guilty of a mistake.

Mozley concludes with a decisive summary of the facts in favour of the view which indentifies Thomas Matthew with John Rogers. No one with the name of Thomas Matthew is known as a leader of the Reformation at all, but John Rogers was the companion and disciple of Tyndale in the last months of his freedom. Rogers would treasure the unpublished translation of a substantial part of the Old Testament and may have been disappointed when it did not find a place in Coverdale's translation. He did not feel himself called to translate and he never engaged in such activity once the Matthew Bible had been published; but he was a Cambridge man and a good scholar, and he might well edit materials left in his hands and see them through the press. He would learn both French and German while in Antwerp, and this would be in full accord with the use of French and German sources in the Matthew Bible. It would not be wise to use the name of Tyndale, since he had been condemned and burnt; nor could he use Coverdale's name, since his share in the work was so much less. Least of all could he use his own name, for his own contribution was minute in comparison. No one can say why he chose the name of Thomas Matthew; perhaps the fact that the printer's name was Matthew Cron would put the idea into his mind. It is not strictly correct to say that Matthew is Rogers, though sometimes one can scarcely avoid that manner

[1] Mozley, op. cit., p. 138.   [2] Ibid., p. 139.

of speaking: rather Matthew stands for Tyndale, plus Coverdale, plus (to a very small degree) Rogers.[1] Bale and Foxe both identify Thomas Matthew with John Rogers, and their statements have been confirmed by the official documents which dealt with the case of Rogers when he was in trouble under Mary. On August 16th, 1553, when the Privy Council confined him to his house, he was described as "John Rogers, alias Matthew".[2] This phrase was used in the sentence of condemnation pronounced by Gardiner on January 29th, 1555.[3] There could be no reason for the second name of Matthew unless it was believed that he had been responsible for the Matthew Bible.

Bonner's list of prohibited books in 1542 refers to the Matthew Bible as one that was "printed beyond the sea".[4] It was in fact printed at Antwerp by Matthew Cron in July 1537, nine months after Tyndale's death at Vilvorde. It was a large folio edition, making up a volume of no less than 1,110 pages, with 78 wood-cuts. It was printed in bold and black letters, and there were two columns, each of sixty lines, for each page. The pen-name of Thomas Matthew is found on the title-page and at the foot of the Dedication, and the initials of John Rogers and of William Tyndale are found at the bottom of a preface and at the end of Malachi. It seems strange that Coverdale's initials do not appear, and this must lead to the question whether Rogers was in sympathy with Miles Coverdale. Coverdale's translation in 1535 had been the first complete printed version of the English Bible; the Matthew Bible in 1537 was the second. Coverdale's Prologue had argued that it is a good thing to have many versions; each may improve on the other and bring new truth to light.[5] But the Coverdale translation had not preserved all the materials left by Tyndale and the Matthew Bible may have been meant by John Rogers as a rival. This may explain why there is no sign of Coverdale's initials in the Matthew Bible; it may also explain why there is no reference to John Rogers in the works of Coverdale. This is conjectural; what is certain is that Rogers achieved his great object. He was able to print the one section of Old Testament translation which might have been lost to the world,

[1] Mozley, op. cit., pp. 140–141.　　[2] Chester, op. cit., p. 113.
[3] *Foxe*, Vol. VI, p. 601.
[4] Mozley, op. cit., p. 130.　　[5] Ibid., p. 69.

and to reprint in one volume all that Tyndale had ever published in separate translations of the Pentateuch and New Testament. Thus the Matthew Bible did what Coverdale's translation did not, for it preserved Tyndale's work in its full integrity. Tyndale's New Testament was printed in England for the first time during 1536, and a stream of reprints was to follow in the next thirty years. "But his influence is not to be measured by reprints of the Testament alone; it is of even greater moment that his work was caught up into Matthew's Bible and has passed into every English Bible that has since been printed."[1]

The full title of the Matthew Bible, printed in red and black, fills the centre of a woodcut which had been used in Luther's low-German Bible printed at Lubeck in 1533–1534. On the reverse side of this page there is a short table of the contents. A Calendar and Almanac in red and black letter fills the next four pages. It was borrowed with slight changes from Tyndale's third New Testament and it covered the years from 1538 to 1555; this was to prove the exact number of years that still lay before Rogers himself. The next page set out "An Exhortation to The Study of the Holy Scripture"; this was eight plain texts of Scripture to commend the reading of the Bible. The foot of this page had two large and flourished capitals, "I.R.", the one direct trace of Rogers in the volume. Then two pages followed with "The Sum and Content of all the Holy Scripture", or a list of the chief doctrines therein contained. The Dedication to Henry VIII took the next three pages, and an alphabetical "Table of the Principal Matters contained in the Bible" took twenty-six pages. "The names of all the books of the Bible" required one page, and the reverse side held a large woodcut of Adam and Eve in Paradise which was also taken from the Lubeck Bible. The text of the Bible was in four parts, each with its own title and foliation; the text itself was divided into chapters and paragraphs, but not into verses. The first section was from Genesis to Solomon's Ballet in 493 pages. A blank page then appeared before the new title in red and black, "The Prophets in English", and the reverse bore a half-page woodcut of Isaiah's call from the Lubeck Bible. The flourished capitals, "W.T.", stand at the end of this section in 188 pages. The title-page of the Apocrypha

[1] Mozley, *William Tyndale*, p. 293.

came next, and the reverse had a preface to the reader which explained the inferior authority of the Apocrypha. The text required 160 pages, and then a blank page came before the title of the New Testament in red and black and in the same woodcut as was used for the title of the Old Testament. There was one more blank page and then the text in 217 pages with the books in the same order as in Luther and Tyndale. Then came a Table of the Epistles and Gospels after the Salisbury Use, and on the last leaf of all stood the words: "The end of the New Testament and of the whole Bible. To the honour and praise of God was this Bible printed and finished in the year of our Lord God, anno 1537."[1]

Rogers did not try to translate from the texts in Hebrew and Greek, although it is clear that he had a sound working knowledge of both.[2] His great object was to edit and publish the work of Tyndale, and to supplement it where necessary from the text of Coverdale. There were minor alterations in which Rogers allowed Coverdale's rendering to replace a Tyndale reading or in which he followed Olivetan; but such alterations did not deflect him from his main purpose, and the Matthew Bible is the text of Tyndale and Coverdale. It used to be thought that Rogers was the author of the prefatory material and the notes or comments in the margins throughout the text. Thus Bonner's Register described them as "Thomas Matthew's doing" and condemned them in 1542; John Daye also described them as the work of "Thomas Matthew" and restored them in 1549.[3] Mozley's research has now thrown new light on the whole question and proved that he borrowed freely from new Continental sources. Thus he derived nearly all the prefatory material and the chapter headings from the two French scholars, Lefèvre and Olivetan, and in lesser degree from Tyndale and Bucer. He used Lefèvre's translation published at Antwerp in 1534 and Olivetan's translation published at Neuchatel in 1535. Mozley reckons that there are more than two thousand notes in the Bible as well as cross-references to other passages. "They are of all kinds, long and short, simple and learned, linguistic and expository, theological

---

[1] Mozley, *Coverdale and his Bibles*, p. 145. For whole paragraph, see Mozley, pp. 142–145; Chester, op. cit., pp. 57–59.
[2] Ibid., pp. 161–162.　　　　　　[3] Chester, op. cit., p. 48.

and practical, peaceable and controversial".[1] Mozley has traced nearly all of them, in whole or in part, to some contemporary author, and he concludes that not more than ten per cent could have been the work of Rogers himself. The main quarry for his notes in the Old Testament was Lefèvre and Olivetan, and in the New Testament, Tyndale and Erasmus; but he also drew from Pellican and Coverdale, from Luther and Bugenhagen, from Bucer and Oecolampadius, and he printed in full Tyndale's Prologue to The Romans in his third edition of the New Testament. "The short notes are often taken over verbatim, but he sometimes alters the wording, enlarges what he has received, combines the opinions of two or three interpreters, adds a sentence of his own. And all this is done with the equipment of a good scholar; he is at home in the Bible and its commentators, understands the points at issue, selects with judgment, has a linguistic capacity equal to its task".[2] Thus his work was not an original contribution, but it was a remarkable accomplishment.

How did Rogers provide for the cost of printing this large folio edition of the Bible? It was financed by Richard Grafton and Edward Whitchurch, who were members of the Grocers' Company in London and the House of Merchant Adventurers in Antwerp. They thought of it as a business venture as well as a godly undertaking, and they brought out fifteen hundred copies which they hoped to sell in England. On the half-page woodcut which precedes the section on the Prophets, the capitals "R.G." stand above and "E.W." below in their honour as the publishers. They would know that Cranmer had issued a series of Injunctions in connection with the Ten Articles, and that the Seventh Injunction required every parish priest to get a copy of the Bible in English and Latin before August 1537. This plan had been deferred at the time when the new Matthew Bible came off the press, but a copy of this Bible was at once placed in the hands of Cranmer, who could hardly tell his delight. On August 4th, 1537, Cranmer wrote to Cromwell and sent him a copy of the Matthew Bible which he declared was more to his liking "than any other translation heretofore made". "And for as much as the book is dedicated unto the King's Grace, and also great pains and labour taken in setting forth of the same, I pray you my

[1] Mozley, op. cit., p. 157.   [2] Ibid., p. 157.

Lord that you will exhibit the book unto the King's Highness, and to obtain of his Grace, if you can, a licence that the same may be sold and read of every person . . . until such time that we the bishops shall set forth a better translation which I think will not be till a day after doomsday."[1] Cromwell took the Bible to the King, who agreed that it should be "allowed by his authority to be bought and read within this realm".[2] Cranmer could not hide his joy when the King's consent was thus obtained, and on August 13th he wrote to thank Cromwell for his great help: "My lord, for this your pain taken in this behalf, I give unto you my most hearty thanks: assuring your Lordship for the contentation of my mind, you have shewed me more pleasure herein than if you had given me a thousand pound: and I doubt not but that hereby such fruit of good knowledge shall ensure that it shall well appear hereafter what high and acceptable service you have done unto God and the King."[3]

It is true that Cranmer's letters do not refer to the Matthew Bible by name; but there was no other Bible to which they could refer. Thus at the foot of the title-page, but outside the woodcut border, there stood in large letters the words: "Set forth with the Kinges most gracyous lycēce."[4] It was the first authorised translation of the English Bible ever published. Cranmer declared that the Dedication to the King was "very well done" and begged Cromwell "to read the same".[5] The first sentence was borrowed from Olivetan and was to the effect that it was an ancient custom to pen such a Dedication to some great prince.[6] Rogers then struck out on his own and went on to declare: "It is no vulgar or common thing which is offered to your Grace's protection, but the blessed word of God: which is everlasting and can not fail, though heaven and earth should perish. So precious a thing requireth a singular good patron and defender, and findeth none other unto whom the defence thereof may so justly be committed as unto your Grace's Majesty."[7] It was only a few years since Henry had threatened to destroy Tyndale and had condemned all his writings; but there had been

[1] Cranmer, *Miscellaneous Writings and Letters*, p. 344.
[2] Mozley, op. cit., p. 125.
[3] Cranmer, op. cit., pp. 345–346.　　[4] Chester, op. cit., p. 57.
[5] Cranmer, op. cit., p. 344.　　[6] Mozley, op. cit., p. 143.
[7] Chester, op. cit., pp. 377–378.

a vast change in circumstances as a result of the Act of Supremacy and the whole breach with Rome. Thus the Coverdale translation had been allowed to go into circulation in 1535, and Tyndale's New Testament had been printed in London itself by Thomas Godfray in 1536. But the Matthew Bible which bore the King's licence as no other Bible had done had now gathered up all Tyndale's work on the Old Testament and on the New Testament alike. His genius for translation, once so widely feared and maligned, was now enshrined in a Bible which had the King's sanction; it had triumphed at last through the efforts of Rogers and Grafton and Whitchurch, of Cranmer and Cromwell and Henry. The royal licence granted to the Matthew Bible in August 1537 was the superlative answer to the prayer of William Tyndale at the hour of his death ten months before: "Lord," he had cried, "open the King of England's eyes!"[1]

It so happened that the Matthew Bible was launched just when the plague swept through London. The Court retired to the country, but Cromwell was eager to have further copies of the Bible and wrote to ask Grafton to send him six more as soon as he could. On August 28th, Grafton's servant arrived in London from Antwerp with fresh supplies and was at once sent to Cromwell with six copies and a letter asking him to have it licensed under his own privy seal as well as in the King's name. This would have been equivalent to the promise of a monopoly, and its object was to secure Grafton from his business rivals. Cromwell said in reply that such action was not necessary, but Grafton wrote again to press his point: "Forasmuch as this work hath been brought forth to our most great and costly labours and charges, which charges amount above the sum of £500, and I have caused of these same to be printed to the sum of fifteen hundred books complete: which now by reason that of many this work is highly commended, there are that will and doth go about the printing of the same work again in a lesser letter, to the intent that they may sell their little books better cheap than I can sell these great, and so to make that I shall sell none at all, or else very few, to the utter undoing of me your orator and of all those my creditors that hath been my comforters and helpers therein."[2] He had vested his whole fortune in the project and he

[1] *Foxe*, Vol. V, p. 127.   [2] Mozley, op. cit., p. 127.

asked for a Royal Proclamation that would require every curate to purchase a copy. We do not know Cromwell's answer to his request, but we may read between the lines. Printers were warned not to meddle with the Matthew Bible, and there were no pirate reprints; but Nicholson brought out a new quarto edition of the Coverdale Bible before the year came to an end and it also received the royal licence. Thus both translations were accorded the royal licence during 1537, and the publishers were left "to compete on equal terms".[1] But this was no concern of John Rogers nor of Miles Coverdale.

The three copies of the Matthew Bible in the British Museum are a standing witness to the careful work of Rogers. It is not known whether it was brought out again in the reign of Henry VIII, but there were three reprints under Edward VI. The first was by John Daye and William Seres in August 1549, and the second by Thomas Raynalde and William Hyll two months later. The last reprint was by Nicholas Hyll in May 1551.[2] The first attempt to revise the Matthew Bible was by Richard Taverner at the request of Thomas Berthelet, who published it in 1539. Taverner knew no Hebrew and his alterations in the Matthew text of the Old Testament were based on the Vulgate or on Pagninus. But he was a good Greek scholar and a leading merit of his work lay in his diligent attention to the details of the Greek text of the New Testament.[3] But the Matthew Bible and the Taverner revision were both superseded almost at once by yet another translation: this was to be known as the Great Bible. Cromwell knew that the two Bibles printed during 1537 by royal licence would be inadequate to meet the needs of the whole realm, and he commissioned Coverdale to revise the Matthew Bible as the text most favoured by men such as Cranmer. Cranmer's deferred Injunction of 1536 was confirmed by Cromwell's Injunction of 1538, and the order was now issued to all clergy: "Ye shall provide, on this side the Feast of All Saints next coming, one book of the whole Bible of the largest volume in English."[4] It was printed partly in Paris, partly in London, and was published by Grafton and Whitchurch in April 1539. This was the last authorised translation in the reign of Henry VIII and its size

[1] Mozley, op. cit., p. 129. [2] Ibid., p. 179 fn.
[3] Ibid., p. 347. [4] Ibid., p. 172.

gave it the name of the Great Bible. Henry VIII himself said with regard to this Bible: "In God's name, let it go abroad among our people."[1] It was ordered that a copy should be placed in every church of the realm, and six more editions with a preface from the pen of Cranmer appeared in 1540 and 1541. Thus the work of Tyndale was caught up through the skill of his devoted disciples in the Matthew Bible and in the Great Bible; and these in turn formed the basis of the Bishops' Bible in 1568 and of the Authorised Version of King James I in 1611.

Rogers had read widely and must have worked night and day since he had come to Antwerp. He had survived the plot against Barnes and Joye as well as against Tyndale because his care for the Reformation was still unknown, and it was not disclosed to the authorities even after Tyndale's death or when the Matthew Bible appeared. He had carried on his work as Chaplain to the House of Merchant Adventurers without interference, and his mind was confirmed in its grasp of Reformation truth and theology. His breach with Rome became final with his marriage, for like Frith he found a wife in the Low Countries. This was Adriana de Weyden or Adriana Pratt of Antwerp; the two names are synonymous and their meaning is a "meadow". She was a kinswoman, perhaps a sister, of Jacob van Meteren's wife; her sons were to be on close terms with Jacob's son Emanuel who was to call them his cousins.[2] Little is known of her apart from a remark by Foxe in the Latin edition of 1559 to the effect that she was "more richly endowed with virtue and soberness of life than with worldly treasures".[3] On his return to England in 1548, Rogers brought eight children with him.[4] When he appeared before Gardiner on January 29th, 1555, he declared that he had been married "these eighteen years".[5] Thus his marriage must have taken place in 1536 or in 1537. But marriage meant exile; it would shut him out of England during the last years of Henry VIII. Coverdale and Barnes had been allowed to return and had grown in favour with Cromwell; but they had not added to their faults by marriage. When Rogers was summoned before the Privy Council on January 22nd, 1555, and told them that he had broken no law, Bourne exclaimed: "A married priest

---

[1] Bruce, *The Books and the Parchments,* p. 214.   [2] Mozley, op. cit., p. 74.
[3] Chester, op. cit. p. 14.   [4] *Foxe*, Vol. VI, p. 596.   [5] Ibid., p. 603.

and have not offended the law!" But he said in reply that he had
not broken the Queen's law nor any other law of the realm; "for
I married where it was lawful". But the members of the Privy
Council did not think that it was lawful in any country and they
all cried out: "Where was that?" Rogers told them that it was in
"Dutchland".[1]

Rogers spent some years at Antwerp and then went to Wittenberg, where he matriculated on November 25th, 1540, We
cannot fix the date when he left the Merchant Adventurers in
Antwerp for the German theologians at Wittenberg, but affairs
in England had turned sharply against the Reformation in 1540.
Rogers would learn of the final collapse of the efforts by the
German Divines to come to an understanding with the English
leaders. He would hear how Cromwell had been sent to the
block and Barnes to the stake in July, and he may have heard
how Coverdale had ventured to marry and then fled to Strass-
burg. The friendship of Tyndale and Coverdale in his early
months at Antwerp was now matched by that of Luther and
Melancthon in Wittenberg. Foxe states that "he with much
soberness of living did not only increase in all good and godly
learning, but also so much profited in the knowledge of the
Dutch (Deutsch?) tongue that the charge of a congregation was
orderly committed to his cure".[2] His intercourse with Melancthon seems to have been very fruitful and he was to translate
four of his books into English. Bale notes that three of these
were the *Homelias*, *Locos Communes*, and *In Danielem*, which
may have been among the books burnt at Paul's Cross on
September 26th, 1546.[3] The fourth was the only volume which
has survived; this was his translation of a work by Melancthon
on *The Interim*. There is little information about his work or his
movements during these years and it has been assumed that he
remained in Wittenberg or Saxony until the death of Henry
VIII. But Foxe has an account of Henry of Zutphen who was
cruelly done to death in 1524 while preaching at Dietmarsh in
the far north-west of Germany, and a footnote to this account
provides brief but valuable information: "In this rude country
of Dithmarsch, Master Rogers our countryman was superin-

[1] *Foxe*, op. cit., p. 596. [2] Ibid., pp. 591–592.
[3] Mozley, op. cit., pp. 131 fn., 346.

tendent at the time of the Six Articles; where he with great danger of his life did very much good."[1]

Mozley has now shown that this was correct, for it is proved by a letter from Melancthon which was printed as early as 1565. Henry of Zutphen was martyred at the hands of a mob, primed with drink and egged on by monks; but his death was not in vain. The whole Dietmarsh country was won over to the Reformation and the Church was served by four Superintendents. Late in 1542, the pastor at Meldorf, one of the four Superintendents, died, and the church was offered to John Dursten. But he declined as he had just gone to a church in Wittenberg. Then on September 18th, 1543, Melancthon proposed the name of John Rogers for the vacant living. He put forward his name in a letter to John Schneck, one of the four Superintendents; he may have been identical with the John Schneck who in 1524 had been active in the murder of Henry of Zutphen.[2] "We have exhorted Master John an Englishman (Joannes Anglus) to go to you," wrote Melancthon; ". . . He has just had an invitation in this neighbourhood to the pastorate of a church, but for the sake of peace he prefers to go to you. At first you will make some allowances for his pronunciation, but that will be corrected by association with the people of your country. By my advice and that of N. (Luther?), he has been induced to undertake the journey; I urged him to it out of a true and sincere zeal for the good of your church. He is an Englishman, but he has lived long in Germany, and his integrity, trustworthiness and constancy in every duty make him worthy of the love and support of all good men. Therefore I most earnestly implore you for Christ's sake, the Son of God, to give a loving welcome to this stranger and to commend him to your people so that they may entrust him with the ecclesiastical office. It is of great moment in a church that colleagues should live in concord. Since this John well understands this and since he is by nature a lover of peace, he will aid you in every way in preserving the general tranquillity; and you should therefore greatly desire to have such a colleague."[3]

There is no doubt that this Joannes Anglus was John Rogers,

---

[1] *Foxe*, Vol. IV, p. 354 fn.   [2] Ibid., pp. 353–360.
[3] Mozley, op. cit., pp. 132–133.

and this distinctive reference to his natural origin finds an echo
in his own words at the close of his life: "I am an Englishman
born, and God knoweth, do naturally wish well to my country."[1]
He was mentioned in the same way in a letter from Cruciger to
Camerarius on June 5th, 1543: "Johannes Anglus qui aliquot
annos versatus est in nostra academia."[2] Both his surname and
the mention of his ultimate martyrdom have been found in
records in the Dietmarsh archives. It is clear that Melancthon's
proposal was put into effect, and that Rogers became pastor of
Meldorf and Superintendent of the Meldorf district in the latter
part of 1543. He exercised this ministry until the first part of
1548, but only one distinct reminiscence has been preserved. On
the ninth day after Easter 1547, a conference of ministers in the
Dietmarsh country was held in his house at Meldorf. Three
articles were considered with regard to murder, wedding banns
and private baptisms, and a statement on these questions was
drawn up and signed by all who were present. Rogers' name
appears as "Johannes Rogerus, pastor at Meldorf".[3] But the
people of Meldorf were troubled: what was meant by wilful
murder, and was it just to put a man to death if he had killed in
self-defence? Rogers discussed these points in the only letter
of his that has survived; it was dated at Meldorf on June 8th,
1547, and it argued that true justice must draw lines of demarca-
tion between wilful murder and a killing in self-defence.[4] Such
facts provide a faint picture of the moral problems in a primitive
area which faced those who followed in the steps of Henry of
Zutphen. Rogers was godly and zealous in the eyes of his flock
and "preached with singular piety on the end of the world and
the nearness of the last day".[5] The words of Foxe ought to be
kept in mind: "he with great danger of his life did very much
good".[6]

Rogers had secured a strong grasp of Reformed theology while
in Antwerp under the guidance of Tyndale, the study of Scripture, and the reading of authors like Olivetan. This is clearly
illustrated in *The Sum and Content of all the Holy Scripture*, which
was borrowed from Lefèvre and published as a preface in the

[1] *Foxe*, Vol. VI, p. 606.
[2] Mozley, op. cit., p. 133 fn.
[3] Ibid., pp. 133–134.
[4] Ibid., p. 134.
[5] Ibid., p. 133.
[6] *Foxe*, Vol. IV, p. 354 fn.

Matthew Bible. "While the fathers looked for salvation and deliverance promised," he wrote, "because man's nature is such that he not only can not, but also will not confess himself to be a sinner, and specially such a sinner that hath need of the saving health promised, the Law was given where through men might know sin and that they are sinners.... And yet this Law was given to the intent that sin and the malice of men's heart being thereby the better known, men should the more fervently thirst the coming of Christ which should redeem them from their sins.... In the New Testament therefore it is most evidently declared that Jesus Christ, the true Lamb and Host, is come to the intent to reconcile us to the Father, paying on the Cross the punishment due unto our sins; and to deliver us from the bondage of the devil ... and to make us the sons of God.... For that faith is the gift of God, whereby we believe that Christ is come into this world to save sinners: which is of so great pith that they which have it desire to perform all the duties of love to all men after the example of Christ.... By that faith and confidence in Christ which by love is mighty in operation and that sheweth itself through the works of love, stirring men thereto, by that (I say) we are justified: that is, by that faith Christ's Father (which is become ours also through that Christ our Brother) counteth us for righteous and for His sons: imputing not our sins unto us, through His grace."[1] This is a clear statement of the objects of the Law of Moses and the Gospel of Christ; man's sin and Christ's death on the Cross; the gift of faith and the ground of personal acceptance with God; the non-imputation of sin and the imputed righteousness of Christ. Rogers had in fact grasped all the salient elements of the Reformed theology before he left Antwerp.

But there can be little doubt that residence in Wittenberg, fellowship with Melancthon, and the friendship of the German Divines must have helped to shape and strengthen his faith. Perhaps this can be traced in his attitude to the Sacrament of the Body and Blood of Christ, the one subject with which Tyndale had urged Frith not to meddle. Rogers had used Olivetan's Table in the Matthew Bible, and its dogmatic article on the Mass had caused great offence to men like Gardiner.[2] But he found in Luther a guide who seems to have displaced Olivetan, and like

---

[1] Chester, op. cit., pp. 372–373. [2] Mozley, op. cit., pp. 144, 347.

Barnes he seems to have held Lutheran opinions on the nature of the Sacramental Presence. There is one short paragraph on "the Sacrament of Christ's body and blood" in his translation of *The Weighing of the Interim*: "In this matter are not our churches against the book (i.e. the Emperor's Interim); but if there be any further declaration demanded of any man as touching this Article, him we suffer to speak thereof through his own confession and acknowledging."[1] He then went on to speak strongly against private Masses and all who taught that Mass "deserveth forgiveness of sins".[2] But in England he would feel the impact of Ridley and Bradford, and this was to reflect itself at his trial in January 1555. He was examined by the Chancellor and his record illuminates the scene: "After many words, he asked me what I meant by the Sacrament; and stood up and put off his cap, and all his fellow bishops, of which there were a great sort new men which I knew not—many of them asking whether I believed in the Sacrament to be the very body and blood of our Saviour Christ that was born of the Virgin Mary and hanged on the Cross, really, substantially, etc. I answered that I had oft times told him that it was a matter in which I was no meddler, and therefore suspected of my brethren to be of a contrary opinion: but seeing the falsehood of their doctrine in all other points, and the defence thereof only by force and cruelty, thought their doctrine in this matter to be as false as the rest; for Christ could not be corporally there, and I could not otherwise understand really and substantially to signify than corporally, and so could not Christ be there and in heaven also."[3] Rogers would not quarrel with true brethren like Ridley and Bradford on the nature of the Presence of Christ; but he was at one with them in indignant rejection of the mediaeval doctrine. When he was pressed again to say what he thought of their doctrine on this subject, he threw out his hands and answered in one word: "False."[4]

Henry VIII died on January 28th, 1547, and the exiles for conscience' sake began to turn their eyes towards England. But Coverdale did not return until June nor Rogers until July 1548; and the reason is found in the words of Rogers to the Privy Council on January 22nd, 1555: "If ye had not here in England

---

[1] Chester, op. cit., p. 398.
[2] Ibid., p. 398.
[3] Ibid., p. 308, cp. *Foxe*, Vol. VI, 598.
[4] *Foxe*, Vol. VI, p. 599.

made an open law that priests might have had wives, I would never have come home again."[1] But events moved slowly; it was November 1547 before Convocation met and resolved to ask for the repeal of all statutes against the marriage of clergy. An Act to this effect was passed by the House of Commons, but lapsed because it failed to reach the House of Lords until the last day of the year's session. Nevertheless Rogers was in England by the end of July 1548, and he brought with him a translation of the little tract by Melancthon called *A Weighing of the Interim*. The Interim was an edict published by Charles V in the Diet of Augsburg on May 15th, 1548, requiring Protestants to conform to Catholic practices; and the tract in reply was written and published by Melancthon in Germany, translated and printed by Rogers in England within three months. There is a plain statement in the Preface to the Reader: "At London in Edward Whitchurch house, by John Rogers. 1 August 1548." And the book ends with the observation: "Imprinted at London in Fleet Street at the Sign of the Sun over against the conduit by Edward Whitchurch the VI day of August, the year of our Lord, MDXLVIII."[2] Did he bring his wife and children with him, or had he come alone to explore the situation? We do not know; but his statement to the Privy Council seems to imply that he must have left them in Meldorf or Antwerp. On October 11th, 1548, he was inducted to the rectory of St. Matthew, Friday Street, and a new sphere of work was assured. But it was not until the 1548–1549 session of Parliament that an Act was passed which gave its grudging recognition to the marriage of priests. Perhaps it was only then that Rogers would feel it safe to bring his wife and eight children into England: "Which thing", he said, "ye might be sure that I would not have done if the laws of the realm had not permitted it before."[3] In April 1552 he secured a special Act of Parliament to naturalise his wife and the children born in Germany.[4]

Nicholas Ridley, who must have known Rogers as a fellow member of Pembroke Hall twenty-five years before, was enthroned as Bishop of London on April 12th, 1550. Ridley soon drew round him men like Edmund Grindal, Bradford, Rogers

[1] *Foxe*, op. cit, p. 596. [2] Chester, op. cit., p. 406.
[3] *Foxe*, Vol. VI, p. 596. [4] *D.N.B.*

and John Lever to help in the Reformation of his great see. On May 10th, Rogers was inducted to the rectory of St. Margaret Moses in Friday Street, and on May 13th to the vicarage of St. Sepulchre "without Newgate" or "in the Bayley". These two churches were Crown livings, and the second indeed was one of the most lucrative in the gift of the Crown. The Great Fire of 1666 destroyed both these churches, and the living of St. Margaret Moses was then annexed to that of St. Mildred, Bread Street. Thus he held three livings with an assured income and a strategic ministry in the heart of London, and his constant preaching from three well-known pulpits would be of the highest value in those years of far-reaching transition. On August 24th, 1551, Ridley gave Rogers the valuable Prebend of St. Pancras, and Bradford that of Kentish Town in St. Paul's Cathedral. As a result Rogers resigned his two livings in Friday Street a few days later; but he retained the vicarage of St. Sepulchre, and the Dean and Chapter of St. Paul's chose him as "the reader of the Divinity lesson there".[1] The list of Acts to which Edward VI and the Privy Council gave their consent in June 1553 includes one for "A Presentation to the Bishop of London to admit John Rogers within the Cathedral Church of St. Paul in London".[2] This gave him a residence in the Cathedral Close which stretched from Paternoster Row and Ave Maria Lane on one side to Old Change, Carter Lane and Creed Lane on the other. The Latin edition of *Foxe* states that his house was near that of Bonner in the angle formed by Paternoster Row and Ave Maria Lane.[3] Ridley was to recall with deep pleasure the fact that he had brought Rogers into the very centre of London, and on February 10th, 1555, he told Augustine Berneher: "And yet again I bless God in our dear brother . . . Rogers, that he was also one of my calling to be a prebendary preacher of London."[4]

Ridley thought highly of Rogers and named him with Edmund Grindal and John Bradford in a letter to Sir John Gate and Sir William Cecil on November 18th, 1552. "Now good Mr. Vice-Chamberlain and Mr. Secretary," he wrote, "ye know both how I did bestow of late three or four prebends which did fall in my time and what manner of men they be unto whom I gave

---

[1] *Foxe*, Vol. VI, p. 592.   [2] Chester, op. cit., pp. 89–90.
[3] Ibid., pp. 118–119.   [4] Ridley, *Works*, p. 381.

them, Grindal, Bradford, and Rogers, men known to be so
necessary to be abroad in the Commonwealth that I can keep
none of them with me in my house."[1] Rogers had a zealous
spirit, and it did not always appear to his credit. On May 2nd,
1550, Joan of Kent was burnt at the stake after much heart-
searching and long delay. Both Cranmer and Ridley had been
deeply concerned with the course of the trial, and at one stage
Rogers had been asked to appeal to Cranmer to prevent her
death. He had refused, and he told the friend who made the
request that death by fire would be a gentle punishment. Joan
was a poor deluded fanatic, but nothing can excuse the harsh
response of John Rogers to that appeal and he deserved the grim
reply: "Well, perhaps you may yet find that you yourself shall
have your hands full of this so gentle fire."[2] The same zealous
spirit may be traced in certain other events. On November 10th,
1554, he was arraigned in the vicar-general's court on a charge
of having helped the wardens of St. Sepulchre's to destroy the
rood-loft without consent.[3] Like Cranmer and Ridley, he was
deeply perturbed by the misuse of the abbey lands and suppressed
monasteries, and he denounced the greed of the Northumberland
faction in a sermon at Paul's Cross so bold that he was required
to appear before the Privy Council. He had also declined to wear
the priest's coat and square cap prescribed by Convocation and
Parliament, and he was suspended from his duties as Reader in
Divinity at the Cathedral; but the Register of the Privy Council
in June 1553 shows that he was quickly restored.[4] But his days
of freedom were then numbered and his courage would soon be
put to a supreme ordeal.

On the death of Edward VI on July 6th, 1553, the horizon
grew ominous for the leaders of the Reformation. On July 9th,
Ridley preached by order of the Council at Paul's Cross, to
denounce the claims of the Princess Mary, but the crowd listened
with an unwonted surliness. On July 16th, in the growing uncertainty of a troubled city, Rogers was the preacher, and he
confined himself to the passage from the Gospel. On July 19th,
Mary was proclaimed Queen, and on August 3rd, she rode
through the cheering crowds of London. Three days later, on

[1] Ridley, op. cit., p. 336.
[2] *D.N.B.*
[3] Mozley, op. cit., pp. 134-135.
[4] *D.N.B.*

August 6th, Rogers preached once more at Paul's Cross, and was therefore the first preacher to fill this most important position after the Queen had reached London. He knew that it was a momentous occasion; was the trumpet to give an uncertain sound? Rogers did not shrink in such a crisis, and he boldly proclaimed "such true doctrine as he and others had there taught in King Edward's days".[1] He was at once summoned before the Queen's Council, but was dismissed when he argued that he had only set forth the religion established by law. He was never to preach again, and this sermon was brought against him at his trial. Rogers asked Gardiner on January 28th, 1555, why he had been sent to prison and was told that it was because he preached against the Queen. "I answered that it was not true," he wrote later; "and I would be bound to prove it, and to stand to the trial of the law, that no man should be able to disprove it, and thereupon would set my life. I preached, quoth I, a sermon at the Cross after the Queen came to the Tower, but therein was nothing said against the Queen." Gardiner fell back on the assertion that he had read lectures against orders from the Council, but he replied: "That did I not; let that be proved, and let me die for it."[2] Rogers' sermon was in fact the last of its kind as well as the last that he preached, for the sermon at Paul's Cross on the next Sunday was to bring in a new order in Church and realm.

On August 11th, an old man, "impatient with the impatience of age that dare not be content to wait", celebrated Mass in the church of St. Bartholomew; this was as yet against the law and caused something of a public riot.[3] On August 12th, Mary told the magistrates of London that while her own conscience was firm, she did not mean to put constraint on that of her subjects; she hoped that they would soon agree with her as they listened to the men of godly learning whom she would ask to preach. Her first choice was Gilbert Bourne, who had been Bonner's chaplain and had held a Prebend at the Cathedral. On August 13th, he preached on the Gospel for the Day at Paul's Cross in the presence of the Lord Mayor, and he indulged in some fulsome praise of Bonner, who was also present. Then there broke out "a great uproar and shouting at his sermon, as it were like

[1] *Foxe*, Vol. VI, p. 592.   [2] Ibid., p. 598.   [3] Prescott, *Mary Tudor*, p. 190.

mad people. . . . as hurly burly and casting up of caps".[1] Some of the crowd began to climb on to the stage on which Bonner had been standing, and he started back in panic to find himself beside Rogers and Bradford. It was clear that the Lord Mayor could not quell the crowd and an ugly situation was fast developing. Rogers and Bradford stepped forward to shout above the din: "For Christ's sake and for the love of Christ to be quiet again."[2] But while they spoke, someone flung a dagger; it touched Bradford's sleeve and buried its point in the woodwork of the pulpit. Rogers and Bradford with great difficulty dragged the frightened man back into the school-house. Lord Courtenay, the Marquis of Exeter and Bonner then hurried him through the Cathedral to safety, while the Lord Mayor and aldermen broke up the crowd which was shouting: "Kill him! kill him!"[3] The Queen's Council was in session the same day at the Tower, and it knew that this was the first challenge from the mob in London to the Queen's faith. But Rogers and Bradford had acted with moderation, coolness, judgment and great boldness.

The Queen's Council was disturbed and began to plan severe measures. It gave the Lord Mayor three days in which to decide whether he could keep the peace and order of the city; if he could not, he was to yield up his sword of office. On the third day, August 16th, the Lord Mayor took action; he placed five or six men under arrest as the authors of the riot. Yet who were these but the very men who had helped him to quell it? Rogers and Becon were placed under house arrest; Bradford and Veron were imprisoned; Hooper and Coverdale were confined to the Fleet. Rogers was brought before the Queen's Council in the Tower of London, and the Council minute cites his case in significant language: "John Rogers, alias Matthew, a seditious preacher, ordered by the Lords of the Council to keep himself as prisoner in his house at Paul's without conference of any person other than such as are daily with him in (his) household until such time as he hath contrary commandment."[4] This was two days before a new proclamation by the Queen which forbade any preaching except by those whom the Queen had licensed.

[1] Prescott, op. cit., p. 191. [2] Ibid., p. 191.
[3] Ibid., p. 191. [4] Chester, op. cit., p. 113.

This plainly showed Rogers and the others what they might now expect; he found himself at once deprived of his emoluments and in effect of his livings. On October 10th, a new Prebend of St. Pancras was appointed; no successor to the vicarage of St. Sepulchre was named until after his death. Many of his friends fled abroad, and he might have escaped; this may even have been the real object of house arrest rather than his immediate imprisonment. But he refused all chances of escape and stood his ground. "He did see the recovery of religion in England for that present desperate; he knew he could not want a living in Germany; and he could not forget his wife and ten children, and to seek means to succour them. But ... after he was called to answer in Christ's cause, he would not depart ... and for the trial of that truth, was content to hazard his life."[1] The months were to drag by while he remained indoors at home, deprived of his income and cut off from his friends; but he knew that, like St. Paul, he was set for the defence of the Gospel.

Rogers owes his fame to the fact that he was the author of the Matthew Bible and was destined to be the first martyr of the second generation. His life story revolves round these two great focal issues, and it is in their light that his character must be considered. Melancthon's evidence in his letter to John Schneck is most valuable: "This Master John the Englishman is a learned man, sound in the doctrine of Christ's Church, and not infected by any evil opinions. And we know that he is gifted with great ability, which he sets off with a noble character; and since he is most anxious to promote the general peace, he will be careful to live in concord with his colleagues."[2] Mozley has shown from the internal evidence of the Matthew Bible that he was an able linguist: he must have been at home in the use of Latin since his days at Cambridge, and his use of foreign writers proves his skill in French and German; and there are signs of his knowledge of Greek as well as of Hebrew and Aramaic.[3] He was in fact a sound scholar as the German Divines declared: and when Convocation met in October 1553 and a bitter debate broke out on a Catechism which taught Transubstantiation, Philpot argued that "Ridley and Rogers and two or three more" should be brought

[1] *Foxe*, Vol. VI, p. 592.   [2] Mozley, op. cit., p. 132.
[3] Ibid., pp. 161-162.

into Convocation and heard.[1] Philpot's demand was not allowed, for they were in prison or under house arrest; but it proves that Rogers was a leading figure in the eyes of the friends of the Reformation. Rogers always had a cheerful spirit: "he was merry and earnest in all he went about".[2] Deprived of his income, compelled to pay for his own food, without books, and cut off though he was from his wife, he was never unnerved. He was willing to live on one meal a day in prison so that others even less fortunate might have at least one meal as well. He was a man of strong family affections, and the taste of death was only acid because of his wife and children. He was also a man of great courage: this had been proved in the troubles which led to his imprisonment, and it was to receive the most shining proof of all at his death.

Towards Christmas 1553, Rogers sent his wife, who was "great with child", and eight "honest women" to petition Gardiner at Richmond for his release from house arrest.[3] This request was refused, and on January 27th, 1554, he was transferred from his home to Newgate. Foxe in his Latin edition said that "Bonner had long striven with his utmost power to accomplish this result as he could not abide such an honest neighbour".[4] We know very little of his life in Newgate during the year 1554; he was allowed neither to see his wife nor use his pen. He was not told when his last child was born and he did not know how his wife had fared until the day on which he died; but he did know that she had gone "many times" to petition Gardiner on his behalf and that there were others who had laboured for him as well.[5] All the leaders of the Reformation who had not fled were in prisons such as the Tower, the Fleet, the King's Bench, Newgate and the Marshalsea: "not as rebels, traitors, seditious persons, thieves or transgressors, ... but alonely for the conscience we have to God and His most holy Word and truth".[6] On February 12th, Lady Jane Grey's execution took place, and a few days later, Bradford expressed the hope that God might yet spare them as He had spared Peter from the hands of Herod: "Even so, dear Lord," he wrote, "break the dream of Thy combined enemies

---

[1] Chester, op. cit., p. 125.
[2] *Foxe*, Vol. VI, p. 609.
[3] Ibid., p. 599.
[4] Chester, op. cit., p. 120.
[5] *Foxe*, Vol. VI, p. 599.
[6] Bradford, *Sermons*, p. 367.

with us, and save Thy servants, Latimer, Cranmer, Ridley, Hooper, Crome, Rogers, Saunders, Bradford, Philpot, Coverdale, Barlow, Cardmaker, Taylor, etc which are appointed to die if Thou by Thy mighty power deliver them not."[1] In April, Cranmer, Ridley and Latimer were sent from the Tower to Oxford for a formal Disputation on the Sacramental controversy; it was a hollow and academic affair in which they were baited, browbeaten and interrupted in a disgraceful performance. They were imprisoned in the Bocardo, but Ridley still contrived to send letters to friends; he was always eager for news of their affairs. Thus in April he wrote to Bradford: "We long to hear of Father Crome, Doctor Sandys, Master Saunders, Veron, Becon, Rogers etc."[2] Bradford was well informed of the treatment which Ridley had received in the Disputation: he "could not be permitted to declare his mind and meaning of the propositions and had oftentimes half a dozen at once speaking against him".[3] It was Ridley's counsel which Bradford and Rogers followed when their time came.

Early in May, it was proposed that Rogers, Bradford, and perhaps others should be sent to Cambridge for a further Disputation. Thus Ridley told Cranmer: "It is said that . . . Master Rogers, Doctor Crome and Master Bradford shall be had to Cambridge and there be disputed with as we were here; and that the Doctors of Oxford shall go likewise thither as Cambridge men came hither."[4] But in conformity with Ridley's advice, they refused on the ground that the court would be partial. On May 8th, Hooper, Ferrar, Rogers, Bradford, Saunders, Taylor, Philpot and Crome signed a Declaration which was smuggled out of prison to set out their reasons. "In that we purpose not to dispute otherwise than by writing except it may be before the Queen's Highness and her Council, or before the Parliament Houses," they wrote, ". . . we have thought it our bounden duty now, whilst we may, by writing to publish and notify the causes why we will not dispute otherwise than is above said."[5] They gave six reasons: it was well known that the determinations of the Universities in matters of religion were

---

[1] Bradford, op. cit., p. 290.   [2] Bradford, *Letters*, p. 83.
[3] Bradford, *Sermons*, p. 369.   [4] Ridley, *Works*, p. 363.
[5] Bradford, op. cit., p. 367.

against God's Word; the prelates and doctors would seek neither the truth nor the welfare of those who joined in the Disputation; the censors and judges would be manifest enemies to the truth which they would defend—"that they be such, their doings of late at Oxford and in the Convocation House in October last past do most evidently declare";[1] they had been in prison for eight or nine months without books or writing materials or freedom for study; they would not be allowed to engage in debate without being interrupted "as was done to the godly learned fathers, especially Doctor Ridley, at Oxford"; and the secretaries who would record the whole Disputation would be "such as either do not or dare not favour the truth".[2] Then the Declaration went on to say: "If they will write, we will answer, and by writing, confirm and prove out of the infallible verity, even the very Word of God, and by the testimony of the good and most ancient Fathers in Christ His Church, this our faith and every piece thereof; which hereafter we in a sum do write and send abroad purposely that our good brethren and sistern in the Lord may know it; and to seal up the same, we are ready through God's help and grace to give our lives to the halter or stake or otherwise as God shall appoint."[3]

On November 12th, Mary's third Parliament began to sit. Doubtless it was Bradford who drew up a Supplication to Mary and Philip and their assembled Parliament in the name of those who were in prison. It was a strong protest at the illegal character of their imprisonment and a sturdy request that they should be brought up for trial. "In most humble and lamentable wise complain unto Your Majesties and to your high court of Parliament your poor, desolate and obedient subjects, Hooper, Ferrar, Taylor, Bradford, Philpot. Rogers, Saunders, etc, that whereas your said subjects living under the laws of God and of this realm in the days of the late most noble King Edward VI did in all things show themselves true, faithful and diligent subjects according to their vocation... your said subjects nevertheless contrary to all laws of justice, equity and right are in very extreme manner not only cast into prison where they have remained now these fifteen or sixteen months; but their livings also, their houses and possessions, their goods and books taken from them,

---

[1] Bradford, op. cit., p. 368.   [2] Ibid., p. 369.   [3] Ibid., p. 370.

and they slandered to be most heinous heretics, their enemies themselves being both witnesses, accusers and judges, belying, slandering and misreporting your said subjects at their pleasure: whereas your said subjects, being straitly kept in prison, can not yet be suffered to come forth and make answer accordingly. In consideration whereof, it may please your most excellent Majesties and this your high court of Parliament, graciously to tender the present calamity of your said poor subjects, and to call them before your presence, granting them liberty either by mouth or writing in the plain English tongue to answer before you or before indifferent arbiters to be appointed by your Majesties unto such articles of controversy in religion as their said adversaries have already condemned them of as of heinous heresies: provided that all things may be done with such moderation and quiet behaviour as becometh subjects and children of peace, and that your said subjects may have the free use of all their own books and conference together among themselves.... And if your said subjects be not able by the testimony of Christ, His Prophets, Apostles, and godly Fathers of His Church, to prove that the doctrine of the Church Homilies and Service, taught and set forth in the time of our late most godly Prince and King Edward VI is the true doctrine of Christ's Catholic Church and most agreeable to the articles of the Christian faith, your said subjects offer themselves then to the most heavy punishment that it shall please your Majesties to appoint."[1]

Such a Supplication was doomed from the outset in a Parliament which had knelt in submission to a Papal Legate, and the only response was an Act to revive the old Lollard laws passed in the reigns of Richard II, Henry IV, and Henry V. These penal statutes came into effect as from January 20th, 1555, and on January 22nd, the first official proceedings began. Various prisoners were brought before the Lord Chancellor and the Privy Council in Gardiner's official residence at Southwark; the main object at this stage was to see if there were one or two who would submit. Eleven prisoners came from Newgate, but the only men whose names were mentioned were Hooper, Rogers, Edward Crome and Harold Tomson. Crome seems to have yielded and Tomson was discharged; the nine others stood

[1] Bradford, op. cit., pp. 403-404.

firm. Rogers wrote an account of his experience dated "ye 27th of January at night";[1] it was hidden in his prison quarters and found by his wife and his son after his death. Chester found the identical copy which had been used by Foxe; but Foxe did not transcribe it in every detail and this makes it necessary at times to quote from the original.

Gardiner introduced matters with an account of Pole's absolution of both Houses of Parliament and their recognition of the Pope as Head of the Church. "How say ye?" he then asked Rogers; "are ye content to unite and knit yourself to the faith of the Catholic Church with us in the state in which it is now in England? Will ye do that?" Rogers replied: "The Catholic Church I never did nor will dissent from." But he was told that it was that Church which had now received the Pope as Supreme Head, and he replied: "I know none other Head but Christ of His Catholic Church, neither will I acknowledge the Bishop of Rome to have any more authority than any other Bishop hath by the Word of God." He went on to say that he had never allowed Henry VIII supremacy in things spiritual such as the forgiveness of sins, and they began to laugh. "Yea," they said, "if thou hadst said so in his days, thou hadst not been alive now."[2] There was further word-play; then he was asked: "What sayest thou? Make us a direct answer whether thou wilt be one of this Catholic Church or not, with us, in that state in which we are now?" And he replied: "My Lord, I can not believe that ye yourselves do think in your hearts that he is supreme head in forgiving of sin etc, seeing you and all the bishops of the realm have now twenty years long preached, and some of you also written, to the contrary."[3]

Gardiner interposed, and "a desultory debate" followed in which Rogers "held his own with some dexterity".[4] At length he was asked what he would do: would he enter into the one Church with the whole realm, or not? "No", he said; "I will first see it proved by the Scriptures. Let me have pen, ink, and books and I shall take upon me plainly to set out the matter so that the contrary shall be proved to be true; and let any man that will confer with me by writing." The Lord Chancellor retorted:

[1] Chester, op. cit., p. 305, cf. *Foxe*, Vol. VI, p. 597.
[2] *Foxe*, Vol. VI, p. 593. [3] Ibid., p. 594. [4] *D.N.B.*

"Nay, that shall not be permitted thee. Thou shalt never have so much proffered thee as thou hast now, if thou refuse it. . . . Here are two things, mercy and justice: if thou refuse the Queen's mercy now, then shalt thou have justice ministered unto thee." Rogers said that he had never offended nor been disobedient to the Queen's Grace; yet he would not refuse the Queen's mercy. But Gardiner was insistent: "If thou wilt not receive the Bishop of Rome to be supreme head of the catholic church, then thou shalt never have her mercy." Scripture itself, he said, forbade him to confer with a man like Rogers, for it forbade intercourse with a heretic.[1] Rogers at once replied: "My Lord, I deny that I am a heretic; prove ye that first, and then allege the text." There was violent argument, and the room was filled with noise and clamour. It was clear that he would not be reformed, and at last the Lord Chancellor overruled the din. "Away, away," said he; "we have more to talk withal." Rogers, who had knelt all this time, now stood up and heard Sir Richard Southwell say with a scoff. "Thou wilt not burn in this gear when it cometh to the purpose, I know well that." Rogers lifted up his eyes to heaven and said: "Sir, I can not tell; but I trust in my Lord God, yes." Thirlby alone spoke to him with genuine courtesy and tried to explain the Queen's policy. Rogers answered that he would not refuse the Queen's mercy though he had been guilty of no offence. There was immediate uproar. "A married priest", they cried, "and have not offended the law!" But he declared that he had not broken the Queen's law, for he had married where it was lawful; nor would he have come home at all had not the law of England allowed priests to marry. There were angry remarks all round, and the serjeant seized his arm to lead him out of the room as they shouted at him.[2] Somehow he finished his account five days later at night with the warning that he should "the next morn come to further answer".[3] And he ended in haste with tears: "If I die, be good to my poor and most honest wife, being a poor stranger, and all my little souls, hers and my children: whom with all the whole faithful and true catholic congregation of Christ the Lord of life and death save, keep and defend. . . . Amen! Amen!"[4]

[1] *Foxe*, Vol. VI, p. 594.   [2] Ibid., pp. 595–596.
[3] Chester, op. cit., p. 305, cp. *Foxe*, Vol. VI, p. 597.   [4] *Foxe*, Vol. VI, p. 597.

On January 28th, Gardiner's Commission for the trial of imprisoned heretics began to sit. Hooper, Cardmaker and Rogers, in that order, were examined that afternoon in St. Marye-over-ye-waye, now St. Saviour's, Southwark. The hearing was public, and many were present. Rogers was asked again if he would join with all the realm in the one Church, and a lengthy debate ensued when he made a dignified refusal. His self-defence was so able that the people began to laugh, and there was an abrupt change in tactics. Gardiner suddenly plunged into a discussion of the Sacrament, and Rogers in reply denied that the real and substantial presence of Christ can be elsewhere than in heaven.

At length Rogers passed from defence to make his own attack. "My Lord, quoth I, ye have dealt with me most cruelly; for ye have put me in prison without law, and kept me there now almost a year and a half. For I was almost half a year in my house where I was obedient to you, God knoweth, and spake with no man. And now have I been a full year in Newgate at great costs and charges, having a wife and ten children to find; and I had never a penny of my livings, which was against the law." Gardiner said that Ridley, who had conferred them on him, had himself usurped the see and that Rogers was wrongly in possession of them. Rogers lost no time to retaliate: "Was the King then a usurper which gave Dr. Ridley the bishopric?" Gardiner fell into the trap as he answered "Yea", and began to list the wrongs which the King had done to Bonner and to himself. Then he hastily corrected himself: "But yet I do misuse my terms", he said, "to call the King usurper."[1] Rogers saw that Gardiner's confusion exposed him to further attack, but he had made his point and let it drop. He went back to his first question and asked again why he had been kept in prison. Gardiner fell into fresh confusion when he said that it was because Rogers had preached against the Queen and had read his lectures in spite of the Council's orders. "That did I not", Rogers declared; "let that be proved, and let me die for it. Thus have you now against the law of God and man handled me, and never sent for me, never conferred with me, never spoke of any learning till now that ye have gotten a whip to whip me with and a sword to cut

[1] *Foxe*, Vol. VI. p. 598.

off my neck if I will not condescend to your mind. This charity doth all the world understand."[1]

At four o'clock Gardiner determined to adjourn the hearing until the next morning, saying that this would give Rogers time to repent and return to the true Catholic Church. Rogers at once declared: "I was never out of the true catholic Church, nor ever would be; but into his Church would I by God's grace never come."[2] Gardiner asked him if he considered that Church false and anti-Christian, and he said "Yea"; he then asked him what he thought of the doctrine of the Sacrament, and he said "False". And with that word he was dismissed until morning.[3] Hooper went out into the street under guard ahead of Rogers; but he waited for him and said as soon as he appeared: "Come, brother Rogers, must we two take this matter first in hand and begin to fry these faggots?" Rogers answered with quiet simplicity: "Yes, Sir; by God's grace." Hooper's reply was one of brave encouragement: "Doubt not but God will give us strength."[4] Then the sheriffs marched them to the Compter instead of to Newgate, and a great crowd thronged all about "so that we had much to do (ado) to go in the streets".[5] But the three had now shrunk to two, for Cardmaker had temporised. Rogers grieved at his fall and wrote of him with deep regret: he "forsook us and stuck not to his tackle, but shrank from under the banner of our Master and Captain Christ: the Lord grant him to return and fight with us".[6] It was not long before that prayer received a full answer, for through Lawrence Saunders, Cardmaker was to recover his poise; he was arraigned again on May 25th and was burnt at the stake on May 30th. Meanwhile Rogers also lifted up his heart in earnest prayer for Hooper and for himself: "The Lord grant us grace to stand together, fighting lawfully in His cause, till we be smitten down together, if the Lord's will be so to permit it. For there shall not a hair of our heads perish againt His will, but with His will. Whereunto the same Lord grant us to be obedient unto the end; and in the end, Amen, sweet, mighty and merciful Lord Jesus, the Son of David and of God! Amen! Amen!"[7]

---

[1] *Foxe*, Vol. VI., pp. 598–599.   [2] Chester, op. cit., p. 312, cf. *Foxe*, Vol. VI, p. 599.   [3] *Foxe*, Vol. VI, p. 599.   [4] Chester, op. cit., p. 178.   [5] *Foxe*, Vol. VI, p. 599.   [6] Chester, op. cit., p. 311.   [7] *Foxe*, Vol. VI, p. 599.

On January 29th, the doors were shut and the public was not allowed in as on the first day. The trial began at nine o'clock, for the court hoped to end matters quickly. Hooper came first and was condemned; Rogers was then summoned and his final hearing began. Gardiner introduced the point at once. "Rogers," he said, "here thou wast yesterday, and we gave thee liberty to remember thyself this night, whether thou wouldst come to the holy catholic Church of Christ again or not. Tell us now what thou hast determined."[1] Rogers replied at length until he was interrupted and told to take his seat. Gardiner mockingly said that "I was sent for to be instructed of them, and I would take upon me to be their instructor". But he refused to sit, saying: "Shall I not be suffered to speak for my life?" Gardiner's impatience was now self-evident; he stood up and refused to let Rogers resume his self-defence. He plied him with taunts and insults, but he could not make him afraid. He poured ridicule on his earnestness: "See what a spirit this fellow hath!" Rogers answered: "I have a true spirit, agreeing and obeying the Word of God."[2] He could not make himself heard in further protest, and his condemnation was read before the court. He was styled "John Rogers, priest, alias called Matthew", and was condemned for two "damnable opinions", namely, "that the catholic Church of Rome is the Church of Antichrist; that in the Sacrament of the Altar there is not substantially nor really the natural body and blood of Christ".[3] He was therefore excommunicated as an "obstinate heretic" and was handed over to the State for secular punishment.[4] When this sentence had been pronounced, Rogers spoke in reply: "Well, my Lord, here I stand before God and you and all this honourable audience, and take Him to witness that I never wittingly or willingly taught any false doctrine; and therefore have I a good conscience before God and all good men. I am sure that you and I shall come before a Judge that is righteous, before Whom I shall be as good a man as you: and I nothing doubt but that I shall be found there a true member of the true catholic Church of Christ, and everlastingly saved. And as for your false church, ye need not to excommunicate me forth of it. I have not been in it these twenty years, the Lord be thanked there-for."[5]

[1] *Foxe*, Vol. VI. p. 599.   [2] Ibid., p. 600.   [3] Ibid., p. 601.
[4] Ibid., p. 602.   [5] Ibid., p. 602.

Rogers made one parting request: "Now ye have done what
ye can, my Lord, I pray you yet grant me one thing." Gardiner
was suspicious and demanded: "What is that?" Rogers replied:
"That my poor wife, being a stranger, may come and speak
with me so long as I live: for she hath ten children that are hers
and mine, and somewhat I would counsel her what were best
for her to do." He was brusquely refused. "No," he said; "she is
not thy wife."[1] Rogers answered: "Yes, my Lord, and hath
been these eighteen years." Gardiner retorted: "Should I grant
her to be thy wife?" Rogers could not restrain his deep indignation: "Choose you whether ye will or not, she shall be so nevertheless." Gardiner rejected his plea: "She shall not come at thee."
It was at that moment and under such provocation that Rogers
uttered a scathing rebuke to which no one dared to reply. "Then
I have tired out all your charity", he said. "You make yourself
highly displeased with the matrimony of priests, but you maintain open whoredom; as in Wales where every priest hath his
whore openly dwelling with him and lying by him: even as
your holy father suffereth all the priests in Dutchland and in
France to do the like."[2]

How soon Gardiner recovered his poise we do not know;
Rogers was at once led away at the Sheriff's hands "which were
much better than his".[3] He and Hooper were placed in the Clink,
the prison of the Clink Liberty or Manor of Southwark which
belonged to the Bishops of Winchester. They were held in the
Clink until nightfall; then they were led through the Bishop's
manor, and the church yard of St. Marye-over-ye-waye,
through Southwark and over the bridge back to Newgate.
It was feared that there would be an uproar; therefore the streets
had been darkened and the very torches on the costermongers'
stalls had been put out. But the streets were lined with men and
women holding lighted candles in their hands and cheering as
they went by.

Rogers did not know how long he still had to live; only five
days in fact remained. But he managed to elude his jailors and
prepare a hurried account of his trial and condemnation. He went
on to add what he had "devised the night before" to say if he
had been allowed; and he had planned it "with sighing and

[1] *Foxe*, Vol. VI. p. 602.   [2] Ibid., p. 603.   [3] Ibid., p. 601.

tears" as well as with much prayer.[1] The last sentence in Foxe breaks off hurriedly: "Some shall have their punishment here in this world and in the world to come; and they that do escape in this world shall not escape everlasting damnation. This shall be your sauce, O ye wicked Papists! Make ye merry here as long as ye may."[2] But the manuscript adds a few last hasty words and ends with one short sentence: "For lack of time I conclude: God's peace be with you. Amen."[3]

On Sunday, February 3rd, Rogers drank a toast to Hooper, who was below, and sent to tell him that "there was never little fellow better would stick to a man than he would stick to him".[4] But they were not to die together: Hooper was sent back to his own Cathedral city and was burnt at Gloucester on February 9th. Meanwhile Rogers was roused from a deep sleep by the jailer's wife on Monday morning, February 4th, and told to make haste as he was to die. He heard the news coolly and said as he began to dress: "If it be so, I need not tie my points."[5] He was taken to the prison chapel where his canonical dress was torn from him and he was formally degraded at the hands of Bonner. Rogers then asked Bonner, as he had asked Gardiner, for one indulgence: "Nothing but that I might talk a few words with my wife before my burning." Bonner refused and he could only reply: "Then you declare your charity, what it is."[6] The two City Sheriffs, Woodroofe and Chester, took control. Woodroofe asked if he would revoke "his evil opinion of the Sacrament", and he replied: "That which I have preached, I will seal with my blood."[7]

He was led to Smithfield through streets thronged with people who were rejoicing at his constancy. Nor were they all strangers: "His wife and children, being eleven in number, and ten able to go, and one sucking on her breast, met him by the way."[8] There were eight sons and three daughters, and this was his first glimpse of the last child in his wife's arms. They stood at the roadside to comfort and strengthen him in his great ordeal, and this was the only farewell he was allowed. He loved them and longed to enjoy their sweet companionship; but "this sorrowful

[1] Chester, op. cit., p. 319.
[2] *Foxe*, Vol. VI, p. 609.
[3] Chester, op. cit., p. 337.
[4] *Foxe*, Vol. VI, p. 611.
[5] Ibid., p. 609.
[6] Ibid., p. 609.
[7] Ibid., p. 611.
[8] Ibid., p. 612.

sight" could not shake his purpose and he went on to die.[1] The stake was set up at Smithfield a few yards from the gate of St. Bartholomew's. He was offered a pardon if he would recant, but he firmly refused. There was a great concourse, but he was not allowed to speak. The faggots were kindled while "he showed most constant patience"[2] and with cheerful faith "quenched the violence of fire" (Heb. 11:34). And when the fire took hold of his legs and shoulders, "he as one feeling no smart, washed his hands in the flame as though it had been in cold water; and after lifting up his hands unto heaven, not removing the same until such time as the devouring fire had consumed them, most mildly this happy martyr yielded up his spirit".[3]

We learn nothing more of his wife apart from her visit to the prison and her discovery of his papers; she may have been able to return to Antwerp, and her eldest son was educated at Wittenberg. Rogers himself was "the proto-martyr of all the blessed company that suffered in Queen Mary's time",[4] and his death made a tremendous impression. The French Ambassador, Count Noailles, wrote to Montmorency: "This day was performed the confirmation of the alliance between the pope and this kingdom by a public and solemn sacrifice of a preaching doctor named Rogers who has been burned alive for being a Lutheran; but he died persisting in his opinion. At this conduct, the greatest part of the people took such pleasure that they were not afraid to make him many exclamations to strengthen his courage. Even his children assisted at it, comforting him in such a manner that it seemed as if he had been led to a wedding."[5] On February 8th, Bradford wrote to Cranmer, Ridley and Latimer at Oxford: "Our dear brother Rogers hath broken the ice valiantly."[6] It was a curious metaphor for such a death, but the perfect adverb to describe his bearing. Ridley was inspired by Rogers' splendid courage, and it may have been in reply to this letter that he wrote to Bradford some time about February 10th: "We do look now every day when we shall be called on, blessed be God! I ween I am the weakest many ways of our company; and yet I thank our Lord God and heavenly Father by Christ that since I heard of our dear brother Rogers' departing and stout confession of

---

[1] *Foxe,* Vol. VI., p. 612.   [2] Ibid., p. 609.   [3] Ibid., p. 611.
[4] Ibid., p. 612.   [5] *D.N.B.*   [6] Bradford, *Letters,* p. 190.

Christ and His truth, even unto the death, my heart—blessed be God!—so rejoiced of it that since that time, I say, I never felt any lumpish heaviness in my heart as I grant I have felt sometimes before.[1] Ridley also wrote to Augustine Berneher: "I bless God with all my heart in His manifold merciful gifts given unto our dear brethren in Christ, especially to our brother Rogers whom it pleased Him to set forth first, no doubt but of His gracious goodness and fatherly favour towards him."[2] Bradford wrote his *Admonition to Lovers of the Gospel* between February 9th and March 30th. "Take up your cross", he wrote, "and follow your Master as your brethren M. Hooper, Rogers, Taylor and Saunders have done. . . . The ice is broken for you; therefore be not afraid, but be content to die for the Lord."[3] Rogers, who "gave the first adventure upon the fire", left his brethren an inspiring example,[4] while, like Bunyan's Faithful, he was "carried up through the clouds, with sound of trumpet, the nearest way to the celestial gate".[5]

[1] Ridley, *Works*, p. 378.   [2] Ibid., p. 380.
[3] Bradford, *Sermons*, p. 410.   [4] *Foxe*, Vol. VI, p. 612.
[5] Bunyan, *Pilgrim's Progress* (Everyman's Edition), p. 115.

BIBLIOGRAPHY

JOHN FOXE, *The Acts and Monuments of John Foxe;* edited by Stephen Cattley (8 vols.), 1841

Dictionary of National Biography, John Rogers (Vol. XVII), 1950

JOSEPH LEMUEL CHESTER, *John Rogers: The Compiler of the First Authorised English Bible; the Pioneer of the English Reformation; and its First Martyr,* 1861

JOHN CHARLES RYLE, *John Rogers: Martyr* (Chapter IV in *Light from Old Times*), 2nd Edition, 1898

J. F. MOZLEY, *William Tyndale,* 1937

J. F. MOZLEY, *Coverdale and his Bibles,* 1953

F. F. BRUCE, *The Books and the Parchments* (Revised Ed.), 1953

E. G. RUPP, *Studies in the Making of the English Protestant Tradition,* 1949

H. F. M. PRESCOTT, *Mary Tudor* (Reprint), 1958

M. L. LOANE, *Masters of the English Reformation,* 1954

THOMAS CRANMER, *Miscellaneous Writings and Letters* (Parker Society Edition), 1846.

NICHOLAS RIDLEY, *Works* (Parker Society Edition), 1843.

JOHN BRADFORD, *Sermons, Meditations, Examinations, etc.* (Parker Society Edition), 1848

JOHN BRADFORD, *Letters, Treatises, Remains* (Parker Society Edition), 1853

JOHN BRADFORD

JOHN BRADFORD

1510–1555

"Master Bradford, nowe in prison at the Compter in the Poultrie for the truthe's sake, hath wryt to one that is friende to a cousyn . . . which were marvellous comfortable epystells. She spake of him as a manne that was more devoute and godlye than anie she dyd ever knowe, being one that dyd leade not onelye a hevenlye lyfe hym selfe, but dyd verie earnestlye and hertily labour to perswade others thereto."—R. FALKENBRIDGE, *Ephemeris—Leaves from the Journal of Marian Drayton* (1592).

JOHN BRADFORD WAS BORN AT BLACKLEY in the parish of Manchester about the year 1510. His Farewell to Lancashire and Cheshire declares: "In Manchester was I born."[1] His Farewell to the City of London observes: "Hourly I look when I should be had hence to be conveyed into Lancashire there to be burned and to render my life by the providence of God where I first received it by the same providence."[2] He was to write in his prison Meditations of "the particular benefits" which he had received in "infancy, childhood, youth, middle age, and always hitherto";[3] and this supports the view that his birth took place about the year 1510. The Latin edition of Foxe's *Acts and Monuments* in 1559 says that he was "of his gentle parents brought up in virtue and good learning even from his very childhood".[4] But the very little we know of his parents and home is gleaned from his *Letters*. It seems likely that his father was dead by the time when he went up to Cambridge, for one of his early letters puts forward a request in which this is implied: "If my mother has not sold the fox fur which was in my father's gown, I would she would send it me."[5] He wrote of and to his mother both from Cambridge and from London, and he cherished the most tender concern for her to the close of his life.[6] He twice referred to his brother-in-law Roger Beswick who had married his sister Margaret and shared his own spiritual ideals;[7] and there were two other sisters, Elizabeth who was also married, and Ann.[8] Perhaps it was Ann to whom he referred on February 16th, 1555: "My poor and most dear sister to me that ever I had, with whom I leave this letter, I commend unto you all and every of you, beseeching you and heartily praying you, in the bowels and blood of Jesus Christ, to care for her as for one which is dear in God's sight."[9] And at the end of June 1555, he wrote

[1] Bradford, *Works*, Vol. I, p. 448.
[2] Ibid., Vol. I, p. 434.
[3] Ibid., Vol. I, p. 162.
[4] Ibid., Vol. II, pp. XI–XII.
[5] Ibid., Vol. II, p. 28.
[6] Ibid., Vol. II, pp. 41, 72, 74, 249.
[7] Ibid., Vol. II, pp. 76, 250.
[8] Ibid., Vol. II, p. 76.
[9] Ibid., Vol. II, p. 197.

again: "Commend me to my most dear sister for whom my heart bleedeth: the Lord comfort her and strengthen her unto the end."[1] Bradford himself was never to marry, although marriage was not out of his mind; but he never forgot the strong ties of family affection, and his parents, his sisters, his brother-in-law, were in his heart to live and die with him (2 Cor. 7:3).

Foxe said that he was brought up in learning from his childhood;[2] he may in fact have been educated in the grammar school at Manchester. "I can not but say", he was to recall, "that I have most cause to thank Thee for my parents, school masters, and others, under whose tuition Thou hast put me. . . . O how good a Lord hast Thou declared Thyself to me which in them and by them hast nourished, fed, instructed, corrected, defended and most graciously kept me. I could reckon innumerable behind me and but few before me, so much made of and cared for as I have been hitherto."[3] Foxe was to add that "he attained such knowledge in the Latin tongue and skill in writing that he was able to gain his own living in some honest condition".[4] He entered the employ of Sir John Harrington of Exton in Rutland who was responsible for the army camps and buildings at Bolougne under Henry VIII. He was thus a confidential clerk or secretary, handling the King's money under Sir John's control, and in 1544, when the Duke of Norfolk carried out the siege of Montreuil, he was deputy paymaster of the English forces.[5] He proved himself so adept in writing, so expert in figures, and so reliable in his conduct, that Sir John not only trusted him in public affairs, but leant on him in his private business "in such sort that above all others he used his faithful service".[6] Bradford remained in his employ until April 1547; then he retired with some kind of pension which was only discontinued as a result of his radical conversion. Bradford's life was to move into a new orbit, but he never lost the Harrington connection. Sir John's third son, Robert, was to be one of his close friends to the end of his life, and was surnamed by him Nathanael as one in whom there was no guile.[7] But the bond with Sir John himself did not survive the great spiritual change in Bradford.

[1] Bradford, Vol. II, p. 252.　　[2] *Foxe*, Vol. VII, p. 143.
[3] Bradford, Vol. I, p. 162.　　[4] *Foxe*, Vol. VII, p. 143.
[5] Bradford, Vol. II, p. xiii.　　[6] *Foxe*, Vol. VII, p. 143.
[7] Bradford, Vol. II, p. 55 fn.

On April 8th, 1547, Bradford entered the Inner Temple to engage in the study of Common Law. Thomas Sampson was his friend and fellow student, and soon turned his thoughts from the Law to the Gospel. Twenty-seven years later, in 1574, Sampson published Bradford's *Sermon on Repentance* with a Preface which contains a valuable sketch of his life. "I did know", wrote Sampson, "when and partly how it pleased God by effectual calling to turn his heart unto the true knowledge and obedience of the most holy Gospel of Christ our Saviour; of which God did give him such an heavenly hold and lively feeling that as he did then know that many sins were forgiven him, so surely he declared by deeds that he loved much."[1] Bradford was to paint his unconverted life in colours which were as dark as they could be. "God might have caused me long before this time to have been cast into prison," he wrote, "as a thief, a blasphemer, an unclean liver and an heinous offender of the laws of the realm."[2] This was hyperbole; but there is no doubt that his whole character underwent a change and his life was filled with a new sense of value. "After that God touched his heart with that holy and effectual calling," Sampson wrote, "he sold his chains, rings, brooches, and jewels of gold which before he used to wear, and did bestow the price of this his former vanity in the necessary relief of Christ's poor members which he could hear of or find lying sick or pining in poverty."[3] Thus he exemplified in his own life what it meant to repent, and it was from his own experience that he declared: "Repentance should contain a sorrowing for our sins, a trust of pardon which otherwise may be called a persuasion of God's mercy by the merits of Christ for the forgiveness of our sins, and a purpose to amend or conversion to a new life."[4] And the central statement was filled out in words that rang true in his own heart: "In heaven and in earth was there none found that could satisfy God's anger for our sins or get heaven for man, but only the Son of God, Jesus Christ, the Lion of the Tribe of Judah, Who by His blood hath wrought the work of satisfaction and alonely is worthy all honour, glory and praise."[5]

In Lent, 1548, Bradford heard a sermon from the eloquent

[1] Bradford, Vol. I, p. 30. [2] Ibid., Vol. II, p. 75.
[3] Ibid., Vol. I, p. 30.   [4] Ibid., Vol. I, p. 45.   [5] Ibid., Vol. I, p. 48.

Latimer in the presence of Edward VI "in which he did earnestly speak of restitution to be made of things falsely gotten".[1] On March 10th, 1550, Latimer was to preach his last sermon before Edward VI and he referred to the earlier occasion in 1548 to enforce his warning on covetousness. "I have now preached three Lents", he said. "The first time I preached restitution. 'Restitution', quoth some, 'what should he preach of restitution?' Let him preach of contrition', quoth they, 'and let restitution alone; we can never make restitution.' Then say I, if thou wilt not make restitution, thou shalt go to the devil for it. Now choose thee either restitution or else endless damnation. But now there be two manner of restitutions; secret restitution and open restitution: whether of both it be, so that restitution be made, it is all good enough. At my first preaching of restitution, one good man took remorse of conscience and acknowledged himself to me that he had deceived the king: and willing he was to make restitution: and so the first Lent came to my hands twenty pounds to be restored to the king's use. I was promised twenty pound more the same Lent, but it could not be made, so that it came not. Well, the next Lent came three hundred and twenty pounds more. I received it myself and paid it to the King's Council. So I was asked, What he was that made this restitution? But should I have named him? Nay, they should as soon have this wesant (windpipe) of mine. Well now this Lent came one hundred and four score pounds ten shillings which I have paid and delivered this present day to the King's Council: and so this man hath made a godly restitution."[2] The sums mentioned by Latimer are confirmed by entries in the Council Book for 1549 and 1550.[3] But who was the "good man" who was filled with remorse because he had deceived the King? This was Bradford, and it marked a further turning point in his life.

An element of mystery is still attached to the details of this affair, and it is not easy to disentangle the details at this distance of time. Latimer's anecdote seems to ascribe direct blame to Bradford for an act of fraud or peculation against the Crown. Sampson's statement in 1574 confirms this point of view. Latimer's words, he said, "did so strike Bradford to the heart for

[1] Bradford, Vol. 1, p. 32.   [2] Latimer, *Sermons*, p. 262.
[3] Darby, *Hugh Latimer*, p. 179.

one dash with a pen which he had made without the knowledge of his master, as full often I have heard him confess with plenty of tears, being clerk to the treasurer of the king's camp beyond the seas, and was to the deceiving of the king, that he could never be quiet till by the advice of the same Master Latimer a restitution was made".[1] But when Bradford was examined by Gardiner and others on January 30th, 1555, there was a sharp exchange which has been thought to prove that he was not an interested party. Gardiner was reminded that Bradford had been in the employ of Sir John Harrington. "True", quoth the Lord Chancellor, "and did deceive his master of seven score pounds; and because of this, he went to be a gospeller and a preacher." Bradford replied at once with a dignified denial. "My Lord", he said, "I set my foot to his foot, whosoever he be, that can come forth and justly vouch to my face that ever I deceived my master. And as you are chief justicer by office in England, I desire justice upon them that so slander me, because they can not prove it."[2] But this explicit denial refers to a supposed offence against Sir John himself; it has no real bearing on the graver issue of fraud against the Crown. Gardiner's confusion was so complete that he dropped the question altogether; it throws no light at all on the peculation which occurred at Boulogne. Bradford's sorrow for that offence was so personal and so emphatic that we cannot doubt his complicity and guilt. He had carried out or covered up some fraudulent transaction with a dash of the pen, either with or without Harrington's direction; and his conscience would not excuse him when he heard Latimer's vigorous sermon, and he sought the preacher's advice.

This is borne out by his letters to and from John Traves of Blackley, and the grief and difficulty in which he found himself may still be traced in their guarded language. The first letter was in February 1548 from Traves, to whom Bradford had first opened his heart. "Ye shall understand," wrote Traves, "that after the receipt of your letters I declared to Master Latimer the sum of that ye writ to me concerning your matter with your master."[3] Bradford himself then saw Latimer and was encouraged to take up the matter with Sir John Harrington; he

[1] Bradford, Vol. I, pp. 32–33.   [2] Ibid., Vol. I, p. 487.
[3] Ibid., Vol. II, p. 1.

was to tell Sir John that the money fraudulently obtained must be restored or else he would lay the matter before the King's Council. His first letter to Traves in March 1548 declares: "Sithens my coming to London I was with Master Latimer whose counsel is as you shall hear; which I purpose by God's grace to obey (if it be Thy will, O Lord, fiat). He willed me, as I have done, to write to my master who is in the country and to show him that if within a certain time which I appointed, fourteen days, he do not go about to make restitution that I will submit myself to my Lord Protector and the King's Majesty's Council, to confess the fault and ask pardon."[1] On March 22nd he wrote again to say that Sir John had come to London and had promised payment in full; but not until he had become convinced that Bradford would definitely lay the matter before the King's Council. On May 12th he could tell Traves: "Concerning the great matter you know of, it hath pleased God to bring it to this end, that I have a bill of my master's hand wherein he is bound to pay the sum afore Candlemas next coming" (February 2nd 1549). "This thinks Master Latimer to be sufficient."[2] In November 1549, Bradford referred to it again: "You know how that God hath exonerated the loaden conscience of the great weighty burthen, for so I did write to you: yea, the Lord hath in manner unburthened me of the lesser burthen also, for I have an assurance of the payment of the same by Candlemas" (February 2nd, 1550). "Lo, thus you see what a good God the Lord is unto me. O Father Traves, give thanks for me and pray God to forgive my unthankfulness."[3] And in February 1550, he wrote that God had "wrought the restitution of the great thing you know of, the which benefit should bind me to all obedience".[4]

Bradford remained at the Inner Temple from April 1547 until June 1548. We may trace the effect of his reading in law in the lucid thought and cogent speech which ran right through his defence before his examiners in January 1555. He had triumphed in the test to which his faith and integrity had been exposed, and his mind was turning more and more to Divinity. He had occupied himself with a translation of selected passages from Artopoeus and John Chrysostom, and he wrote a Preface for their publica-

---

[1] Bradford, Vol. II, pp. 5–6.   [2] Ibid., Vol. II, p. 17.
[3] Ibid., Vol. II, p. 27.   [4] Ibid., Vol. II, p. 33.

tion by Lynn in May 1548 with a stringent attack against the
Mass. "Repent," he wrote, "and embrace by faith that only
sacrifice which Christ Himself made once for all: or else, I will
be so bold to say, you shall never be saved."[1] His chief source of
income had been withdrawn as a result of Sir John's "sore displeasure: the which hath brought me", he wrote, "—God, I
should say, through it—unto a more contempt of worldly
things through the sequestration of such his business as tofore I
had ado withal",[2] He could scarcely have been surprised at this
result; Sir John indeed felt that he had threatened him with ruin.
Bradford was not disturbed by the loss of worldly prospects,
and a letter to Traves in May 1548 describes his plans. "I have
moved my master therein already by letters", he wrote, "to
see if I shall have any living of him as hitherto I have had; but I
have thereof no answer, nor, as our natural speech is, any likeli-
hood of any grant. Yet that I have already, I trust, will be able
for me for three years: you look what my purpose meaneth, I am
so long afore I come to it. Therefore I do it, because my long
babbling should be less tedious. Now shall you have it. If God's
will be, whereunto pray I may be obedient, I am minded afore
midsummer to leave London to go to my books at Cambridge,
and if God shall give me grace, to be a minister of His Word."[3]

Thus, as Sampson wrote, "he changed not only the course of
his former life, . . . but even his former study".[4] It was late in
May or early in June when he sent the next news to Traves:
"This present day by God's grace I take my journey towards
Cambridge where, I pray God, and so earnestly pray you to
pray for me, that I may circumspectly redeem this time which
God hath appointed, to me unknown, to lend me."[5] And he
went on to say: "My master which was hath denied me all his
beneficence; but I have for this life more than enough, thanks be
to God. . . . I will lie, God willing, this summer at Catharine's
Hall in Cambridge."[6] His next letter to Traves, dated August
15th, was written from "Catharine's Hall in Cambridge".[7]
Little more than twelve months elapsed before he was asked by

---

[1] Bradford, Vol. I, p. 8.   [2] Ibid., Vol. II, pp. 17–18.
[3] Ibid., Vol. II, p. 18.   [4] Ibid., Vol. I, p. 30.
[5] Ibid., Vol. II, p. 20.   [6] Ibid., Vol. II, p. 21.
[7] Ibid., Vol. II, p. 24.

Ridley to become a Fellow of Pembroke Hall, and he wrote to Traves on October 22nd, 1549: "My master has in all his affairs disowned me; and he has now refused to pay what he had before allowed. . . . I write not this that you should think me to be in poverty or straits. No, father, the Lord giveth me all things in abundance, and will do. I trust I shall shortly here have a Fellowship; I am so promised, and therefore I have taken the degree of Master of Art, which else I could not have attained."[1] It was Ridley's offer to make him a Fellow which had allowed him to proceed to his degree on October 19th, and the entry in the University Grace Book describes him as "a man of mature age and approved life" who for eight years had been engaged in the study of literature, arts and the Holy Scriptures.[2] He next wrote to Traves from Pembroke Hall in November: "Where you know the sun, the moon and the seven stars did forsake me and would not shine upon me—you know what I mean, through my master and my master's friends—yet the Lord hath given me here in the University as good a living as I would have wished. For I am now a Fellow of Pembroke Hall, of the which I nor any other for me did ever make any suit; yea, there was a contention betwixt the Master of Catharine's Hall and the Bishop of Rochester who is Master of Pembroke Hall whether should have me. Thus you may see the Lord's carefulness for me."[3]

Bradford was so tender-hearted that he grieved to lose the goodwill of his "master"; but he never wanted for friends. He had a most winning nature and warmed to the friendship of young and old alike. Sampson was with him both in the Inner Temple and at Cambridge, and he lived to declare: "I which did know him familiarly must needs give to God this praise for him that among men I have scarcely known one like unto him."[4] And "good father Traves" had helped him with wise counsel and calm encouragement. "There is none whose company and talk I more desire than yours," Bradford wrote on December 1st, 1549; "I speak it before God."[5] He stood high in Latimer's confidence as a result of his faithful dealing on the point of restitution. "I thank him I am as familiar with him as with you", he

---

[1] Bradford, Vol. II, pp. 25–26.
[2] Ibid., Vol. II, p. 26 fn.; cf. *D.N.B.*
[3] Bradford, Vol. II, p. 27.
[4] Ibid., Vol. I, p. 30.
[5] Ibid., Vol. II, p. 31.

told Traves in February 1550; "yea, God so moveth him against me that his desire is to have me come and dwell with him whensoever I will, and welcome."[1] Edwin Sandys, a fellow Lancastrian, was the Master of St. Catherine's Hall while he was in residence and would gladly have appointed him to a Fellowship. Bishop Ridley chose him as a Fellow of Pembroke Hall and grew to love him with a father's love for his son. Edmund Grindal was a Fellow of Pembroke Hall at the same time and was also marked out for high service. Whitgift entered Pembroke Hall in the Michaelmas term of 1550 and had Bradford as his tutor. It has been said that "the severe austerity and selfless unflagging devotion to duty that marked the whole course of Whitgift's life were beyond doubt fired by sparks caught from the spirit of John Bradford".[2] And one more name must be mentioned. Martin Bucer had become Regius Professor of Divinity at Cambridge in 1549, and Bradford soon became "right familiar and dear unto him".[3]

Sampson's account of Bradford at Cambridge depicts him as a man of "high moral ideals and intense personal self-discipline".[4] "He did not count himself to have prayed to his contentation unless in it he had felt inwardly some smiting of heart for sin, and some healing of that wound by faith. . . . He used in the morning to go to the common prayer in the College where he was, and after that he used to make some prayer with his pupils in his chamber; but not content with this, he then repaired to his own secret prayer . . . as one that had not yet prayed to his own mind."[5] Another exercise from which he sought encouragement was this: "He used to make unto himself an ephemeris or a journal in which he used to write all such notable things as either he did see or hear each day that passed. But whatsoever he did hear or see, he did so pen it that a man might see in that book the signs of his smitten heart."[6] Thus he noted his own need for strength and virtue, or asked God for grace and mercy He would sometimes lose himself in a reverie, regardless of others, and would sit in deep and prolonged silence. Sometimes

---

[1] Bradford, Vol. II, p. 34.
[2] P. M. Dawley, *John Whitgift and the Reformation*, p. 39.
[3] Bradford, Vol. I, p. 31.   [4] Dawley, op. cit., p. 39.
[5] Bradford, Vol. I, pp. 33–34.   [6] Ibid., Vol. I, p. 35.

his eyes would fill with tears; sometimes his face was lit with smiles. "I did perceive", Sampson wrote, "that sometimes his tears trickled out of his eyes as well for joy as for sorrow."[1] But he was not always so self-absorbed. "He would freely reprove any sin and misbehaviour which appeared in any person. . . . And this he did with such a divine grace and Christian majesty that ever he stopped the mouths of the gain-sayers."[2] Bradford carried out his studies upon his knees, and prayed as he studied; his one great aim was to bring his "dull heart to love Christ more".[3] He once wrote to Mistress Warcup: "To the Lord our God, to the Lamb our Christ, which hath borne our sins on His back and is our Mediator for ever, do I send you."[4] He would have her go where he had been himself.

"Cambridge in the reign of Edward VI was in the throes of change", and this reflects something of the incoherence in the realm as a whole.[5] Henry's Visitation in 1535 had not only suppressed the old monastic houses, but had also changed the academic emphasis. Canon Law was suppressed, and Chairs had been endowed for Divinity, Hebrew and Greek. But this early flame of promise had died away in the darker years of faction towards the close of the reign of Henry VIII, and in 1549 a new Visitation took place "to establish God's Word and good learning".[6] Martin Bucer was the central figure in the group of Cambridge scholars who were wedded to the Reformation; Matthew Parker, Edwin Sandys, Edmund Grindal and John Bradford were the four men who "held a more particular converse with that great learned foreign divine".[7] They were opposed by Masters and Fellows who were entrenched in "the well-worn grooves of the centuries";[8] no one could tell when or how such new wine would burst the old wine-skins.

One slight glimpse of Bradford's close friendship with Bucer is found in Humfrey's Life of Jewel. Humfrey says that "Bucer, accompanied beside others by John Bradford, . . . one of his most dear and intimate friends, went to Oxford to see that University and Peter Martyr a little before St. Mary Magdalen's

---

[1] Bradford. Vol. I, p. 36.
[2] Ibid., Vol. I, p. 36.
[3] Ibid., Vol. I, p. 559.
[4] Ibid., Vol. II, p. 163.
[5] Dawley, op. cit., p. 40.
[6] Ridley, *Works*, p. 328.
[7] Bradford, Vol. II, p. xxi.
[8] Dawley, op. cit., p. 41.

Day (July 22nd) 1550".[1] Little more than six months later, Bucer sustained his last illness. Bradford constantly ministered to him and was named with Sampson in a codicil to his will as the one whom his wife was to consult for the ordering of his burial. Bucer died on February 28th, 1551, and Nicholas Car wrote to Sir John Cheke: "I remember when John Bradford, a holy young man and especially beloved by this our friend, . . . exhorted him to consider who he was, what he had taught, and what steadfastness, faith and devotion he had always exercised, and when most troubled, then above all to cast his whole mind, thought and care upon God; for He alone it was that paid the price of our sins, Who could restore from darkness to light, from despair to hope, from death to life—I remember, I say, that Bucer then became rather more disturbed and replied with some warmth that he wished his mind not to be drawn aside from the meditation which engaged it by any man's address or exhortation; that his eyes were fixed upon Christ crucified, that God dwelt in his heart and that he was contemplating nothing but heaven."[2]

John Foxe says that Bucer "so liked" Bradford that he counted him as "most dear" among his friends and urged him "to bestow his talent in preaching". Bradford always replied that he was not ready for that office because of his "want of learning". Bucer used to reply: "If thou have not fine manchet bread, yet give the poor people barley bread or whatsoever else the Lord hath committed unto thee."[3] Bradford had in fact gone up to Cambridge to fit himself for the preaching of the Gospel,[4] and the time came at length. Ridley, who had discerned his worth and made him a Fellow of Pembroke Hall, now called him to London. On August 10th, 1550, he ordained him at Fulham as a Deacon and gave him a licence to preach. He made him one of his chaplains,[5] and gave him a lodging in his own house.[6] All that Frith had meant to Tyndale, Bradford was to prove for Ridley. Frith and Bradford were both destined to die before the men whom by nature they might well have outlived; yet it was true that the faith and courage of Tyndale and Ridley

[1] Bradford, Vol. II, p. xxii.   [2] Ibid., Vol. II, pp. xxiii–xxiv.
[3] *Foxe*, Vol. VII, p. 143.   [4] Bradford, Vol. II, p. 18.
[5] Ridley, *Works*, p. 331.   [6] Ibid., p. 380.

were born afresh and lived again in the lives of Frith and Bradford. On July 23rd, 1551, Ridley wrote to Sir John Cheke: "I have gotten the good will and grant to be with me of three preachers, men of good learning, and as I am persuaded, of excellent virtue; which are able both with life and learning to set forth God's Word in London and in the whole Diocese of the same, where is most need of all parts in England."[1] He went on to say that one of them was "Master Bradford, a man by whom, as I am assuredly informed, God hath and doth work wonders in setting forth of His Word".[2] And on August 24th, 1551, Ridley offered Bradford the Prebend of Kentish Town and Rogers the Prebend of St. Pancras in the Cathedral Church of St. Paul.

Some months later, in December 1551, Bill, Harley, Perne, Grindal, Knox and Bradford were made Chaplains in Ordinary to Edward VI. Two were to be at Court and four always in the country; they were to be "itineraries, to preach sound doctrine in all the remotest parts of the kingdom, for the instruction of the ignorant in right religion to God and obedience to the King."[3] Bradford was to itinerate in Lancashire and Cheshire, and his Farewell to those counties shows the extent of his preaching. "Turn unto the Lord, yet once more I heartily beseech thee", he wrote, "thou Manchester, thou Ashton-under-Lyne, thou Bolton, Bury, Wigan, Liverpool, Mottram, Stockport, Winstanley, Eccles, Prestwick, Middleton, Radcliffe, and thou city of (West) Chester, where I have truly taught and preached the Word of God."[4] He also preached widely both in London and at Saffron Walden, and wrote Farewells to his hearers in these centres. "When I remember how that by the providence and grace of God", he wrote, "I have been a man by whom it hath pleased Him through my ministry to call you to repentance and amendment of life, something effectually as it seemed, and to sow amongst you His true doctrine and religion . . . ."[5] It was agreed among all that Bradford was a master in the art of preaching, and Foxe said that "many parts of England" heard him proclaim the truth "by the space of three years".[6] On November 18th, 1552,

[1] Ridley, op. cit., p. 331.
[2] Ibid., p. 331.
[3] Bradford, Vol. II, p. xxv.
[4] Ibid., Vol. I, p. 454.
[5] Ibid., Vol. I, p. 455.
[6] *Foxe*, Vol. VII, p. 144.

Ridley wrote of Grindal, Bradford and Rogers as "men known
to be so necessary to be abroad in the commonwealth that I can
keep none of them with me in my house."[1] Bradford was in
Lancashire for the last time during Christmas that year and his
sermon on St. Stephen's Day was not soon forgotten.[2] Gardiner
tried to ridicule his gifts: "I know thou hast a glorious tongue,
and goodly shows thou makest."[3] He mocked his "eloquent
tongue" and his "gay glorious words".[4] But his ordinary hearers
knew the truth: he was in at their hearts before they were aware,
winning them as he would for God.

Bradford was a preacher of righteousness and repentance, and
his sermons have the ring of "passionate earnestness".[5] Perhaps
his most famous sermon was one which dealt with this subject
during the summer of 1552 while he was preaching in the
country.[6] Many asked him for a copy of this sermon, but he
had not written it out. "When no way would serve but I must
promise them to write it as I could", he said, "I consented to
their request that they should have it at my leisure."[7] Thus in
July 1553, it was published with a Preface in which he said that
it had "lien by me half a year at the least for the most part of it".[8]
Bradford knew that God speaks sometimes in the thunder of
judgment, sometimes in the music of mercy, and that both by
mercies and by judgments He calls men to repent. Never for a
moment did he slacken his energy or narrow his objective; he
spared the sins neither of rich nor poor, and he rebuked the
wordliness of courtiers with an intrepid singleness of mind.
Ridley's *Piteous Lamentation* makes it clear that Bradford was
most forthright in his attacks on the greed and the self-seeking of
men in power under Edward VI: "As for Latimer, Lever, Bradford and Knox, their tongues were so sharp, they ripped in so
deep in their galled backs, to have purged them no doubt of
that filthy matter that was festered in their hearts of insatiable
covetousness ... that these men of all other, these magistrates
then could never abide."[9] Sampson says that Bradford preached
before Edward VI in Lent 1553 when his reign was nearing its

---

[1] Ridley, *Works*, p. 336.
[2] Bradford, Vol. I, p. 453.
[3] Ibid., p. 466.   [4] Ibid., p. 467, 476.
[5] *D.N.B.*
[6] Bradford, Vol. I, p. 41.
[7] Ibid., Vol. I, p. 41.
[8] Ibid., Vol. I, p. 41.
[9] Ridley, *Works*, p. 59.

end, and cried with the mighty spirit of a Hebrew prophet: "I summon you all, even every mother's child of you, to the judgment of God; for it is at hand."[1] John Knox may have had this sermon in mind when he wrote his *Godly Letter to the Faithful* in 1554 and declared: "Master Bradford, whom God for Christ His Son's sake comfort to the end, spared not the proudest, but boldly declared that God's vengeance should shortly strike them that then were in authority. . . . Judicium Domini, Judicium Domini, lamentably cried he, with weeping tears."[2]

Bradford carried on his work as Prebendary of St. Paul's and Chaplain-in-Ordinary with growing success, but none of his letters between February 1550 and August 1553 have been preserved. Late in 1552 there were plans to divide Durham into two sees and to translate Ridley from London to Durham. This was not to eventuate, but on November 18th, Ridley wrote to Sir John Gate and Sir William Cecil on the subject. He referred to "Master Bradford whom in my conscience I judge more worthy to be a bishop than many a one of us that be Bishops already to be a parish priest".[3] Ridley had singled out Bradford as a future bishop just as he had chosen Grindal, and his appointment to a diocese was barred only by the death of Edward VI. Edward's bright star set on July 6th, 1553; Bradford's *Preface to his Sermon on Repentance* was dated July 12th. He was able to insert a moving passage in the printed sermon with regard to Edward which shows how the leaders of the Reformation felt at the time. "And here with me a little look on God's anger," he wrote, "yet so fresh that we can not but smell it. . . . I mean it forsooth, for I know you look for it, in our dear late Sovereign Lord, the King's Majesty. You all know he was but a child in years: defiled he was not with notorious offences. Defiled! quoth he? Nay rather, adorned with so many goodly gifts and wonderful qualities as never prince was born from the beginning of the world. Should I speak of his wisdom, of his ripeness in judgment, of his learning, of his godly zeal, heroical heart, fatherly care for his commons, nursely solicitude for religion etc.? Nay, so many things are to be spoken in commendation of

---

[1] Bradford, Vol. I, p. 31.   [2] McCrie, *Life of Knox*, p. 341.
[3] Ridley, *Works*, p. 337.

God's exceeding graces in this child that ... I had rather speak nothing than too little, in that too much is too little ... Oh, if God's judgment be begun on him, which as he was the chiefest, so I think the holiest and godliest in the realm of England; alas, what will it be on us whose sins are overgrown so our heads that they are climbed up into heaven! ... God save England and give us repentance! My heart will not suffer me to tarry longer herein."[1]

Bradford had no illusions as to the future, but he did not approve of the attempt to crown Lady Jane Grey. He thought that the King's last illness must have weakened his mind,[2] and he wrote of those who subscribed to his last will as men who had done that "for the which they beshrewed themselves".[3] On July 19th, Mary was proclaimed; on August 3rd, she arrived in London. It was during this lull that he composed his first extant letter since February 1550. He saw that men would be required to yield to the Papal demands: else "our bodies are like to be laid in prisons, and our goods given, we can not tell to whom".[4] "I trust you all", he went on to say, "will consider this gear with yourselves, and in the cross see God's mercy, which is more sweet and to be set by than life itself."[5] His own buoyant faith shone through his words of encouragement: "This mercy of God should make you merry and cheerful. ... Few love God better than their goods; but I trust yet you are of this few."[6]

Bradford chose this time to publish his *Translation of Melancthon on Prayer* with a Preface which shows what his feelings were in that dark uncertain interval. "These perilous days of necessity so nip us and provoke us to pray," he wrote, "and by prayer to fetch down help from above, that if now we will not with diligence use it ... surely we needs must feel that which we can not be able to bear." He looked upon the death of "our late Lord and most dear King" as a mark of judgment; and when judgment began with the King, "I can not believe it will stay there: though he was Adam's child ... yet am I persuaded that it was not his but our sins which hath procured God to take him away from us."[7] "To the intent therefore that God might turn

---

[1] Bradford, Vol. I, pp. 61–62.   [2] Ibid., Vol. I, p. 62.
[3] Ibid., Vol. II, p. 87.   [4] Ibid., Vol. II, p. 35.   [5] Ibid., Vol. II, p. 37.
[6] Ibid., Vol. II, p. 37.   [7] Ibid., Vol. I, p. 19.

His favourable countenance towards us, in that the means thereunto is hearty repentance and prayer; because I can not be everywhere to stir up men thereunto by preaching, I have thought it my duty to signify my good will by writing that which something God might use as a mean to help thereunto. Unto a Sermon therefore of Repentance which even presently I have put forth, I have also put forth this Treatise of Prayer, the which hath been a good space translated; as a good part more of the Common Places of this Master Melancthon which one day may fortune to come abroad if I shall perceive any commodity by this to come to the Church of Christ."[1]

Bradford went on preaching, but his time was now short and the climax came on Sunday morning, August 13th. That day Gilbert Bourne, the Rector of High Ongar in Essex and future Bishop of Bath and Wells, preached at Paul's Cross and a riot ensued. He was rescued by Rogers and Bradford in a dramatic episode. They were standing behind him when the storm burst round his head and he begged them "for the Passion of Christ" to take his place and speak to the people.[2] Bradford was to recall the scene in a vivid account when he was examined by the Lord Chancellor: "There he sitteth by your Lordship (I mean my Lord Bishop of Bath) which desired me himself for the Passion of Christ I would speak to the people: upon whose words, I, coming into the pulpit had like to have been slain with a naked dagger which was hurled at him, I think; for it touched my sleeve."[3] Foxe adds further details which Bradford did not mention and describes the swift response of the people to a favourite orator: "So glad they were to hear him that they cried with a great shout: Bradford! Bradford! God save thy life, Bradford!"[4] Order was soon restored and the crowd began to break up. But Bourne was so unnerved that he clung to Bradford: "He eftsoons prayed me I would not leave him; and I promised him as long as I lived, I would take hurt that day before him; and so went out of the pulpit and entreated with the people and at length brought him safe to a house."[5] Foxe says that while the Mayor and the Sheriffs were his escort, "Bradford

---

[1] Bradford, Vol. I, p. 20. [2] Ibid., Vol. I, p. 485.
[3] Ibid., Vol. I, p. 485. [4] *Foxe*, Vol. VII, p. 144.
[5] Bradford, Vol. I, p. 485.

went at his back, shadowing him from the people with his gown".[1] The day was not over for John Bradford, for that afternoon he preached at the Bow Church in Cheapside. "And there," he told the Lord Chancellor, "going up into the pulpit, one willed me not to reprove the people"; for it was said that he would not come down alive if he did. "And yet," he said, "notwithstanding, I did in that sermon reprove their fact and called it sedition at the least twenty times."[2]

Three days later, on Wednesday, August 16th, Bradford and Rogers were summoned before the Queen's Council on a charge of preaching without authority. Bradford was imprisoned in the Tower of London while Rogers was confined to house arrest. In January 1555, Bonner described Bradford's conduct in the riot at Paul's Cross with wilful ingratitude: "I saw him with mine own eyes when he took upon him to rule and lead the people malapertly; thereby declaring that he was the author of the sedition."[3] Gardiner's memory played round the way in which he had behaved at the bar of the Queen's Council: "I have not forgotten how stubborn thou wert when thou wert before us in the Tower."[4] Bradford himself soon found means to write to William Punt in terms which give a graphic picture of his early imprisonment: "God most justly hath cast me now into a dungeon, but much better than I deserve; wherein I see no man but my keeper, nor can see any except they come to me. . . . I thank God, my common disease doth less trouble me now than when I was abroad, which doth teach me the merciful providence of God towards me".[5] What he calls his "common disease" was nothing more severe than "a rheum" and a feeble stomach.[6]

It was not long before he was transferred from this solitary "dungeon" to the "Nun's bower" which he shared with Edwin Sandys for some six months. They found that their keeper was a papist named John Bowler, but he listened to what they had to say and was so drawn by their "gentle using of him" that he began "to favour the Gospel". Thus on Sundays while Mass was said in the Chapel, Bowler brought the Book of Common Prayer, a piece of manchet bread and a glass of wine into their cell: "and

[1] *Foxe*, Vol. VII, p. 144.   [2] Ibid., Vol. I, p. 485.
[3] Ibid., Vol. I, p. 466.   [4] Ibid., Vol. I, p. 466.
[5] Ibid., Vol. II, pp. 38–39.   [6] Stevens, p. 45 fn.

there Doctor Sandys ministered the communion to Bradford and to Bowler".[1] Thus their keeper was like a son born while they were in bonds, and his fellowship with the prisoners was like a new version of the jailer at the feet of Paul and Silas. Bowler no doubt would hear Bradford state the truth which he had proclaimed in his Sermon on the Lord's Supper: "Surely do every of you think when you hear these words, Take, eat; this is My body broken for your sins: Drink; this is My blood shed for your sins, that God the Eternal Father embraceth you, Christ calleth and clepeth (nameth) you most lovingly."[2]

On October 6th Bradford wrote a moving letter to his mother, kinsfolk, Traves, and other friends in reply to a letter which he had just received from his brother. "I am at this present in prison sure enough for starting to confirm that I have preached unto you," he wrote; "as I am ready, I thank God, with my life and blood to seal the same, if God vouch me worthy of that honour."[3] Persecution would spread and its results would be drastic. "Now will God make known His children. When the wind doth not blow, then can not a man know the wheat from the chaff; but when the blast cometh, then flieth away the chaff, but the wheat remaineth and is so far from being hurt that by the wind it is more cleansed from the chaff and known to be wheat."[4] This was a favourite metaphor; thus he assured Joyce Hales: "you are of God's corn: fear not therefore the flail, the fan, millstone nor oven".[5] Meanwhile his first letter had gone on with another metaphor: "Gold when it is cast into the fire is the more precious: so are God's children by the cross of affliction."[6] Then he referred to his preaching at a time when there had never been more knowledge of God and less godly living: "I am most certain it is and was God's truth, and I trust to give my life for it by God's grace. . . . And indeed I thank Him more of this prison than of any parlour, yea than of any pleasure that ever I had, for in it I find God my most sweet good God always."[7] This led him on in the strain of jubilant martyrdom: "Wherefore fear God; stick to His Word though all the world would swerve from it. Die you must once, and when or how you can not tell.

---

[1] *Foxe*, Vol. VIII, p. 593.
[2] Bradford, Vol. I, pp. 104–105.
[3] Ibid., Vol. II, p. 41.
[4] Ibid., p. 41.
[5] Ibid., p. 112; cp. Vol. II, p. 50.
[6] Ibid., p. 41. [7] Ibid., p. 42.

Die therefore with Christ; suffer for serving Him truly and after His Word; for sure may we be that of all deaths, it is most to be desired to die for God's sake . . . You shall see that I speak as I think; for by God's grace, I will drink before you of this cup, if I be put to it. I doubt not but God will give me His grace and strengthen me thereunto. Pray that He would and that I refuse it not. I am at a point, even when my Lord God will, to come to Him. Death nor life, prison nor pleasure, I trust in God, shall be able to separate me from my Lord God and His Gospel."[1]

It was during these months in the Tower that Bradford wrote his *Treatise on The Hurt of Hearing Mass* which was to circulate in manuscript form among his friends.[2] It was a tract for the times, as his first words make quite clear: "At this present, men call this into question, whether it be lawful for a man which knoweth the truth to be present at the celebration of the mass or no."[3] Twelve points were then listed as the reasons which were commonly accepted as to why men might go to Mass. He examined the history of each part of the Mass as Barnes had done,[4] and his references were based on the Sarum Missal which had been most widely used in England. Then he made three primary objections to the use of the Mass: it was an offence against the Priesthood and Sacrifice of Christ, an obstacle to the true worship of God, and a perversion of the New Testament Ordinance. He went on to argue that "Mass is an outward idol and the service of God there used is idolatry".[5] "The Pope and his Prelates say, If thou come not to hear Mass, but disallow it, thou shalt fry a faggot in Smithfield. God almighty saith, If thou keep thee not from the Mass, or if thou come to it and do not openly disallow it, thou shall fry a faggot in hell-fire."[6] Bradford closed his Treatise with a reply to the twelve reasons which had been listed in favour of going to Mass: most men seek to avoid the cross, but this could not make their presence at Mass lawful. This is made still clearer in his *Sermon on the Lord's Supper* which was revised by Ridley at Oxford in 1554 and published by Sampson in 1574. Bradford would not allow

---

[1] Bradford, Vol. II, p. 43.
[2] Ibid, Vol. II, pp. 116, 126, 236.
[3] Ibid., Vol. II, p. 300.
[4] Barnes, *Works*, pp. 356–358.
[5] Bradford, Vol. II, p. 317.
[6] Ibid., Vol. II, p. 324.

the old title, "the Sacrament of the Altar", but spoke of "the Supper of the Lord, or the Sacrament of Christ's body".[1] And he affirmed his faith with a ringing declaration: "The presence which we believe and confess is such a presence as reason knoweth not and the world can not learn, nor any that looketh in this matter with other eyes or heareth with other ears than with the ears and eyes of the Spirit and of faith."[2]

On February 6th, 1554, there was a change in the prison arrangements as a result of the necessity to make room for scores of Wyatt's Rebels. Edwin Sandys was sent to Marshalsea while Bradford was transferred to a room in the Tower which he shared with Cranmer, Ridley and Latimer. The four men were housed in this room for a little more than six weeks and they rejoiced at the chance to strengthen their faith. Latimer was to recall this with gratitude in his Disputation at Oxford on April 18th: "Behold the providence of God . . . did bring this to pass that where these famous men, viz., Mr. Cranmer, Archbishop of Canterbury, Mr. Ridley, Bishop of London, that holy man Mr. Bradford, and I, old Hugh Latimer, were imprisoned in the Tower of London for Christ's Gospel preaching, and for because we would not go a massing, every one in close prison from other; the same Tower being so full of other prisoners that we four were thrust into one chamber as men not to be accounted of, but God be thanked, to our great joy and comfort, there did we together read over the New Testament with great deliberation and painful study; and I assure you as I will answer at the tribunal throne of God's Majesty, we could find in the Testament of Christ's body and blood no other presence but a spiritual presence."[3]

The two leading spirits were Ridley with his learning and logic and Bradford with his fervour and passion, and they were a tonic to Cranmer and Latimer, who were braced and refreshed by fellowship and discussion. They all knew that they were living in days of dark uncertainty, and the execution of Lady Jane Grey and Lord Guilford Dudley on February 12th was a sombre warning of what was in store for others. Bradford wrote that very day to Robert Harrington: "Now God will try

[1] Bradford, Vol. I, p. 85.   [2] Ibid., Vol. I, pp. 96–97.
[3] Latimer, *Sermons and Remains*, pp. 258–259.

you to make others to learn by you that which ye have learned by others; and by them which suffered this day ye might learn, if already ye had not learned, that life and honour is not to be set by more than God's commandment. They in no point, for all that ever their ghostly fathers could do, ... would consent or seem to consent to the popish mass and papistical God otherwise than in the days of our late King they had received; and this their faith they have confessed with their deaths to their great glory and all our comforts if we follow them."[1] Two days later he wrote again: "What way is so sure a way to heaven as to suffer in Christ's cause? If there be any way on horseback to heaven, surely this is the way."[2]

On the eve of Easter, March 24th, 1554, Bradford was transferred to the King's Bench prison where he was to remain for ten months in constant uncertainty. The Knight-Marshal was Sir William Fitzwilliam, who was known as "a good man and a lover of the Gospel",[3] and he allowed Bradford a remarkable degree of freedom. Robert Ferrar, Rowland Taylor and John Philpot were all in the King's Bench, and John Bradford was to become their spokesman and leader.[4] Ferrar had succumbed to pressure and had agreed to receive the Sacrament on Easter Day in one kind only. Bradford was at once made aware of this, and was able to persuade him to revoke his promise. This was a true turning point for Ferrar; he would "never after yield" to any kind of pressure at all.[5] Taylor told his friends that he could only rejoice to have found in Bradford "such an angel of God" to cheer him in prison.[6] The Marshalsea was adjacent to the King's Bench and there was some contact between men in the two prisons. Edwin Sandys had been discharged from the Marshalsea, but good Lawrence Saunders was there; and Foxe records that Bradford and Saunders used to meet and confer "on the backside" of the prisons as often as they would.[7]

Foxe's account makes the astonishing statement that John Bradford preached twice a day in the King's Bench and ministered the Sacrament to those who came: "and through his means, the keepers so well did bear with him, such resort of good folks

[1] Bradford, Vol. II, p. 63.   [2] Ibid., Vol. II. p. 69.
[3] Strype, *Ecclesiastical Memorials*, Vol. III. Part 1, p. 124.
[4] Bradford Vol. II, p. 96.   [5] *Foxe*, Vol. VII, p. 146.
[6] Ibid., Vol. VI, p. 684.   [7] Ibid., Vol. VII, p. 146.

was daily to his lecture and to the ministration of the Sacrament that commonly his chamber was well nigh filled therewith".[1] This is confirmed by Bradford's own remark in a letter on August 8th, 1554: "I break up this abruptly because our common prayer time calleth me."[2] Once a week he used to visit that part of the prison where the criminal element was housed; he would exhort them to amend their lives and would relieve their wants by gifts and goodwill. Sometimes he was allowed to go out on parole and "there was no day but that he might have escaped" had he so wished.[3] He told a friend that if he were released, he would marry, stay in England, teach those whom he could in private, and serve God in that way; but he knew that there was little prospect of his release, and he was on spiritual tiptoe for his ultimate martyrdom.

Bradford was in fact to assume the real leadership of the Reformers who were then in prison and to achieve more for his cause in this role than ever he had in his days of freedom.[4] His great reputation as a preacher, his attractive gentleness and singular holiness, the fire of his dauntless courage, and his martyr spirit were the marks of a man who had "outstripped the age in which his lot was cast".[5] We are told by Foxe that he was "tall and slender, spare of body, of a faint sanguine colour, with an auburn beard. He slept not commonly above four hours in the night; and in his bed, till sleep came, his book went not out of his hand."[6] "Preaching, reading, and praying was all his whole life. He did not eat above one meal a day, which was but very little when he took it; and his continual study was upon his knees."[7] He wept much in secret, but he was so pleasant when others were present that they might have thought he did not know what it was to shed a tear. "Very gentle he was to man and child";[8] his tenderness and affection are the shining virtue of his letters. "Good mother and right dear to me in the Lord", he wrote on February 24th, 1554, "I wish to you for ever God's peace in Christ."[9] He did not count the hour well spent in which he had not done some good with his pen or his voice, on his knees or

[1] *Foxe*, Vol. VII, p. 145.
[2] Bradford, Vol. II, p. 116.
[3] *Foxe*, Vol. VII, p. 146.
[4] J. Ridley, *Cranmer*, p. 361.
[5] Bradford, Vol. II, p. xi.
[6] *Foxe*, Vol. VII, p. 145.
[7] Ibid., p. 145.   [8] Ibid., p. 145.
[9] Bradford, Vol. II, p. 72.

his feet, and the impression which his character made on his own generation was to reflect itself in the universal praise of posterity. Thus Strype said that he was "a man of great learning, elocution, sweetness of temper, and profound devotion towards God".[1] Even a Catholic and Jesuit such as Robert Parsons said that he was "of a more soft and mild nature than many of his fellows".[2] But those who read his works must be conscious that there was as well an intolerance and an intensity in his nature which were just as vivid as his gentleness or his piety. This strand in his nature was the result in part of his firm grasp of the Reformed Theology, and in part of his clear knowledge of God's grace in his own experience. The key is found in the beautiful tradition which has survived the lapse of time and which records that when he saw evil-doers on their way to execution, he was wont to exclaim: "But for the grace of God, there goes John Bradford."[3]

Bradford's writings fill more than nine hundred pages in two volumes prepared for the Parker Society by the Rev. Aubrey Townsend. They were mostly occasional pieces such as sermons, letters, meditations and prayers. They were largely written while he was in prison, often in haste and with difficulty to meet some need of the moment. Sometimes writing materials were hard to get; sometimes he could only write "by starts and stealth".[4] Perhaps nothing that he wrote has been more widely read or highly valued than his letters; they came straight from his heart and were always warm and self-revealing. Thus on February 24th he wrote to his mother, and it is a letter which affords the clearest picture of his life in prison. "You shall know, good mother, that for my body though it be in a house out of the which I can not come when I will, yet in that I have conformed my will to God's will. I find herein liberty enough, I thank God; and for my lodging, bedding, meat, drink, godly and learned company, books and all other necessaries for mine ease, comfort and commodity, I am in much better case than I could wish."[5] It was for Christ's sake that he was called to suffer; therefore he should be both merry and glad. "And

---

[1] Strype, op. cit., Vol. III, Part I, p. 363.
[2] *D.N.B.*   [3] Bradford, Vol. II, p. xliii.
[4] Ibid., Vol. I, p. 434.   [5] Ibid., Vol. II, pp. 74–75.

indeed, good mother, so I am as ever I was; yea, never so merry and glad was I as I now should be, if I could get you to be merry with me, to thank God for me and to pray on this sort."[1] Yet in spite of brave words, there were rigours which in the end he could not hide from her: "Now therefore will I make an end, praying you good mother to look for no more letters; for if it were known that I have pen and ink and did write, then should I want all the foresaid commodities I have spoken of concerning my body, and be cast into some dungeon in fetters of iron: which thing I know would grieve you: and therefore for God's sake, see that these be burned, . . . for perchance your house may be searched for such gear when you think little of it; and look for no more, sweet mother, till either God shall deliver me and send me out, either you and I shall meet together in heaven."[2]

The great merit of all his work was the warmth and freshness with which he dealt with the life of God in the soul. He was not a formal theologian like Cranmer and Ridley, and he did not engage in works of great learning. Tracts such as *The Hurt of Hearing Mass* were meant for the plain reader; but they revealed a sound instinct for true theology. His early translations from Artopoeus and Chrysostom were followed by further translations from the Common Places of Melancthon and the Comment-aries of Martin Bucer. He sought Ridley's advice in his *Sermon on The Lord's Supper*[3] and his *Defence of Election*.[4] Ridley wrote with regard to the former in May 1554: "Sir, what shall best be done with these things now ye must consider: for if they come in sight at this time, undoubtedly they must to the fire with their father. . . . Blessed be God that hath given you liberty in the mean season that you may use your pen to His glory and to the comfort as I hear say of many."[5] Ridley for his part sent Bradford his own manuscript narrative of the Oxford Disputation[6] and his reply to the work of Cuthbert Tunstall on the Eucharist;[7] Ridley had written in Latin and left it to Bradford to "translate and order them as he should think might best help to open the eyes of the simple".[8] Bradford's strength lay in the thrust of his

[1] Bradford, Vol. II, p. 75.   [2] Ibid., Vol. II, p. 76.
[3] Ibid., Vol. II, p. 93.   [4] Ibid., Vol. II, p. 170.
[5] Ibid., Vol. II, p. 93; Ridley, *Works*, pp. 363–364.
[6] Bradford, Vol. II, p. 136.   [7] Ibid., Vol. II, p. 159.
[8] Ibid. Vol. II, pp. 159–160.

pen and the drive of his words both in rebuke and in encouragement. Thus he wrote to Robert Cole and Nicholas Sheterden
and gave them the plainest counsel: "I believe that faith and to
believe in Christ is the work and gift of God. . . . If you feel not
this faith, then know that predestination is too high a matter
for you to be disputers of it until you have been better scholars
in the school-house of repentance and justification."[1] There
were other prison writings which were treasured by his friends
and published after his death. Perhaps the most moving of all is
a series of short Meditations which were found in his handwriting in a copy of Tyndale's New Testament. The initials
I.B. and I.H. for John Bradford and Joyce Hales were written
on the back of the last fly-leaf and were engraved in gilt letters
on each side of the cover. A few manuscript lines on the reverse
of the title-page were dated February 8th, 1555, and were
addressed to "mine own most dearly beloved sister in the Lord".
It seems likely that the book was bound for Joyce Hales after his
death, for the writing was cut by the binder.[2]

In May 1554, Bradford composed *A Declaration Concerning
Religion* which was signed by Ferrar, Taylor, Philpot and Bradford in the King's Bench, Saunders in the Marshalsea, Hooper and
Rogers in Newgate, and by certain others as well. In November,
he prepared the *Supplication to Their Majesties and the Houses of
Parliament* in the name of the same persons. He drew up his
Exhortation to the Brethren in England a little later; it ends with a
moving request: "Pray for all your brethren which be in prison
and in exile, and so absent from you in body but yet present with
you in spirit; and heartily pray God once to prove us and trust
us again with His holy Word and Gospel; that we may be
suffered to speak and you to hear His voice. . . . He remember
His mercy towards us in His time, we beseech Him. Amen.
Your own in the Lord, John Bradford."[3] On January 16th, 1555,
royal assent was given to the recent Act which revived the old
Lollard statutes for punishment of heresy. Gardiner established
a Commission to examine the men who had been in prison for
non-comformity to the Queen's faith, and their trials soon began.
Bradford appeared before the Lord Chancellor on three oc-

[1] Bradford, Vol. II, pp. 133–134.   [2] Ibid., Vol. I, p. 248.
[3] Ibid., Vol. I, p. 433.

casions late in January and was closely questioned on doctrine
and conduct. He wrote his own account of each Examination,
and his answers show that he was imperturbable. He was calm,
self-possessed, swift and lucid in thinking and speaking; and he
proved his mettle in such a way that the court was all but baffled.
Bradford's account was forwarded in manuscript to Grindal
at Strasburg; Grindal sent it to Foxe in November 1557, and it
appeared in the Latin edition of *The Acts and Monuments* in 1559.
It was printed separately by Griffith in 1561 and it appeared again
in Foxe's English edition of 1563. Griffith alone preserved
Bradford's account in the exact form in which he penned it,
and Aubrey Townsend in the Parker Society volumes followed
Griffith. Bradford's defence won the whole-hearted approval of
Ridley, who declared: "Blessed be the Holy Trinity, the Father,
the Son and the Holy Ghost, for your threefold confession. I have
read all three with great comfort and joy and thanksgiving unto
God for His manifold gifts of grace wherewith it is manifest . . .
that God did assist you mightily."[1]

On January 22nd, 1555, Bradford was brought before the
Lord Chancellor and the Privy Council at Gardiner's residence
in Southwark. Gardiner instructed him to stand up and tried to
stare him out; this was in vain. He then told him that his imprisonment was due to his conduct in the riot at Paul's Cross
when he had presumed to preach without authority. "But now",
he said, "the time of mercy is come: and therefore the Queen's
Highness, minding to offer unto you mercy, hath by us sent
for you to declare and give the same, if so be ye will with us
return."[2] Bradford declared that he had long been in prison
without justice, for he had sought "peace and all godly quietness
both in going about to save the Bishop of Bath that now is . . .
and in preaching for quietness accordingly."[3] Gardiner rejected
Bradford's statement as "a loud lie", and Bradford then declared:
"My Lord, as I said, I say again, that I stand, as before you, so
before God; and one day we shall all stand before Him; the
truth then will be the truth, though you will not now so take it.
. . . I took nothing upon me undesired, and that of Master
Bourne himself, as if he were here present, I dare say he would

[1] Ridley, *Works*, p. 369.   [2] Bradford, Vol. I, p. 465.
[3] Ibid., Vol. I, p. 466.

affirm it; for he desired me both to help him to pacify the people and not to leave him till he was in safety."[1]

Gardiner then broke off this discussion and turned to his real point. "Well," he said, "to leave this matter; how sayest thou now? Wilt thou return again and do as we have done? And thou shalt receive the Queen's mercy and pardon." Bradford replied: "My Lord, I desire mercy with God's mercy; but mercy with God's wrath, God keep me from!" Gardiner then ridiculed his "babbling rolling" tongue with the warning: "If thou . . . wilt not receive mercy offered to thee, know for truth that the Queen is minded to make a purgation of all such as thou art." Bradford was not perturbed. "The Lord tofore whom I stand as well as before you knoweth . . . His mercy I desire, and also would be glad of the Queen's favour to live as a subject without clog of conscience: but otherwise the Lord's mercy is to me better than life. And I know to Whom I have committed my life, even to His hands which will keep it, so that no man may take it away before it be His pleasure. There are twelve hours in the day; and as long as they last, so long shall no man have power thereon: therefore His good will be done. Life in His displeasure is worse than death; and death in His true favour is true life." Gardiner reacted strongly: "I knew well enough we should have glorious talk enough of thee."[2]

Tunstall tried to turn the case in another direction and asked: "Tell me what you say by the ministration of the Communion as you now know it is?" Bradford would not discuss it on the ground that he had six times sworn that he would in no case consent to the jurisdiction of the Bishop of Rome in the realm of England. Sir John Bourne, the Secretary of the Council, asked him: "Hast thou been sworn six times? What offices hast thou borne?" Bradford ignored an interjection by Gardiner that it was a lie and answered: "Forsooth I was thrice sworn in Cambridge; when I was admitted Master of Art, when I was elected Fellow in Pembroke Hall, and when I was there, the Visitors came thither and sware the University. Again I was sworn when I entered into the ministry, when I had a prebend given unto me, and when I was sworn to serve the King a little before his death."[3]

---

[1] Bradford, Vol. I, pp. 466–467.   [2] Ibid., Vol. I, p. 467.
[3] Ibid., Vol. I, p. 468.

Sir John Bourne then observed that the Earl of Derby had complained that Bradford had "done more hurt by letters and exhorting those that have come to him in religion than ever he did when he was abroad by preaching". Bradford would only say: "That I have written, I have written."[1]

Gardiner finally discoursed at length about the false doctrine taught in the reign of the late King and asked Bradford: "How sayest thou?" "My Lord," Bradford replied, "the doctrine taught in King Edward's days was God's pure religion, the which as I then believed, so do I now believe more than ever I did: and therein I am more confirmed and ready to declare it by God's grace ... than I was when I first came into prison."[2] There was a pause; Gardiner asserted that such doctrine bred heresy and rebellion. Then he offered Bradford the Queen's mercy, only to receive the reply: "Mercy with God's mercy should be welcome: but otherwise he would none." Gardiner rang a bell and the Under Marshal came in. "You shall take this man", Gardiner directed, "and keep him close without conference with any man but by your knowledge; and suffer him not to write any letters etc; for he is of another manner of charge unto you now than he was before." And so Bradford went out; "and as God knoweth, with as merry a heart and so quiet a conscience and ever I had in all my life."[3] It was that night or the next that Saunders wrote to the four men in the King's Bench and asked for their prayers. He then added: "I would gladly meet with my good brother Bradford on the backside about an eleven of the clock. Before that time I can not start out, ye have such out-walkers: but then they will be at dinner."[4] Were they able to meet? We do not know.

On January 29th, after Rogers had been condemned, Bradford was brought before Gardiner's Commission which was sitting in St. Marye-over-ye-waye. He was offered the Queen's pardon if he would now return: "There is yet space and grace", Gardiner exhorted, "tofore we so proceed that you be committed to the secular power, as we must do and will do if you will not follow the example of Master Barlow and Cardmaker."[5] Bradford replied: "At this present, I stand before you guilty or

[1] Bradford, Vol. I, p. 469. [2] Ibid., Vol. I, p. 471.
[3] Ibid., Vol. I, p. 472. [4] Ibid., Vol. II, p. 179. [5] Ibid., Vol. I, p. 473.

guiltless; if guilty, then proceed and give sentence accordingly; if guiltless, then give me the benefit of a subject which hitherto I could not have."[1] There was protracted argument as to whether his oath sworn six times meant that he could not answer further questions lest it were to admit papal jurisdiction. At last he said: "If you of your honour shall tell me that you do not ask me anything whereby my answering should consent to the practising of the Bishop of Rome's jurisdiction, ask me wherein you will and you shall hear that I will answer you as flatly as ever any did that came before you. I am not afraid of death, I thank God; for I look and have looked for nothing else at your hands of long time."[2] Gardiner was indignant and resentful and protested that the oath against the Bishop of Rome was against charity. Bradford replied: "Saving mine oath, I will answer you in this behalf, that the oath against the Bishop of Rome was not nor is not against charity."[3] Gardiner's argument on this point came to a climax in the statement: "Thou goest about to deny obedience to the Queen which now requireth obedience to the Bishop of Rome." "No, my Lord," said Bradford, "I do not deny obedience to the Queen if you would discern between genus and species." Gardiner retorted: "I will none of those similitudes." And Bradford then rejoined: "I would not use them if that you went not about to persuade the people I mean that which I never meant."[4]

Bradford made a telling appeal to the argument used by Gardiner in his book *De Vera Obedientia:* "Vincat modo Domini verbi veritas: Let God's Word and the reasons thereof bear the bell away." Gardiner angrily fell back on the charge that Bradford had written seditious letters to subvert the people and did not dare to make reply. Bradford denied the charge and said: "That which I have written and spoken, that will I never deny, by God's grace. And where your Lordship saith I dare not answer you; that all men may know I am not afraid, saving mine oath, ask me what you will and I will plainly make you answer, by God's grace, although I now see my life lieth thereon." Gardiner had won this long manoeuvre in the meanest fashion and he at once began with his questions: "Well then, how say

[1] Bradford, Vol. I, p. 474.   [2] Ibid., Vol. I, p. 476.
[3] Ibid., Vol. I, p. 477.   [4] Ibid., Vol. I, p. 479.

you to the blessed Sacrament? Do you not believe there Christ to be present concerning His natural body?" But Bradford would allow that He was there present only to faith. "Unto faith!" exclaimed Gardiner; "we must have many more words to make it more plain."[1] Bradford agreed, but asked leave to make a statement. "I have been now a year and almost three quarters in prison," he said, "and of all this time you never questioned with me hereabouts, when I might have spoken my conscience frankly without peril: but now you have a law to hang up and put to death, if a man answer freely and not to your appetite; and so you now come to demand this question. Ah, my Lord, Christ used not this way to bring men to faith: no more did the prophets or the apostles." Gardiner asserted that this was not of his doing, while Bonner and others urged that he had ever been "too mild and too gentle". "My Lord." said Bradford, "I pray you stretch out your gentleness that I may feel it; for hitherto I never felt it." Gardiner chose to interpret this as though it were an appeal, and said that not only he but the Queen herself would stretch out mercy if he would now return. "Return!" exlaimed Bradford; "my Lord, God save me from that going back! I mean it not so; but I mean that I was three quarters of a year in the Tower without paper, pen or ink; and never in all that time nor sithen did I feel any gentleness from you."[2] But the court broke up for dinner while he was still speaking. "And so was he had into the vestry, and was there all that day till dark night: and so was conveyed again to prison, declaring by his countenance great joy in God."[3]

Thomas Hussey, once a servant of the Duke of Norfolk, had come into the church about four o'clock on the pretext that he was in search of someone who was not there. He made himself known to Bradford, who with Taylor was still in the vestry, on the ground that he had known him at the siege of Montreuil and said that he would pay him a further visit in the morning. Thus on January 30th, at seven o'clock in the morning, Hussey came to Bradford's prison and was allowed to see him by himself. Hussey said that Bradford had so behaved before Gardiner's Commission the day before that his "veriest enemies" could see

---

[1] Bradford, Vol. I, p. 480.   [2] Ibid., Vol. I, p. 481.
[3] Ibid., Vol. I, p. 482.

that they had no real case; therefore Hussey advised him that when he appeared again that day, he should ask for time and men with whom to confer. Bradford answered that he neither could nor would make such a request lest it should lead people to think that he stood in some doubt of his doctrine. While they were talking, the door was unlocked and in came a certain Doctor Seyton who saw Hussey and expressed some surprise. "What, Sir," he said, "are you come before me?" Bradford then knew the truth. "Yea, thought I, goeth the matter thus? And he told me, no man knew of his coming. . . . I see these men be come to hunt the matter that the one may bear witness with the other."[1] Seyton argued that as Cranmer had expressed a desire to confer with Tunstall, Bradford should do likewise. There was a great deal of conversation with much flattering argument. Bradford stuck to his point; he was certain of the doctrine which he had held and taught. At last he told Seyton that he had never found the least justice, much less charity, at the hands of the Lord Chancellor; he had long been held in prison although they had no charge except what they could wring out of his own statements. Bradford would not argue further, for he saw that they had come to trap him into something which would allow it to be said that there was cause to keep him in prison. He gleaned from their remarks that he was to appear in court again that day, and after much ado he got them to leave him as he wished to spend time alone in prayer.[2]

Bradford was soon summoned again to St. Marye-over-ye-waye, but he was not called to appear in court until eleven o'clock, after Saunders had been condemned. Gardiner told him that he had been granted time to recant the heresy which he had voiced about the Sacrament the day before. "My Lord," Bradford declared, "you gave me no time of any such deliberation, neither did I speak anything of the Sacrament which you did disallow; for when I had declared a presence of Christ to be there to the faithful, you went from the matter to purge yourself that you were not cruel, and so went to dinner."[3] There was vigorous argument about his oath against the Bishop of Rome, and Bradford kept him at bay, citing his own book to prove that

[1] Bradford, Vol. I, p. 494.   [2] Ibid., Vol. I, p. 496.
[3] Ibid., Vol. I, p. 483.

the oath had been lawful. Finally Gardiner declared: "You may see how this fellow taketh upon him to have more knowledge and conscience than all the wise men of England; and yet he hath no conscience at all." "Well, my Lord," said Bradford, "let all the standers-by see who hath conscience. I have been a year and a half in prison: now, before all this people, declare wherefor I was prisoned or what cause you had to punish me. You said the other day in your own house . . . that I took upon me to speak to the people undesired. There he sitteth by your Lordship (I mean my Lord Bishop of Bath) which desired me himself for the Passion of Christ I would speak to the people. . . . For all which my doing, I have received this recompense, prison a year and a half and more, and death now which you go about. Let all men now judge where conscience is."[1] They tried to cut him short, but he spoke on until he had ended. Gardiner hastily tried to change his ground and said that Bradford had been put in prison because he would not yield to the Queen's religion. "Why," said Bradford, "your Honour knoweth you would not then reason with me in religion; but you said a time should afterward be found out when I should be talked withal. But if it were, as your Lordship saith, that I was put in prison for religion, in that my religion was then authorised by the public laws of the realm, could conscience punish me or cast me in prison therefor? Wherefore let all men judge in whom conscience wanteth."[2]

Gardiner at length began a new line of argument. "Sir," he said, "in my house the other day you did most contemptuously contemn the Queen's mercy, and further said you would maintain the erroneous doctrine in King Edward's days against all men; and this you did most stoutly."[3] Bradford coolly replied: "Well, I am glad that all men see now you had no matter to imprison me afore that day justly. Now say I that I did not contemptuously contemn the Queen's mercy, but would have had it, (though if justice might take place, I need it not), so that I might have had it with God's mercy; that is, without saying or doing anything against God and His truth. . . . I said I was more confirmed in the religion set forth in King Edward's days than

[1] Bradford, Vol. I, pp. 485–486.   [2] Ibid., Vol. I, p. 486.
[3] Ibid., Vol. I, pp. 487–488.

ever I was. . . . So I said then, and so I say again now." Gardiner persisted: "Yesterday thou didst maintain false heresy concerning the blessed Sacrament; and therefore we gave thee respite till this day to deliberate." Bradford answered: "My Lord, as I said at the first, I spake nothing of the Sacrament but that which you allowed; and therefore you reproved it not, nor gave me no time to deliberate." Gardiner demanded: "Didst thou not deny Christ's presence in the Sacrament?" "No," said Bradford, "I never denied nor taught but that to faith whole Christ's body and blood was as present as bread and wine to the due receiver." Gardiner continued: "Yea, but dost thou not believe that Christ's body naturally and really is there under the form of bread and wine?" And he replied: "My Lord, I believe Christ is present there to the faith of the due receiver; as for transubstantiation, I plainly and flatly tell you, I believe it not."[1] Someone asked whether the wicked receive the very body of Christ or no, and he said "No."[2] Altercation broke out; they all declared that he was a heretic and Gardiner proceeded to read out his excommunication. Bradford declared: "God, I doubt not, will give His blessing where you curse."[3] He fell on his knees and thanked God that He had called him to suffer for His Name's sake. The Sheriffs of London led him first to the Clink and then to the Compter in the Poultry which stood in the Grocers' Hall Court. He was closely confined, without friends or books, pen or ink, waiting for an early execution.

It was proposed that the Earl of Derby should conduct Bradford from London to Manchester so that he could die in his own city. It was in this expectation that the early days of February were spent, and he prepared himself accordingly. Somehow he got hold of writing materials and was never so busy in writing. On February 5th, he told Lady Vane: "Now do I begin to be Christ's disciple; now I begin to be fashioned like to my Master in suffering."[4] Two days later, he told Mistress Warcup: "Now I write my farewell to you in this life indeed upon certain knowledge. My staff standeth at the door; I continually look for the sheriff to come for me, and I thank God I am ready for him. Now go I to practise that which I have preached. Now am I

---

[1] Bradford, Vol. I, p. 488.   [2] Ibid., Vol. I, p. 489.
[3] Ibid., Vol. I, p. 492.   [4] Ibid., Vol. II, p. 184.

climbing up the hill: it will cause me to puff and blow before I come to the cliff. The hill is steep and high; my breath is short and my strength is feeble. Pray therefore to the Lord for me that as I have now through His goodness even almost come to the top, I may by His grace be strengthened not to rest till I come where I should be."[1] He wrote his fine little treatise *Against the Fear of Death*; death "at whose door though I have stand a great while, yet never so near, to man's judgment, as I do now".[2] On February 11th, he was hourly looking to be conveyed to Manchester for martyrdom, and he wrote his Farewells to the City of London, to the University and Town of Cambridge, and to Lancashire and Cheshire; and the next day he wrote one more Farewell to the Town of Saffron Walden. "Although the charge is great to keep me from all things whereby I might signify anything to the world of my state," he wrote, "yet having as I now have pen and ink through God's working, ... I thought good to write a short confession of my faith";[3] and he signed himself "your brother in bonds for the Lord's sake".[4] And he affirmed that "the condemnation is not a condemnation of Bradford simply, but rather a condemnation of Christ and His truth: Bradford is nothing else but an instrument in whom Christ and His doctrine are condemned".[5] It was this clear insight which gave him strength and poise through those days of suspense and trial.

On February 8th, Bradford wrote to Augustine Berneher: "Come hither betimes I pray you in the morning. ... Pray Walsh to steal you in, as I hope he will do. ... For I am persuaded I shall into Lancashire there to be burned: howbeit first they say I must to the Fleet. ... Also I pray you, will Robert Harrington, who I hope will go with me, to look for that journey. Visit often my dear sister ... God shall give us to meet in His Kingdom. In the mean season, I will pray for her as my dearest sister. Of truth I never did love her half so well as I now do; and yet I love her not half so well as I would do."[6] On the same day, he wrote to Cranmer, Ridley and Latimer: "Our dear brother Rogers hath broken the ice valiantly; and as this day I think or

[1] Bradford, Vol. II, p. 185.   [2] Ibid., Vol. I, p. 332.
[3] Ibid., Vol. I, p. 434.   [4] Ibid., Vol. I, p. 440.
[5] Ibid., Vol. I, p. 449.   [6] Ibid., Vol. II, p. 187.

tomorrow at the uttermost, Hooper, Saunders and Taylor end their course and receive their crown. The next am I which hourly look for the porter to open me the gates after them."[1] Augustine Berneher saw him the next morning and then wrote to Ridley: "Mr. Bradford moveth to-morrow towards * * * with my Lord of Derby. I have promised him to meet him at Cambridge."[2]

A day or two later, Ridley wrote to Augustine Berneher: "I bless God with all my heart in His manifold merciful gifts given unto our dear brethren in Christ" (i.e. Rogers, Hooper, Saunders, Taylor), "whom it hath pleased the Lord to set in the forebrunt now of battle. . . . And evermore and without end, blessed be even the same our heavenly Father for our dear and entirely beloved brother Bradford, whom now the Lord I perceive calleth for. . . . I do not doubt but that he . . . hath holpen those which are gone before in their journey. . . . The Lord be His comfort, whereof I do not doubt: and I thank God heartily that ever I was acquainted with him and that ever I had such a one in my house."[3] Ridley also wrote to Bradford a most moving farewell which he hoped that Berneher would give him in Lancashire: "O dear brother, seeing the time is now come wherein it pleaseth the heavenly Father for Christ our Saviour His sake to call upon you and to bid you to come, happy are you that ever ye were born, thus to be awake at the Lord's calling. O dear brother, what meaneth this, that you are sent into your own native country? The wisdom and policy of the world may mean what they will; but I trust . . . all thy country may rejoice of thee that ever it brought forth such a one which would render his life again in His cause of Whom he had received it. Brother Bradford, so long as I shall understand that thou art in thy journey, by God's grace I shall call upon our heavenly Father for Christ's sake to set thee safely home. . . . O good brother, blessed be God in thee, and blessed be the time that ever I knew thee! Farewell, farewell."[4]

But the end was not yet; he was kept in prison for five more months. Ridley soon wrote again: "I had thought of late that I had written unto you your last farewell . . . by our dear brother

[1] Bradford, Vol. II, p. 190.   [2] Ridley, *Works*, p. 382.
[3] Bradford, Vol. II, p. 192; Ridley, *Works*, p. 380.
[4] Bradford, Vol. II., pp. 193–194; Ridley, *Works*, pp. 377–378.

Austin, and I sent it to meet you in Lancashire whither it was said here you were appointed to be sent to suffer. But now ... they have changed their purpose and prolonged your death."[1] Immense efforts were now made to win him over, and the lengths to which those in authority went to achieve this end prove how much he meant to the cause of the Reformation. A succession of visitors streamed into his prison: laymen, divines, prelates and two Spanish Friars. It began on February 4th when Bonner came to degrade Rowland Taylor. This was at one o'clock; Rogers had been burnt that very morning. Bradford in the Compter had not yet heard of the death of Rogers who had been in Newgate; nor did Bonner tell him. Bonner sent for Bradford before he saw Taylor, and the conversation began with great civility. "Off went his cap", Bradford wrote, "and outstretched he his hand";[2] and he suavely told him that he perceived that he wished to confer with some man of learning. Bradford told him roundly: "I am not afraid to talk with whom you will; but to say that I desire to confer, that do I not."[3] That night at eight o'clock one of Gardiner's gentlemen came to offer him time to confer if he so wished; but he refused to make such a request, though he would not refuse to confer if any were sent: "because", he said, "I am certain and able, I thank God, to defend by godly learning my faith".[4]

Bonner's visit was the preface to this strange new chapter in the life of Bradford, and it formed the pattern for what was to follow. The approach was always the same; it was implied that he wished to confer and that he was being treated with great favour. He was able to keep fragmentary records of his conversations and they show that he was sought out by an astonishing variety of men throughout February, March and April. There were servants of the Earl of Derby and of the Queen herself who begged him with tears to make suit for her mercy. There were former acquaintances such as Beiche and Cresswell who plied him with plausible suggestions. There were theologians like Harpsfield and Weston who asked what would befall him if he were deceived; and he merely replied as the sun shone through the window: "What if you did say the sun did not

---

[1] Ridley, *Works*, p. 369.
[2] Bradford, Vol. I, p. 496.
[3] Ibid., Vol. I, p. 497.
[4] Ibid., Vol. I, p. 497.

shine now?"[1] Some might threaten; some would cajole; and all strove to shake his faith and resolution. Perhaps Cranmer was the only person besides Bradford to be treated in this manner, and it told at length on Cranmer's will to endure. But it was not so with Bradford; he was serene and light-hearted, willing to live or die as God might will, and his poise could not be ruffled.

The most interesting visits were those of Nicholas Heath and George Day on February 22nd and of Alphonsus a Castro and Bartholomew Carranza three days later. Heath was the Archbishop of York and Day was the Bishop of Chichester; and they behaved "very gently", coming, they said, "of love and charity" and for the sake of old acquaintance.[2] They spent four hours in a persuasive encounter and they only left when called for another appointment; but their soft words did not shake his settled purpose. The two Spanish Friars were by contrast cold and formal; their conversation of necessity was in Latin. They both stood high in the counsels of Philip and Mary and were destined for the highest office in Spain: Alphonsus a Castro was to become Archbishop of Compostella and Bartholomew Carranza, of Toledo. Alphonsus was so impatient with Bradford's clear logic that he began to shout until the whole building caught the echo. Bradford asked him: "What and if that I prove it to you continually for eight hundred years after Christ at the least, the substance of bread to remain in the Sacrament, by the testimony of the Fathers: what will you do?" Alphonsus replied: "I will give place." "Then", said Bradford, "write you how that you will give place if I so prove; and I will write that I will give place if you so prove." This was too much for the Friar. "Lord God," exclaimed Bradford, "how angry he was now, and said that he came not to learn at me."[3] The two Friars stormed out, and did not so much as bid him farewell.

So it went on. On February 17th he was warned that he would set out on the journey to Lancashire in the morning; on February 19th he was told that the writ for his execution had been called in and that he would have all his books again.[4] A month later he was informed by Hugh Weston that the latter had inquired

[1] Bradford, Vol. I, p. 510.   [2] Ibid., Vol. I, p. 518.
[3] Ibid., Vol. II, pp. 536–537.   [4] Ibid., Vol. I, p. 517.

about his conduct while he was at Cambridge. "Your life", he said, "I have learned was such there always as all men, even the greatest enemies you have, can not but praise you and it."[1] Weston also told him that the Bishop of Bath and Wells had urged that some favour towards him should be shown by the Queen and Council,[2] and he told the keeper as he left that he saw no cause why they should burn Bradford.[3] There were many rumours abroad; some of them reached Ridley in prison at Oxford. Thus he wrote to Bradford: "It is said here that you be pardoned your life; and when you were appointed to be banished and to go I can not tell whither, you should say that you had rather here suffer than go where you could not live after your conscience, and that this pardon should be begged for you by Bourne the Bishop of Bath for that you saved his life."[4] But rumour and uncertainly did not disturb the light that shone within that cell, and he answered when asked how he fared in prison: "Well, I thank God: for as men in sailing which be near to the shore or haven where they would be would be nearer; even so the nearer I am to God, the nearer I would be."[5]

But the patience of the authorities was running out; the prisons were emptied as the weeks slipped away. On February 4th, John Rogers died "valiantly" at Smithfield; on the 8th, Saunders was burnt at Coventry; on the 9th, Hooper died at Gloucester and Taylor at Hadleigh. Between that date and March 30th, when Ferrar was burnt in Wales, Bradford wrote *An Admonition to Lovers of the Gospel*. "Take up your cross", he said, "and follow your Master as your brethren M. Hooper, Rogers, Taylor and Saunders have done; and as now your brethren M. Cranmer, Latimer, Ridley, Ferrar, Bradford etc. be ready to do. The ice is broken for you; therefore be not afraid, but be content to die for the Lord."[6] In May or June, Ridley wrote to Grindal: "The Lord hitherto hath preserved above all our expectation our dear brother ... John Bradford. He is condemned and is already delivered unto the secular power, and writs as we have heard say given out for his execution and called in again."[7] Towards

[1] Bradford, Vol. I, p. 547.   [2] Ibid., Vol. I, p. 549.
[3] Ibid., Vol. I, p. 550.   [4] Ridley, *Works*, p. 370.
[5] Bradford, Vol. I, p. 553.   [6] Ibid., Vol. I, p. 410.
[7] Ridley, *Works*, pp. 390–391.

the end of June, Bradford was warned that the end was at hand. He wrote a joint letter to Augustine Berneher and Mistress Joyce Hales. "I have good hope that if you come at night about nine of the clock, I shall speak with you," he told Berneher; "but come as secretly as you can."[1] Claydon, the keeper, "hath been with me an hour this afternoon; he thinks I shall be burned in Smithfield, and that shortly".[2] "Be merry, dear heart," he told Joyce Hales; "God shall give us to meet in His Kingdom. . . . Dear Joyce, thou art His a great deal more than I am. Indeed it is so; praise thy God and Father."[3]

He wrote one more letter "out of prison the 24th of June 1555".[4] This was to his mother, the one letter to her of which we know after February 1554. "My most dear Mother," he wrote, "in the bowels of Christ I heartily pray and beseech you to be thankful for me unto God which thus now taketh me unto Himself. I die not, my good mother, as a thief, a murderer, an adulterer, etc; but I die as a witness of Christ, His Gospel and verity, which hitherto I have confessed, I thank God, as well by preaching as by imprisonment; and now, even presently, I shall most willingly confirm the same by fire. . . . Be mindful of both your daughters, to help them as you can. I send all my writings to you by my brother Roger: do with them as you will, because I can not as I would: he can tell you more of my mind. I have nothing to give you or to leave behind for you; only I pray God my Father for His Christ's sake to bless you and keep you from evil. . . . Thus my dear mother, I take my last farewell of you in this life, beseeching the Almighty and Eternal Father by Christ to grant us to meet in the life to come where we shall give Him continual thanks and praise for ever and ever. Amen."[5]

On Sunday, June 30th, 1555, Bradford and a fellow prisoner were walking in the keeper's chamber when "the keeper's wife came up as one half amazed, and seeming much troubled, being almost windless, said, O Master Bradford, I come to bring you heavy news". He asked what that might be and she replied: "Marry, to-morrow you must be burned; and your chain is now a buying, and soon you must go to Newgate." Bradford took

---

[1] Bradford, Vol. II, p. 251.   [2] Ibid., Vol. II, p. 252.
[3] Ibid., Vol. II, pp. 252–253.   [4] Ibid., Vol. II, p. 251.
[5] Ibid., Vol. II, pp. 249–251.

off his cap and looked up to heaven and said: "I thank God for it; I have looked for the same a long time, and therefore it cometh not now to me suddenly, but as a thing waited for every day and hour; the Lord make me worthy thereof!"[1] He went into his room and spent a long vigil in prayer; then he gave his fellow prisoner all his papers and told him what was in his mind. At length half a dozen of his friends came in and he spent the evening with them in the sustaining fellowship of prayer. It was late at night when he was taken from the Compter to a cell at Newgate, but the prisoners were all alerted as he crossed the court on his way from the Compter; they all had a last word for him and in tears bade farewell. It was nearly midnight as they passed through Cheapside, and it had been hoped that no one would be astir; but the streets were packed with people who wept and prayed for him and "most gently bade him farewell".[2]

Bradford was not to die alone; John Leaf, a "godly young springal", was his fellow martyr.[3] This nineteen-year-old tallow-chandler's apprentice had been arrested and examined by Bonner. He was illiterate, and could not read or write; but he knew well Whom he believed, and he resisted all the arguments with which he was assailed. He was sent to prison and two papers were placed in front of him. One was a full recantation, while the other was a copy of the statements he had made at his trial. When the first had been read to him, he refused to affix his mark. When the second had been explained, he seized a pin, thrust it into his hand, and let the blood drop down as his sign-manual. He was asked if he were one of Rogers' scholars, and he at once affirmed that he was and that he believed all that he had learnt from him and was ready to die for it. This was the true spirit for one that should suffer back to back with Brad-ford; they were gay and happy martyrs who went to their death with cheerful courage and the unshaken conviction that to them would open the gates of life. Yet if these things were done in a green tree, what would be done in a dry? (Luke 23:31).

Thus on Monday, July 1st, 1555, "that holy man Mr. Brad-ford", the friend and disciple of "old Hugh Latimer",[4] the pupil of Bucer, Ridley's chaplain, Whitgift's tutor, was to die at

---

[1] *Foxe*, Vol. VII p. 147.　　　　[2] Ibid., p. 148.
[3] Ibid., p. 192.　　　　[4] Latimer, *Sermons and Remains*, p. 258.

Smithfield. It was rumoured in the City that he was to suffer at four o'clock in the morning before the people were abroad, and the result was that Smithfield was crowded with people from four o'clock onwards. But it was much later before he left Newgate and it was nine o'clock before he reached Smithfield. It seems that his brother-in-law, Roger Beswick, waited for him and took him by the hand as he passed by, but that Woodroofe, one of the two Sheriffs, broke his staff on his head. Bradford looked on with sorrow, bade him farewell, and sent a last message to his mother.[1] Nothing was left to chance, and the guard was so strong that the like had not been "seen at any man's burning"; armed men were on all sides and in every corner of the market.[2] There stood the stake, and there at last, by the grace of God, went John Bradford. He fell flat to the ground on one side of the stake while John Leaf lay on the other, unburdening their hearts in this last tense moment of prayer. Then one of the Sheriffs gave the order: "Arise and make an end; for the press of the people is great."[3]

Bradford and Leaf stood up, put off their clothes, and were chained to the stake. Bradford held up his hands and cried: "O England, England, repent thee of thy sins, repent thee of thy sins!"[4] He was silenced by the Sheriff with the threat that his hands would be tied if he did not refrain. He went on to ask that all the world should forgive him as he forgave all the world, and he prayed the people to pray for him. Then he sought to brace his fellow martyr for the ordeal with words of high courage: "Be of good comfort, brother; for we shall have a merry supper with the Lord this night."[5] He "spake no more words that any man did hear, but embracing the reeds, said thus: Strait is the way and narrow is the gate that leadeth to eternal salvation; and few there be that find it."[6] Fuller says that Bradford endured the flame as if it were no more than a gale of wind in summer,[7] and his "shining integrity" never shone more brightly than that day in Smithfield.[8]

Ridley would soon learn how Bradford had died just as Rogers had died; they had been his chaplains, Prebendaries of

[1] *Foxe*, Vol. VII, p. 148. [2] Ibid., p. 148. [3] Ibid., p. 194.
[4] Ibid., p. 194. [5] Ibid., p. 194. [6] Ibid., p. 194.
[7] Bradford, Vol. II, p. xlii. [8] Rupp, op. cit., p. 204.

St. Paul's, and preachers of the Gospel. Ridley did not yet know what his own fate would be, but he could "never betray the memory of Rogers and Bradford".[1] He was in fact to die the most cruel death of all, back to back with "old Hugh Latimer" on October 16th, 1555, lingering in terrible pain after his fellow martyr had yielded up the spirit; but he was to fulfil his great hope in making up with Rogers and Bradford "the trinity out of Paul's Church to suffer for Christ".[2]

[1] J. Ridley, *Nicholas Ridley*, p. 382.
[2] Bradford, Vol. II, p. 192; Ridley, *Works*, p. 381.

BIBLIOGRAPHY

JOHN FOXE, *The Acts and Monuments of John Foxe;* edited by Stephen Cattley (8 vols.), 1841

WILLIAM STEVENS, *Memoirs of the Life and Martyrdom of John Bradford, M.A.,* 1832

RICHARD HONE, *The Lives of John Bradford, Edmund Grindal and Sir Matthew Hale* (Vol. IV in *Lives of Eminent Christians*), 1843

JOHN CHARLES RYLE, *John Bradford: Martyr* (Chapter VIII in *Light From Old Times,* 2nd Edition), 1898

Dictionary of National Biography, John Bradford (Vol. II), 1950

JOHN STRYPE, *Ecclesiastical Memorials* (Oxford), 1824

JOHN BRADFORD, *Sermons, Meditations, Examinations, etc.* (Parker Society) (Cited as Vol. I), 1848

JOHN BRADFORD, *Letters, Treatises, Remains* (Parker Society) (Cited as Vol. II), 1853

HUGH LATIMER, *Sermons* (Parker Society), 1844

HUGH LATIMER, *Sermons and Remains* (Parker Society), 1845

NICHOLAS RIDLEY, *Works* (Parker Society), 1843

HAROLD S. DARBY, *Hugh Latimer* (Epworth Press), 1953

JASPER RIDLEY, *Nicholas Ridley: A Biography,* 1957

JASPER RIDLEY, *Thomas Cranmer,* 1962

THOMAS MCCRIE, *Life of John Knox* (New Edition), 1880

P. M. DAWLEY, *John Whitgift and the Reformation,* 1954

E. G. RUPP, *Studies in the Making of the English Protestant Tradition,* 1949

Note: Special acknowledgement is due to an unpublished manuscript by Mr. Philip F. Johnston of Wolverhampton Grammar School, entitled *The Life of John Bradford, The Manchester Martyr.* It would have been of great advantage had this manuscript been accessible before the chapter on Bradford in this book was written. It provides a critical assessment of all the materials, old and new, available for a life of Bradford, and it must be hoped that it will soon be published.

INDEX